Racial Formations/Critical Transformations

Racial Formations/Critical Transformations

Articulations of Power
in Ethnic and Racial Studies
in the United States

E. San Juan, Jr.

Humanities Press
New Jersey ▼ London

First published 1992 by Humanities Press International, Inc.,
Atlantic Highlands, New Jersey 07716, and
3 Henrietta Street, Covent Garden, London WC2E 8LU

© 1992, E. San Juan, Jr.

Library of Congress Cataloging-in-Publication Data
San Juan, E. (Epifanio), 1938–
    Racial formations/critical transformations : articulations of
power in ethnic and racial studies in the United States / E. San
Juan, Jr.
      p. cm.
    Includes bibliographical references and index.
    ISBN 0-391-03751-X
    1. Racism—United States. 2. United States—Race relations.
3. United States—Ethnic relations. 4. United States—Race
relations—Study and teaching. 5. United States—Ethnic relations—
Study and teaching. I. Title.
E184.A1S26 1992
305.8'00973—dc20   91–33426
                          CIP

A catalog record for this book is available from the British Library.

Printed in the United States of America

For Delia, Karin, and Eric

I advance it therefore as a suspicion only, that the blacks, whether originally a distinct race, or made distinct by time and circumstances, are inferior to the whites in the endowments both of body and mind.

—Thomas Jefferson, *Notes on the State of Virginia* (1784)

Our goal is that of establishing our common humanity—of striving to remove the barriers that prejudice and limited views of every kind have erected amongst men, and to treat all mankind without reference to religion, nation, or color, as one fraternity, one great community. . . . The recognition of the bond of humanity becomes one of the noblest leading principles in the history of mankind.

—Wilhelm von Humboldt, *Cosmos: A Sketch of a Physical Description of the Universe* (1888)

We of the black American colony must finally take courage, control our fear, and adopt a realistic picture of this world and our place in it. We are not fascist, or Amerikans. We are an oppressed, economically depressed colonial people. . . .
We have a momentous historical role to act out if we will. . . .
I want to leave a world that is liberated from trash, pollution, racism, nation-states, nation-state wars, and armies, from pomp, bigotry, parochialism, a thousand different brands of untruth, and licentious usurious economics. We must build the true internationalism now. . . .

—George Jackson, *Soledad Brother* (1970)

Contents

Acknowledgements

I would like to express my thanks to the editors and publishers of the following journals for permission to use materials which first appeared in different or earlier versions in their publications: *American Literary History*, *Proteus*, *Cultural Critique*, *Rethinking Marxism*, *Journal of Ethnic Studies*, and *The Massachusetts Review*, with special acknowledgement to the Oxford University Press and *The Massachusetts Review*, Inc.

I would also like to acknowledge the invaluable contributions of the following colleagues to the research and writing of the essays in this book: Sam Noumoff, Douglas Allen, Norman and Nancy Chance, Roger Bresnahan, Robert Dombroski, and Evelyn Hu-Dehart. I am also grateful for the support of Bruce Franklin, Fredric Jameson, Paul Buhle, Victor Paananen, and John Beverley; and especially of my colleagues at Bowling Green State University, Karen Gould, director of the Women's Studies Program, and Robert Perry, chair of the Department of Ethnic Studies.

I also wish to take this opportunity to thank my colleagues around the world who are co-workers in the field of comparative cultures for their solidarity, among whom I would like to mention: Dr. Vladimir Makarenko of Moscow State University; Professor Daniel Henri Pageaux of the Université de la Sorbonne Nouvelle; Dr. Reinhart Kössler and the staff of *Peripherie* (Munster, Germany); the editors of *TriContinental* (La Habana, Cuba); Nora Räthzel and the staff of *Das Argument* (Berlin, Germany); Wang Fengzhen of the Institute of Foreign Literature, Academy of Social Sciences, the People's Republic of China; Dr. Erwin Marquit and the staff of *Nature, Society and Thought*; Tom Goodkind and the Editorial Collective of *Forward Motion*; and Csaba Polony, editor of *Left Curve*.

Dr. Delia D. Aguilar of the Department of Ethnic Studies and the Women's Studies Program, Bowling Green State University, provided many ideas and suggestions, as well as timely encouragement, for all of which I am deeply grateful.

E. SAN JUAN, JR.

Introduction

Signs of the times in the last decade: Vigilante gunman Bernhard Goetz catapulted into a folk hero for shooting down four black youth in a New York subway. Fear of Willy Horton, a black inmate, helped elect a president. Blacks killed in Howard Beach in 1986 and Bensonhurst in 1989 in New York City. Racial confrontation in Forsyth County, Georgia. Urban rebellions in 1980, 1982, and 1989 in Miami City, Florida. Antibusing attacks in the early eighties in most big cities. The 1982 murder of Chinese American Vincent Chin mistaken by unemployed Detroit autoworkers for a Japanese. Continuing racist harassment and violence in the universities of Massachusetts, Wisconsin, Michigan, and Connecticut and other prestigious institutions. A man of Ethiopian descent slain in Portland, Oregon, by neo-Nazi skinheads. The scapegoating of the entire Afro-American community in Boston by wife-killer Charles Stuart. The mass murder of five Asian children and wounding of thirty others in Stockton, California, by a white gunman with a hate psychosis. The election to the Louisiana legislature of Republican David Duke, former head of the Ku Klux Klan— our litany of circumstances and events can go on interminably (see Shafer 1990). With the outbreak of war in the Persian Gulf, we witness symptoms of mass hysteria against Arab Americans—in Blissfield, Michigan, to cite one case, a restaurant owned by a Palestinian American couple was first vandalized one week and burned the next (*Time* 4 Feb. 1991). Can one still obscure or dismiss these signs as isolated incidents?

Even Establishment mouthpieces like *Time* and *Newsweek* have repeatedly bewailed the resurgence of blatant racism in the last decade, particularly during the Reagan administration. Once alarming, current trends like the following seem "business as usual": The Justice Department's Community Relations Service (*Time* 2 Feb. 1987) reported that racial attacks have increased from 99 in 1980 to 276 in 1986. Meanwhile, the Boston City Emergency Medical Services Department has amassed data that demonstrate a widespread pattern of racial abuse pervading all sectors of the population (*Newsweek* 5 Jan. 1987), a pattern most quickly apprehended in written/spoken racist vituperation.

Something has gone wrong. Statistical projections indicate that in the first decade of the twenty-first century, the bulk of the U.S. working class will be the racial minorities, peoples of color, who will also be the demographic majority in the big cities. Is the plight of these populations (to use a

1

preferred neutral term)[1] to be gauged by the election of a few black mayors or token Hispanic bureaucrats? Whatever happened to the optimistic prediction in the sixties, after the passage of the Civil Rights Acts and the demise of overt segregation in the South, that the problem of the "color line"—the racial divide that W. E. B. Du Bois invoked as the crucible of Western civilization—would finally be surmounted?

The presidential veto of the 1990 Civil Rights Bill, according to Manning Marable, marks the end of the civil rights movement for democracy in the United States. He cites the shocking deterioration of the situation of African Americans as a whole (1991, 2). Based on data of the National Center for Health Statistics, life expectancy of males has fallen to 64.9 years, below retirement age; black infant mortality rates are twice the white rate; and millions of black women are not receiving adequate prenatal care. Moreover, although blacks comprise only 13 percent of the total population, they now account for 80 percent of all premature deaths (between ages 15 and 44 years) due to abnormally high rates of pneumonia, asthma, bladder infections, and other diseases aggravated by lack of access to regular health care services and affordable health insurance (see *Time* 10 Dec. 1990). Today a black male in Harlem—citizen of one of the most affluent countries in the world—"enjoys" a lower life expectancy than a poor peasant in Bangladesh.

A report by the National Urban League on *The State of Black America* (1985) has documented the persistent and worsening economic gap between blacks and whites: black median income compared to whites' declined from 62 percent in 1975 to 56 percent in 1985. Unemployment of black youth increased from 25 percent in 1960 to 40 percent in 1985. In 1988, 44 percent of all black children and 38 percent of all Hispanic children were living in poverty (Carby 1990, 84). Even more disturbing is the number of blacks in prison. One recent study shows that black males are "incarcerated at a rate four times that of Black males in South Africa [where apartheid is state policy]: 3,109 per 100,000 Black males, compared with 729 under apartheid" (*The Christian Science Monitor* 24 Jan. 1991). These abstractions are further fleshed out in harrowing detail by numerous accounts of "the war on drugs" and "rampant criminality"—code words for the new racism—in the inner cities. We confront a panorama of unmitigated terrorism and deprivation suffered by peoples of color whose logic is trenchantly captured by H. Rap Brown: "Racism is the state religion. Racism is to America what Catholicism is to the Vatican. Racism is the religion, and violence is its liturgy to carry it out" (*Time* 2 Feb. 1987). By "racism" is meant ideas, systems of thought, institutional practices, and all behavior that deterministically ascribe fixed roles and negatively evaluated group characteristics (moral, intellectual, cultural) to peoples on the basis of selected physical attributes whereby their oppression and exploitation are legitimized and perpetuated. I call "racial formation" the sociohistorical field of forces that racism inhabits.

In a recent historical survey entitled *Black Lives, White Lives: Three Decades of Race Relations in America*, Robert Blauner substantiates Rap Brown's rhetoric. He diagnoses how the gains of the sixties and early seventies, despite a temporary material improvement in the lives of African Americans, have not genuinely altered the "common sense" of the majority: whites still reject intermarriage, oppose affirmative action as "reverse racism," and distinguish between "good" (middle-class) and "bad" (poor) blacks (Farber 1990, 31). While many people became exposed to consciousness-raising in the sixties and learned that racial inequality had something to do with slavery, poverty, and institutional discrimination, the vast majority in the seventies had grown tired of "the Black problem" and now blamed individuals belonging to the "underclass" for their continuing degradation. In the eighties, paradoxically, the "color-blind" federal policies of integration had produced a more intense de facto segregation in schools and workplaces. And despite the disguise of racial bias in the more acceptable language of social class, we observe today the "color-blind" life-style of the "silent majority" in the endemic display of bigotry and unrelenting hatred toward peoples of color by middle-class youth in campuses and young working-class whites in urban communities.

Against this background, I interject a personal note: As a Filipino expatriate, an exiled intellectual from a Third World country (the Philippines was the only direct Asian colony of the United States for more than half of this century), I am always warned by ubiquitous circumstances that I exist in a state of permanent indeterminacy. Like more than two million Filipino immigrants and other fellow-traveling "aliens" who share my predicament, I am always asked by the ordinary Euro-American: "Where are you from? Are you going back to the Philippines? Why did you come here?" An intellectual uprooted from the Third World, or from "postcolonial" Commonwealth nations, inhabiting First World sites of confrontation often finds herself straddling boundaries of "elective affinities" and primordial loyalties. We span frontiers of contracts and traditions; we traverse the "no man's land" of the unthinkable, the tabooed and stigmatized; we crisscross borderlines of memories and misrecognitions and hopes. The Third World artist-exile (contradistinguished from the Soviet or East European émigrés) haunts the postmodern map of Western nation-states as a liminal figure as though ironically parodying Joyce, Pound, and Beckett. Nameless, this deracinated figure can transplant herself in almost any environment. Identities can be deconstructed and reconstructed, as the current postmodernist orthodoxy claims, but I think only up to a point. Ineluctable constraints exist, as the latest circulars from the Departments of Justice and of the Treasury would tell you. Not only this. Constraints of the historical pasts, the force of what Bourdieu calls inherited *habitus*, public perceptions maintained by the media and other ideological apparatuses of civil society, the official and received consensus hypostatized as acceptable "commonsense," immigration laws, the routine discourse of business and private occasions— all these no doubt circumscribe the available space and the hospitable occasion in which to invent one's identity by fiat.

In this book I explore the complex interaction between constraints and opportunities and its aesthetic inscriptions in the larger totality. This totality is characterized by a continuous decentering of a still disputed national space, by a condensation of temporal sequences into points of crisis and contestation. Because the Third World consciousness inhabiting U.S. space is an identity always in crisis, the subaltern's presence constantly generates questions about foundational axioms which might strike the law-abiding citizen as merely trendy topics for elite circles. But for "the Others," these are life-and-death questions for beleaguered millions who perform the alienating chores of everyday life in business society. Here are some of them rehearsed in an ad hoc sequence: Is identity simply a matter of positionality, of semiotic/discursive construction? Is ethnic consciousness central or subordinate to the problematic of racial categorization? Should we valorize "lived experience" more than systematic knowledge? Or is this relative to stages and conjunctures of the struggle? Is multicultural or pluralist ideology the way to recuperate sensibilities disintegrated by the labor market? Is the search for roots in ethnic writing still a viable enterprise? Or is that organically indivisible from the overarching project of cultural self-determination for besieged nationalities caught "in the belly of the beast"? How are gender and class determinants calibrated into the quest for cultural autonomy? How can we conceive of difference without fetishizing it by a separatist and ultimately hedonistic, self-canceling politics of identity? Is liberalism bankrupt in overcoming racism? How should peoples of color reaffirm themselves when identity is now supposedly untenable, without any truth-value? What price alterity/Otherness? These questions, articulated in various philosophical contexts and plotted in manifold literary expressions, comprise the most salient themes I address in this book. A few preliminary remarks may be helpful at this juncture in order to establish the parameters of my inquiry.

It is now an acknowledged truism that the configuration of U.S. politics from the time of the early settlement, the struggle over what sector or social bloc will be privileged to articulate the national identity and exercise hegemony over the body politic, has been mediated through the language of race. This has been massively documented in such works like Thomas

Gossett's *Race: The History of an Idea in America* (1963), Reginald Horsman's *Race and Manifest Destiny: The Origins of American Racial Anglo-Saxonism* (1981), in the persuasive writings of Eugene Genovese, Herbert Gutman, George Frederickson, Stanley Lieberson, Howard Zinn, and others. This theme of a racializing national telos and its institutional relay in the disciplinary regime of the humanities serves as one of the organizing principles of the essays collected in this volume. It is presupposed by my principal argument, elaborated in the first two chapters, that race, not ethnicity, is the explanatory and hermeneutic concept needed to describe the heterogeneous terrain of conflicting cultures in the United States. Race, not ethnicity, articulates with class and gender to generate the effects of power in all its multiple protean forms. Ethnicity theory elides power relations, conjuring an illusory state of parity among bargaining agents. It serves chiefly to underwrite a functionalist mode of sanctioning a given social order. It tends to legitimize a pluralist but hierarchical status quo. Ellis Cashmore (1984) correctly points out that while ethnicity designates a collective sense of shared experiences underlying group solidarity, a sense of inclusiveness which grounds identity (*ethnos* etymologically denotes people or nation), race implicates peoples and social structures in historical processes of dissociation and exclusion that have distinguished the trajectory of Western civilization particularly since the European colonization of the Middle East, Africa, Asia, and the Americas.

What orients this disjunction of ethnicity and race in this work is the following fundamental insight. From its inception, the United States has been distinguished as a sociohistorical formation with specific racial dynamics. It was contoured by the expulsion of American Indian nations from their homelands and their genocidal suppression, an inaugural and recursive phenomenon followed by the enslavement of millions of Africans, the dispossession of Mexicans, the subjection of Asians, and so on. The historical origin of the United States as a nation-state, traditionally defined by the revolutionary Enlightenment principles enunciated by the "Founding Fathers," cannot be understood without this genocidal foundation. "Race" came to signify the identities of social groups in struggle for resources: land, labor power, and their fruits. Ultimately then, the struggle for command over time/space and the positioning of bodies in this North American habitat politicized the social order and set the course for the future.

Racial categorization thus became the principle of exclusion and inclusion that continues to inform and reinforce all other social antagonisms. In countering Nathan Glazer's thesis that the United States was a "nation of free individuals" from the very beginning, Ronald Takaki (1987) cogently delineates the "racial patterns" that have shaped the polity from the time the Naturalization Law of 1790 denied citizenship to nonwhites (in effect up to

1952). Contrary to the commonsense belief propagated by mainstream academic scholarship that the experience of white European ethnics is the universal paradigm of success applicable to all racial minorities, Takaki insists on the unequivocal record: "But only blacks were enslaved, only Native Americans were removed to reservations, only Chinese were singled out for exclusion, and only Japanese Americans (not Italian Americans or German Americans) were placed in concentration camps" (7). Whenever the Empire is confronted with challenges from subjugated nationalities and transported subjects, the violence of law and order falls down heavily on racially identified victims who were seized in the periphery or domesticated in the metropolis.

Especially after the Civil War and the making of great fortunes in the late nineteenth-century period of industrialization, the history of the United States has been and continues to be narrated as the success story of white European immigrants. Instead of race, ethnicity is the term used by academic scholars today to codify the conventional belief in the virtue of assimilation, the gradual homogenizing of diverse groups predicated on value consensus ("the American Creed") and the norm of social integration.[2] In this sense, "Americanization" virtually means cultural and psychological suicide for peoples of color. It was not until the urban rebellions of the "internal colonies" (ghetto, barrio, reservation) in the late sixties that the centrality of race in the preservation and reproduction of the U.S. social order came to be recognized in the burning district of Watts, Los Angeles; and in the streets of Detroit, Chicago, New York City, Atlanta, Miami, and elsewhere. (I hasten to interpose here that I use the term "race" in this book to denote a social construct, a historical conceptualization of how the U.S. social formation was structured in dominance by the construction of every inhabitant as a racialized subject. Not to do so is to lapse unconscionably into racist thinking and practice, whatever one's humanitarian intent.) Herman George (1984) inter alia locates the inspiration for the discovery of the race/power nexus in the black struggle for self-determination and cultural autonomy in the sixties and early seventies. From this perspective, conflict was no longer limited to "the quarrels over the distribution of valued attributes within routinized channels" (185); it was now concerned with interrogating hierarchical, monopolized power. In this connection, I explore the ramifications of the "internal colony" paradigm and its interface with the Marxist approach to racism in the third chapter.

One of the seminal insights of a class-conscious black nationalism, as elaborated for instance in the inaugural classic text of Third World insurgency, George Jackson's *Soledad Brother* (1970), is the contradictory nature of a racist formation: while dividing the working class, it also fertilizes the ground for an oppositional cultural practice that would challenge the logic of racial hegemony. By definition, such hegemony implies a degree of "free space," however illusory, conceded to the ruled. Contradictions involve positive and negative forces reciprocally determining each other. Violence cannot suppress the "negative" without which inequality cannot be reproduced. Inequality has thus engendered the resistance of black slaves, of Chinese and Filipino workers, and so forth. Racism begets its opposite. Lucius Outlaw (1990) underscores the complex tradition of black nationalism which has sought to define African Americans as a people by "identifying and nurturing [their] characteristics, and the institutions and practices that generate, shape, sustain, and mediate them" (75). To denounce the struggles of peoples of color for cultural autonomy as a symptom of neo–social Darwinism is as reactionary as to claim that ethnic pluralism or multiculturalism (which I discuss in Chapter 5 and the Afterword) is the single master narrative required to liberate peoples of color from systemic exploitation.[3] Obviously we need a more dialectically nuanced comprehension of the changes in the modality of capital's self-reproductive rule as well as a sophisticated understanding of the metamorphosis of liberal-democratic ideology for countering the racisms of the next century.

With the shift in the social climate beginning with the end of the Vietnam War in 1975, neoconservatism and the New Right forces succeeded in constructing a social bloc that implemented an authoritarian populist program under the banner of "traditional American values." The themes of individual rights, market rationality, anti-statism, and laissez-faire liberalism were deployed in a universalizing strategy to decontextualize race and institute a project of reinforcing the individualist ethos. This is the central argument of Michael Omi and Howard Winant's innovative study *Racial Formation in the United States From the 1960s to the 1980s* (more on this in Chapter 3). This work examines the growth and development of the neoconservative and New Right movements, focusing on their strategies of achieving hegemony through the articulation of race and class in the direction of a neoclassical political economy of individual competition. Omi and Winant (1986) propose a theory of postmodern racial formation, conceiving race as "an unstable and 'decentered' complex of social meanings constantly being transformed by political struggle" (68–69). In their view, the concept of racial formation is the site of political contestation where racial meanings are fought over, negotiated, displaced, and transformed. Race can no longer be considered a fixed, ontological essence or a unitary, transcendental category predicated on the epistemological reasoning supplied by anthropology, biology, and other physical sciences. Rather it is a framework for articulating identity and difference, a process that governs the political and ideological constitution of subjects/agents in history.

We are therefore infinitely far removed from the time when race as a category of classification was first used by eighteenth-century thinkers like Linnaeus, Blumenbach, Cuvier, Buffon, Montesquieu, Voltaire, Kant, and Hume—each adding contingent qualifications—to explain human differences. But we need to go back farther. Even before the rise of modern science in the Renaissance and the Enlightenment, the mythology of Christianity had already established the groundwork for the exercise of dualistic, Manichaean thinking via the symbolism of color ("somatic norm image," in sociological jargon). Roger Bastide is the scholar who has traced the roots of segregation, the "frontier complex" of apartheid, in the Calvinist idea of predestination and the contagiousness of sin connoted by dark pigmentation (1977, 286–97). More influential on such humanists like Voltaire and Goethe was the belief in polygenesis (the myth of the separate origins of Adamite and pre-Adamite races) which prepared the way for the pseudoscientific teachings of the craniologist Dr. Samuel Morton and biological determinists like Louis Agassiz, precursors of contemporary advocates of racial hierarchy like Jensen, Shockley, and Herrnstein (Popkin 1974, 140–53; Banton 1987, 1–18). In the time of the Enlightenment and the Industrial Revolution, a mode of typological thinking emerged that tried to distinguish varieties of *Homo sapiens* employing a logic based on a postulated "natural" hierarchy of groups. This ranking is premised in turn on rationality (as posited by Greek metaphysics), the possession of the rational capacity as what essentially demarcates humans from animals. This conflation of physical and intellectual/moral characteristics becomes systematized later on in Joseph-Arthur de Gobineau's *Essay on the Inequality of Human Races* (1854).[4] With Darwin and Mendel, the notion of stable pure racial types is replaced with organically evolving species influenced by the force of natural selection. Adapted by sociologists Herbert Spencer and Ludwig Gumplowicz to explain social change (the origin of social Darwinism), Darwin's theory served primarily to rank racial groups in an ascending scale based on their supposed development toward successful human adaptation: from primitive to civilized, from underdeveloped to industrially developed or advanced societies.

In the absence of a "utopian moral vision of a racially egalitarian society" informing any social movement in the United States today, some commentators have noted a pervasive climate of neo–social Darwinism. This has allegedly infected a renascent black nationalism growing in the face of an eroded welfare-state liberalism and the ascendancy of white middle-class reaction (Watts 1990, 4). Realizing that integration has only promoted the interest of a tiny fraction of the middle class at the expense of a large disadvantaged majority, black leaders now call for ethnic solidarity, a strategy of self-help to achieve "the group's just aspiration toward self-determination, self-governance and self-respect" (Muwakkil 1990). They call for rebuilding the community's integral institutions and mobilizing politico-economic initiatives of reconstruction. This is definitely not just a reflex reaction to neo–social Darwinism. What we are witnessing here is the urge for a renewal of the dynamic social movements of the sixties which accompanied the incalculably profound revitalization of organized cultural projects for the affirmation of dignity and the fundamental right of self-determination for peoples of color.[5]

We are not, however, returning exactly to the historical conjuncture of the sixties which saw the birth of the Black Panther Party, the Puerto Rican Young Lords, the Chicano La Raza Unida Party, and the American Indian Movement. Suffice it to say that history returns . . . but only with an incommensurable difference. One indication is the appearance of new languages and discourses of racism in consonance with the evolution of a post-Fordist and post-Keynesian dispensation (Harvey 1989, 141–97).

Logos follows praxis. Sometime in the eighteenth century Western rationalism, more precisely scientistic positivism, established the paradigm of modern racism: the reduction of the cultural to the biological, an axiomatics of biologism that operated to legitimize the colonial control and subjugation of Third World peoples. While demystifying new versions of racism as caricatures of rationalism, Christian Delacampagne (1990), however, ascribes to Western culture the invention of rationalism (is there just one?) and the concept of human rights. One can countrapose to this Samir Amin's *Eurocentrism* and his view that Western universalism and its theology of the "free market" has produced and continues to produce genocide (1989, 112–14). In addition, Richard Popkin has painstakingly traced the philosophical basis of modern racism in the supersession of Christian/Biblical dogmas by Enlightenment thought such as John Locke's notion of natural rights based on the human capacity to create property (1974, 126–65; see also Puzzo 1964, 579–86).

From the conception of the putatively unified Cartesian ego to the Lockean property owner, it is only a step to the folk understanding of equality as the "American Creed" popularized by Gunnar Myrdal's often-quoted study *An American Dilemma* (1944). Myrdal's peculiar notion of caste applied to the American scene has been questioned by Oliver Cox, Louis Dumont, and others. While modern social science has repudiated the use of "race" as a scientific concept to measure cultural and intellectual worth—see the various official statements of the United Nations on race—a persistent *habitus* of conceiving group diversity may be discerned whenever moral, ethical, and aesthetic judgments of value are made, as Dumont (1966) reflects:

In the modern Western world not only are citizens free and equal
before the law, but a transition develops, at least in popular mentality,
from the moral principle of equality to the belief in the basic identity of all
men, because they are no longer taken as samples of a culture, a society or
a social group, but as *individuals* existing in and for themselves. In other
words, the recognition of a cultural difference can no longer ethnocentri-
cally justify inequality. But it is observed that in certain circumstances,
which it would be necessary to describe, a hierarchical difference continues to be posited, which is this time attached to somatic characteristics,
physiognomy, color of the skin, 'blood.' No doubt, these were at all times
marks of distinction, but they have now become the essence of it.
How is this to be explained? It is perhaps apposite to recall that we are
heirs to a dualistic religion and philosophy: the distinction between
matter and spirit, body and soul, permeates our entire culture and spe-
cially the popular mentality. Everything looks as if the egalitarian-
identitarian mentality was situated within this dualism, as if once
equality and identity bear on the individual souls, distinction could
only be effected with regard to the *bodies*. What is more, discrimination
is collective, it is as if only physical characteristics were essentially collective whence everything mental tends to be primarily individual.
(Thus mental differences are attributed to physical types.) Is this far-
fetched? It is only emphasizing the Christian ancestry of modern individualism and egalitarianism: the individual has only fellow-men (even
his enemies are considered not only as objects but also as subjects), and
he believes in the fundamental equality of all men taken severally; at
the same time, for him, the collective inferiority of a category of men,
when it is in his interest to state it, is expressed and justified in terms
of what physically differentiates them from himself and people of his
group. To sum up, the proclamation of equality has burst asunder a
mode of distinction centered upon the social, but in which physical,
cultural and social characteristics were indiscriminately mixed. To
reaffirm inequality, the underlying dualism demanded that physical
characteristics be brought to the fore. (255–56)

Because of this fixation in the dualism of mind and body, psychological
research in the cause of racism has often focused on prejudice and attitudes
(see Loewenberg 1989). Anthony Wilden (1972) has shown that the
metaphysical dualism entailed by the transcendental categories of binary
oppositions—inclusion/exclusion, Self/Other, either/or—are fabrications
of what Hegel calls "the understanding" and therefore "illegitimate abstractions from sensuous experience" which are altogether absent in nature and
in the mind (413–29). Binary thinking evinced in racist discourse reflects
"the social ideology of the survival of the fittest" (424) which sustains, at
the same time as it is nourished by, the political economy of class-divided
societies.

I should like to underscore here my caveat that given the sociohistorical contextualization of race relations, racism cannot be judged merely as a psychological reflex, a pattern of conduct induced by wrong ideas, beliefs, and sentiments. Against this psychologistic tendency, which functions as the rationale of virtually all educational reforms sponsoring the ideal of ethnic pluralism, multicultural diversity, and other reformist panaceas, Joel Kovel (1984) points out quite cogently that racist violence (in contrast to recent sociobiological experiments on genetically influenced behavior) cannot be divorced from the structured totality of the U.S. political economy (177–230). He criticizes the reigning ego-dominated psychoanalytic practice that has undercut to some extent the historical thrust of his quite exceptional, provocative study *White Racism*.

In his 1983 preface to a reissue of his work, Kovel reiterates his thesis that the integral American self has been constituted historically by its violation of Others (the fantasized reduction of peoples of color to the sinful, excremental body from which the Self has to be purified). Others are first treated as dirt, beasts, then things to be bought and sold; and, in our intensively and extensively administered society, items to be indexed and filed. The totality of U.S. social relations, for Kovel, is thoroughly racist, but the forms of racism have varied in time and place. Relations with Others are embodied in specific material practices of domination and subordination that constitute the abstractive, dehumanized, property-centered world in which we live. Dominative racism characterizing the antebellum South had been replaced by aversive racism (covert liberal practices) after the Civil War. Today, however, the predominant form is what Kovel calls "metaracism" where social and economic inequalities are rendered normal through bureaucratic, technological, quantifying mechanisms of control. Race as the mystifying logic of Otherness coincides with a programmed centralized system based on exchange-value: the production, circulation, and consumption of commodified Others. Cognizant of the imperial drive of the Western psyche to master nature and in the process subjugate peoples within or outside the metropolis, Kovel concludes that racism in all its varieties is "the subjective reflex of imperialism, the fate of primary tendencies of alienation under the domination of the imperial state" (li). Consequently, to restore peoples' rights to fully determine their own histories, it is imperative to destroy the material foundations that breed and recycle the ideology, discourse, and cultural practices of racism.

In the past two decades, Third World intellectuals like Stuart Hall and Cornel West have made a breakthrough in the theoretical impasse of confining racism simply to economic exploitation. West (1990) has urged a genealogical inquiry into cultural practices of domination/subjugation to supplement macrostructural critiques of political repression. He calls for inter alia "a microinstitutional or localized analysis of the mechanisms that sustain white supremacist discourse in the everyday life of non-Europeans (including the ideological production of certain kinds of selves, the means by which alien and degrading normative cultural styles, aesthetic ideals, psychosexual identities, and group perceptions are constituted) and ways in which resistance occurs." These genealogical investigations into sociocultural practices are designed to complement analyses concentrating on key structural constraints linked to modes of production, the state, bureaucratic modes of control, and so on. West asserts his fundamental premise that "racist practices directed against black, brown, yellow, and red people are an integral element of U.S. history, including present-day American culture and society. This means not simply that Americans have inherited racist attitudes and prejudices but, more importantly, that institutional forms of racism are embedded in American society in both visible and invisible ways" (see Aronowitz 1981, 89–100).

Postmodern critiques of racism have decisively shifted attention away from empirical methodologies to scrutiny of the foundational assumptions of Western rationality. They examine how representation works, how subjects are constituted by power imbricated in the material practice of discourses and institutional structures. They investigate how disciplinary regimes of truth/knowledge production regulate bodies and determine actions. To cite one example: in an ambitious endeavor to anatomize "the social formation of racist discourse" by applying Foucault's archaeological analytic, David Goldberg (1990) discerns the unity of racist discourse to inhere in "differential exclusion" which he considers "the most basic primitive term of the deep structure definitive of racist discourse. As the basic propositional content of racist desires, dispositions, beliefs, hypotheses, and expressions (including acts, laws, and institutions), racial exclusion motivates the entire superstructure of racist discourse" (304). Although qualified by reminders that the rules and norms of such discourse are historically derived (epitomized by South African apartheid and other "adjacencies"), Goldberg's grammar of racist discourse seems partially vitiated by a positivist formalism which also conditions the pursuit of a primordial matrix of racist thought such as Dumont's. Another liability is that Foucault's knowledge/power perspectivism posits the constitution of a subject wholly determined by the antihermeneutic principles of an archaeology open to instrumentalist reduction (Dews 1987, 214–15). It thus forfeits the opportunity of theorizing a historical agent of resistance which Goldberg regards as a desideratum in any research program professing to overthrow racist discourse and practice.

In a recent study on racism (1989), Robert Miles proposes a more historically specific diagnosis of racialization and racism as processes of signification with ethical implications and political consequences. He focuses on "ideological articulation" of racial themes and motifs in various conjunctures, using the vicissitudes of the "White Australia" policy as an illuminating case study. The concept of ideology as one level of an overdetermined social totality, a seminal hypothesis first elaborated by the French philosopher Louis Althusser, has been most fruitfully deployed by Stuart Hall and his colleagues in the Centre for Contemporary Cultural Studies, University of Birmingham, in their action-oriented analysis of racism in Britain and the Caribbean.

While not completely rejecting genealogical and deconstructive modes of analyzing racism, I think we need a dialectical approach to suture history and consciousness together in order to highlight the possibilities of active resistance. Semiotic debunking is highly educational but not enough. Roland Barthes' (1979) semioclastic staging of racist discourse in "Bichon and the Blacks" (35–38) and "African Grammar" (103–9) might prove to be valuable pedagogical weapons, but they lack the circumstantial frames for actualizing their effectivity. Racist discourse can be most concretely grasped only if it is conceived as articulated in a complex differentiated social structure composed of relations of dominance and subordination. This approach requires two interdependent procedures. Racism as an ideological and political phenomenon has to be grounded first "in the material conditions of existence," the network of modes of production and interacting ideological and political levels. Second, the specific form of relations involving racial categories or concepts must be situated in the historical conjuncture that would endow this form with their *differentia specifica*, thus avoiding economistic reductionism, historical relativism, or sociological pluralism. One example of this approach can be illustrated by Errol Lawrence's (1982) analysis of contemporary British racism as an institutional discursive practice in which historical agencies and cultural traditions converge to produce historically specific racisms. Many have noted that contemporary racist practice has replaced biological or genetic invocations with functional equivalents announced in such seemingly innocuous themes and leitmotifs as "our way of life," national heritage, free choices, and so forth (see Barker 1990; Gilroy 1990).

In the United States, following the lead of Glazer, Murray, and other opponents of affirmative action, a new racist discourse has been popularized. Shelby Steele, a black professor of English, has gained notoriety by blaming African Americans for their peculiar syndrome of "racial anxiety-distortion-reenactment" which accounts for their poor performance, low income, etc., in a laissez-faire economy (1989, 51; see Leone 1978, 152–59). This updated version of "blaming the victim" displays both continuity and discontinuity with outmoded discursive forms of racism; its efficacy can only be explained by the uneven, qualitative changes in the milieu which intimate how negotiations of compromises transpire. Its distorted picture of the world where victims are either animalized and robotized, simply mimicking the master's repertoire, has been countered by Walter Rodney (1972), Manning Marable (1983), Arthur Brittan and Mary Maynard (1984, 100–106), and others who all accent the process of self-awakening, mutual cooperation, and revolt. Mapping the itinerary of what Hegel in *The Phenomenology of Spirit* conceives as the master–slave dialectic, and harnessing the notions of hegemony and of the concrete analysis of contradictory forces first crafted by Gramsci, I examine the modernist and postmodernist theories of ethnic literary production in Chapter 4, offering afterward a sketch of my own semiotic model for heuristic, consciousness-raising purposes.

A recent collection of essays entitled *The Invention of Ethnicity* (1989) tries to rehabilitate the prevalent paradigm of "ethnicity" by infusing it with a deconstructive élan. "Ethnicity" becomes the label for an invented, fictional, locally blueprinted process of identification based on "dissociation," "antagonistic acculturation," and so forth (Sollors 1989, x, xv). While this view claims that it seeks neither pure "ethnic consciousness" nor "assimilation," the attempt, I think, is seriously compromised because its paradigm of liberal modernization fails to recognize its limitations, the most fundamental of which is its erasure of the totalizing system of exploitation and its racial dynamics. Likewise, it fails to perceive in literary forms the coding of the operations of power linked to property relations, in particular the racializing of the social order by prejudiced ascription of roles and rights over and beyond ethnic disparities.

In a review of dominant trends in cultural studies today, Richard Johnson (1987) surveys the site of its future development in the cross-fertilizing interaction between three modes: production-based studies, text-based studies, and studies of lived cultures. In the United States, various styles of poststructuralist analysis have explored the linguistics and semiotics of regional discourses: sexuality, ecology, and so on. While orthodox Marxists and the "new historicism" have focused on production in both macro and micro senses, postmodernizing anthropologists (see, for example, Clifford and Marcus 1986) have charted the fraught dialectic between participant observer and target culture, syncopating vocabularies and tonalities in order to foster respect for indigenous differences. What is missing in these approaches is the racial dimension, its potential as a mediating and synthesizing force. Given the specificity of the historical development of the U.S. formation that I have outlined earlier, the articulation of race with class, gender, and other sectoral issues is central to the political struggle for hegemony. That is because Others are constituted racially so as to provide a mode of totalizing the "United States" as a homogeneous nation-state, a self-evident, structured, and cohesive polity. "Ethnicity" is the official rubric to designate the phenomenological plurality of peoples ranked in a hierarchy for the differential allocation and distribution of resources. This hierarchy in turn is guaranteed by the taken-for-granted doctrines of liberal democracy premised on individual competition, the right to acquire property and sell labor power, and so on. It is this liberal ideology that underwrites the theoretical claims of the New Criticism, psychoanalysis, and recent forms of "cultural studies" consorting with feminism, reader response, new pragmatism, and so forth.

As we enter the twenty-first century, the problematic (in Althusser's sense) of ethnicity is bound to be overtaken by a politics of racial articulation sublimated in the proxy languages of "culture," "underclass," "meritocracy," "neo–social Darwinism," and so on. In such an eventuality, literary studies will then have to be oriented around the transfigurations of the racial signifier if a genuinely popular-democratic agenda in the humanistic disciplines is to be addressed. Otherwise, in a time when the demonology of anticommunism can no longer provide an index of national identity—as I suggest in the Afterword—the counterhegemonic project of autonomy may remain a commodified ideal "always already" manipulated for subliminal as well as gross consumption in the global supermall.

From the time of the Elizabethan Age's preoccupation with Moors, Jews, and especially the colonial prototype Caliban in Shakespeare's *The Tempest*, up to Walter Scott's *Ivanhoe*, Cooper's *Leatherstocking Tales*, Melville's *Moby Dick*, and so on, race has served as an obsessive theme in Western writing. But thematics is not the only crucial arena where race intervenes. Alluding to "racially understood ethnicity" exemplified by Afro-American literary criticism, Kwame Anthony Appiah (1990) stresses the irrelevance of ethnicity when he deals with the debate on the standard Eurocentric canon: "The politics of Anglo-Saxonist nationalism excluded Afro-American culture from the official American canon, and the politics of race relations inevitably structures discussion of their *inclusion*" (287). Approximating the commitment of romantic nationalists like Herder and naturalists like Taine, W. E. B. Du Bois dreamed of a revitalized tradition of black letters, a gesture of recuperating submerged African glory which partly anticipates the speculations of Houston Baker and Henry Louis Gates on a vernacular, indigenizing poetics. It is not wholly implausible to construe the extrapolated community of the nation as the crucial link between literary production and racial politics, as Appiah surmises (282). In any case, throughout this book, I argue against the culturalist abuse of "ethnicity" to mask hegemonic domination under the pretext of pluralist tolerance. In Chapter 5, I try to read "race" as an articulation of power relations rendered in specific texts by Asian American writers. In particular, I attempt to show how the production of an antinomic racial identity is mediated through a critique of the episteme of exchange-value, in particular the circuit of production, exchange, and accumulation of symbolic capital. It is this circuit that needs to be elucidated because it functions as the condition of possibility of the world labor market, and thus of immigration, gender and racial differentiation, and class polarity, as well as the enabling motive-force of beliefs concerning individual freedom, private ownership of social wealth, the mystery of the unconscious, and so on.

The issue of exactly what is at stake in the modernism-versus-postmodernism controversy among Western theoreticians (principally Lyotard and Habermas) seems to have eclipsed the return of the repressed: the multiplicity of racial subjects in the United States and in Europe, even in Japan where migrant Third World workers suffer one of the worst treatments on record anywhere. Parallel with this are the emergent narratives of other peoples of color in the peripheries of the "free world" empire. In dissolving the subject as possible agent of critical transformation, postmodernism ignores those developments and apologizes for the status quo. Lyotard's privileging of difference may allow space for aleatory ruptures and novel language games, but his anarchic stance both presumes and ignores the totalizing *grands recits* he is challenging: late capitalist strategies of low-intensity warfare in El Salvador, Palestine, South Africa, and the Philippines, as well as the historically unprecedented high-tech warfare and the U.N.–sanctioned terror of saturation bombing unleashed on Iraq. On the other hand, Habermas' project of revitalizing the Enlightenment ideals of modernity seeks to preserve a vision of a liberating humanistic synthesis of cognitive, moral, and aesthetic discourses. Secular modernism dangles out a seductive prize, indeed. But Habermas' task is undermined by evading or leaping over the historical complicity of modernist thought in the Euro-American imperialist barbarism inflicted on colonial subjects in Africa, Asia, and Latin America. Postmodernism can easily disguise the repressive hegemony of transnational consumerism and the International Monetary Fund (IMF)–World Bank "civilizing mission" concealed in slogans trumpeting "inexhaustible heterogeneity and unassimilated otherness" so facilely celebrated by Baudrillard and his cult (Connor 1989, 50–62). We wonder how these Others, millions of them, are faring in the slums of Mexico City, Rio de Janeiro, Johannesburg, Bangkok, Harlem, and elsewhere.

Coinciding with late capitalist retrenchment and a "New World Order" ushered in the wake of the crumbling of transcendental foundations is the emergence of racial subjects from multiple loci of resistance in the United

States, Britain, South Africa, and in the far-flung outposts of the corporate monopolies' empire. This can be interpreted as a response to the accelerating impact of reification in the world market as well as the persisting commodification of space-time whose mutations have been perceptively described by David Harvey in *The Condition of Postmodernity* (1989, 327–59). Heterogeneity, dialogic "free play," and intractable aporias can be comprehended only as negations of the systematic racial order lived through by the Others: American Indians, African Americans, Chicanos, Asians, Puerto Ricans, West Indians, and countless more. But this dialectical insight presupposes the discovery of community and a subaltern tradition of subversion that informs it. In Chapter 5 and also in the Afterword, I demonstrate what that proposition signifies with the example of the Filipino community and its experience of struggle dramatized in the writings of Carlos Bulosan. In the Philippines itself, a classic Third World neocolony, the refusal of the postmodern "eclecticism" of money underwritten by transnational corporations manifests itself in the insurrectionary praxis of women's collectives, armed cultural activists in the guerilla zones, writers involved in trade union organizing, and artists in the embattled homelands of the Igorot and Moro peoples, more than ten million strong, who daily combat the forces of transnational capital and its native servitors.

A new theorizing of the concept of historic agency is surely needed to discover the asymmetrical Other of a world system produced and reproduced by processes of inclusion and exclusion. Again I envisage here not so much an empirical subject in the making as a whole racial formation, a constellation of forces and processes, which is properly the "bearer" of radical social change. This theoretical task has so far been neglected. I suspect that the main obstacles (as I try to explain in Chapter 3) involve, among others, the economistic and mechanical reductionism of intellectuals burdened with their pragmatic heritage. The task is also inhibited by the obscurantist, superficial, and ultimately trivializing effect of the ethnicity model appraised in Chapters 1, 2, and 4.

One hopes that the theorizing of a racial formation may open up the space for charting new paths of resistance against the disciplinary regimes of a world system of accumulation thriving on fragmentation, nomadic free play, pragmatic relativism, and "acephalous" or "rhizomatic" experiments of all kinds. The praxis of this collective racial subject-in-process (to use Julia Kristeva's phrase) in fact seeks to interrogate the hegemonic discourse of Western postmodernism and its claim to liberate everyone from panoptic power and the metaphysics of logocentrism. The academic slogan of "multi-ethnic literature" addressed in Chapters 1 and 5 can now be replaced with a conceptualization of antiracist discourse as a project of mobilizing versatile agents of transformation (to be distinguished from a politics of identity, inward salvation, narcissistic catharsis, and so forth criticized in Chapter 5). Within the free market of subjectivities and floating signifiers (the most fashionable being the mana of *différance*), the split Other which we have encountered before in Fanon, Sartre, and Lacan can be judged as an outflanking maneuver of transnational capital to adapt itself to a post-Fordist, post-Keynesian accumulation strategy. And around the "weak links" of this strategy, I hold that it is possible to seize conjunctural opportunities for disruption, recovery of lost ground, and carnivalesque renewals of all kinds. I have in mind an agenda whose reach, variety, and scope are exemplified by, among others, the problematizing montage of public and private selves in Maxine Hong Kingston's quasi-allegorical fiction;[6] the prophetic and dissonant realism initiated by Filipino expatriate artists; the visionary pastoral inversions in Chicano and American Indian narratives; and the "multiplex enabling script" of the blues vernacular deciphered and retooled by Houston Baker. All these interventions by peoples of color can be seen to converge as a multipronged campaign to mount a counterhegemonic attack on the sovereign rule of exchange-value, commodity-fetishism, and the liberal marketplace. It is an attack on the racializing machine of the state that paradoxically energizes the postmodern elite's drive for world domination in the name of individual freedom, avant-garde pluralism, laissez-faire desire, and mass fantasies of self-fulfillment through endless consumption.

What are the signs heralding the advent of this new praxis? The most hopeful testimony of a new initiative for a popular democratic program at a time when the "overconsumptionist logic" of the middle strata is nearing exhaustion is Jesse Jackson's Rainbow Coalition experiment. I think this multiracial coalition constitutes a major challenge to the reactionary racial formation of the past three decades whose symptoms are detailed in my opening paragraphs. In *Prisoners of the American Dream* (1986), Mike Davis provides an excellent background to Jackson's challenge. He observes how the end of the Rooseveltian epoch of reform based on the integrative capacities of a Fordist mass consumption economy also spelled the phasing out of the minimal democratic program of the civil rights movement (equal housing, equal employment, equal political representation). Given the tendency of capital accumulation to reproduce the unequal distribution of political and social power and shift resources from social programs to the military and its imperial global needs, the liberal agenda remains unfulfilled. What is required now is a transformation from the grass roots up of the decaying racially stratified order. Davis believes that the revived struggle for equality will follow from the "mobilization of the radical political propensities within the Black—and, perhaps, Hispanic—working classes" (311–12). Any political strategy concentrating on the axial problem of the revolutionary-democratic struggle for equality must be built on the "increasing solidarity between the liberation movement in Southern Africa and Latin America and the movements of the Black and Hispanic communities in the USA" (313).

In the wake of the massive catastrophe visited on the Persian Gulf nations, harbinger of a fragile and precarious "New World Order," I would endorse Davis' foregrounding of Rainbow Coalition politics as the key to any viable, realistic dismantling and overhaul of the moribund system:

> as the shrinkage of the gender gap in the [1984] election indirectly showed, no matter how important feminist consciousness must be in shaping a socialist culture in America, racism remains the divisive issue within class and gender. There can be no such thing as a serious reformist politics, much less an effective socialist practice, that does not frontally address the struggle against racism and defend the full program of a Second Reconstruction. . . . It is no disparagement of the existing anti-nuclear and anti-intervention movements to insist that the real weak link in the domestic base of American imperialism is a Black and Hispanic working class, fifty million strong. This is the nation within a nation, society within a society, that alone possesses the numerical and positional strength to undermine the American empire from within. (299, 313–14)

Impelled by the irreversible flow of enormously complex contradictions, the present racial formation of late transnational capitalism can either regress to fascist barbarism, this time even with "kinder and gentler" visage, or it can stagnate further. . . . Or else it can progress toward a more egalitarian, deracializing stage more responsive to the needs and demands of, as well as more accountable to, peoples of color who will be the majority in the twenty-first century. Do we have another choice?

Finally I conclude with this emergency meditation. In exploring the interaction between Western ideology and the lives of peoples of color, between majority-hegemonic and minority-decolonizing cultures, between Third World writing and the canonical performance of interpretation and critical judgment, I position myself in a planetary ecosystem whose bearings can be calculated from existing landmarks such as: South Africa's still functioning apartheid; the drug traffic between Latin American warlords and their U.S. cabal of accessories; the persistence of popular-democratic nationalist projects in Nicaragua and all over South America; the unprecedented diaspora of labor power from the Philippines, Thailand, Bangladesh, and elsewhere; the breakup of statist "socialism" in Eastern Europe and the Soviet Union; and finally, the explosion of a geopolitical, racialized war (aggravated by tensions among religious fundamentalisms) in the Middle East coalescing with the prospect of a "New World Order" where Germany and Japan and their Middle Eastern middlemen with their moneybags full of petrodollars subsidize the mercenary forces of a new *pax Americana*. In this transitional passage, the wandering subaltern—incarnate specter of all the dispossessed!—can certainly speak. Utterance is hers for, as Marx has pointed out in that still unsurpassed treatise on race and human freedom, "On the Jewish Question," the ambiguous catalyzing power of "the stranger" (Simmel's name for the subaltern) is enabled precisely by the modes of resistance using cunning, humor, and subterfuge recuperable from the inertia and technocratic vertigo of modern civil society. In any case, I submit that the urgent concerns about participation "from below" are succinctly captured by such questions as: If we are to speak, under what conditions? Who chooses the time and place? Who sets up the rules? In what language? For whose interests? And to whom? The following chapters aim to contribute to a reconaissance of the historical conditions required for peoples of color in the United States to be able to speak, act, and make changes on their own terms.

Notes

1. The anthropologist Ashley Montagu prefers the term "population" to "race": "For all general purposes, an 'ethnic group' may be defined as one of a number of breeding populations, which populations together comprise the species *Homo sapiens*, and which individually maintain their differences, physical or genetic and cultural, by means of isolating mechanisms such as geographic and social barriers" (1982, 62). The maintenance of differences, however, disrupts the claim of the term "population" as antiseptic, neutral, and value-free.
2. Even in this postmodern age of "flexible accumulation," Anglo assimilationism is still alive, as attested to by a 1986 testimony to the Joint Economic Committee of Congress cited in *Population Bulletin* (November 1986): 35.
3. Cultural pluralism should not be mistaken for the theoretical concept of the "plural society" developed by J. S. Furnivall (*Netherlands India: A Study of Plural Economy*, 1944) to designate colonial formations like Dutch Indonesia where multiple racial groups lived side by side without any real contact except through transactions in the marketplace, a socioeconomic arrangement that guaranteed the colonizer's extraction of surplus value and insured its political hegemony through divide-and-rule techniques inscribed in laws, state apparatuses, institutions of civil society, customs, and practices of everyday life. For a contemporary application, see Smith (1986, 187–225); for criticism of its explanatory validity, see Rex and Mason (1986a, 69–71) and Jenkins (1986, 178–82).
4. Gobineau rivals Kant for the title of inaugural founder of modern racism (Poliakov 1982, 59).
5. Even mainstream political scientists could acknowledge the cognitive-psychological imperative of cultural autonomy, for example: "The breaking of the dominant group's [Anglo-European] psychological hold over the subordinate group is a critical first step if the latter is to build resources, mobilize its members, and achieve a degree of solidarity in contesting against dominant group power" (Baker 1983, 200).

6. Apropos of her hyphenated situation, the Chinese-American writer Maxine Hong Kingston delivered the following remarks to a Chinese audience when she visited China in 1988: "One of the paradoxes that interests me is that I am a Han person, a member of the largest race on Earth, and in my country, the U.S.A., I am a minority person. How does a minority writer speak in America, and still be true to her smaller community? . . . The U.S. has treated its minorities shamefully, and is regretting it. There have been policies of slavery, genocide, relocation, quarantine. Artistically, minorities have been excluded from literature, both as creators and as sympathetic characters" (1988, 42).

1

Race and Literary Theory:
From Difference
to Contradiction

Like all passageways between past and present, the threshold to the twenty-first century conceived as a crisis point presents both a danger and an opportunity: a danger of the solid gains of the civil rights struggles in the sixties being dissolved in an unprecedented social amnesia, and an opportunity to learn from experience and advance race relations in an emancipatory, counterhegemonic direction. Change, as everyone knows, always proceeds unevenly. Despite the call for a return to the old dispensation, with the Great Books of the Western World summoned to fill the gaps in the national "cultural illiteracy," progress toward liberating us from Eurocentric, male-dominated learning can be discerned in such reforms as, for example, the presence in recent textbooks of black women writers (Walker, Petry, Morrison) and token American Indian and Chicano writers.[1] This would not have been possible without such collective efforts as *Radical Teacher*, the Project on Reconstructing American Literature, and numerous individual initiatives. The agenda then was to problematize the canon and transform it—but for whose benefit? on what grounds?

In his introduction to *Reconstructing American Literature* (1983), Paul Lauter observes that in the last decade or so a growing consensus has emerged for revising/transforming the canon established by the aesthetic standard of the New Criticism which has privileged a white/male normative "paradigm of experience." The modernist patriarchal pantheon of Hemingway, Faulkner, Bellow, and Mailer, questioned by women and minorities, can no longer claim a transparent foundational superiority when its rationale has been undermined. Nor can the New Critical norms and habits—the dismissal of readers' sensibility, the discounting of the artists' milieu—be taken for granted as truisms. Amid the transvaluation of Establishment values, Lauter envisages the possibility of opening up the canon in consonance with radical social changes whose impact is to compel us to ask not just "how to apply a given and persisting set of standards, but where standards come from, whose values they embed, whose interests they serve." At stake is the function or role of the teaching profession in a world of alienated labor and mass reification.

The strategy of this new "Reconstruction" is manifestly one of compromise and piecemeal reforms. While lauding the virtues of oral texts like the American Indian chant, Lauter and colleagues seem unable to forsake such New Critical virtues as "complexity," irony, and so on; what they are pleading for is latitude, pluralism, and diversity. But reforms have been won, the Establishment has made concessions: Douglass' *Narrative* and Linda Brent's *Incidents in the Life of a Slave Girl* (in full or excerpts), for example, are now often mandatory for introductory courses; Kate Chopin's *The Awakening* is on the way to enshrinement. Now I don't mean to discount those necessary critiques of the old formalist standard, but the targeting of the New Criticism (now eclipsed by poststructuralist approaches like reader response, semiotics, deconstruction, and so on) and the espousal of a more militant liberalism have been overtaken by the larger sociocultural changes in the latter half of the Reagan era.

In the sphere of racial conflicts, some experts have suggested that the issue of "racism" has already been resolved by the civil rights victories of the sixties so that it no longer figures in the public debate on what the American community is and should be. Jeffrey Prager, for example, argues that race as a social construction, that is, "the projection of socially created difference" organized by racial category, has been displaced by other collective or social representations which mediate reality for individual subjects. He contends that the resurgent tradition of expressive and utilitarian individualism, now dominant over the biblical and civic republican variants (following Bellah's findings in *Habits of the Heart*), at present articulates race in terms of private virtue, not collective responsibility. Using Durkheim's concept of "collective representations," Prager (1987, 63), however, holds that "the shifting meaning of race is a function of its negotiated and contingent public character."[2] While this may sound like a recap of Gunnar Myrdal's thesis in *An American Dilemma* (1944) which Oliver Cromwell Cox has effectively criticized in *Caste, Class and Race* (1948), Prager does not perceive any discordance between ideals and actuality. In fact he believes that the quest for the meaning and purpose of the American community cannot be accomplished except through the mediation of racial difference as part of "the American tradition," the preservation of which (he thinks) is "critical in a democratic society." Now why and how this collective representation of racial difference acquires permanent status as a necessary and constitutive element in American society is not demonstrated but simply assumed. In any case, what Prager points out as the mutations of racial discourse under the varying pressures of "historical circumstance and social negotiation" may explain, to some extent, why Douglass (but not George Jackson) and Walker (but not Angela Davis) can be assimilated or integrated into the canon. But if so, has racism (as the lived experience of millions with real material consequences) been effectively abolished or even neutralized in the pacification of the ghettos and minority enclaves?[3]

Since the seventies, the repudiation of New Critical dogmatism found in such volumes as *The Politics of Literature* (1970), Richard Ohmann's *English in America* (1976), and the writings of feminists and Third World activists (e.g., Paulo Freire's intervention was catalyzing at one stage of pedagogical reflection) may be regarded as symptomatic of the widespread dissatisfaction not with the racial problematic but chiefly with the exhausted pedagogical scholasticism of Ransom, Tate, and Brooks which did not and could not address the urgent concerns of women and blacks, and particularly students being drafted for the Vietnam War. Academic minds, as usual, lagged behind events. We know that from its genealogy in the agrarian reaction against the capitalist rehabilitation of the South, the New Critics were successfully incorporated into monopoly capital's hegemonic order as required by an expansive state engaged in surmounting the depression, fighting fascism, and asserting post-war global leadership. It was also supplanting Europe in its imperial tutelage/domination of the Third World. New Critical discourse was in effect instrumentalized to articulate the national identity even as the trope of the melting pot yielded to the rhetoric of integration.

In line with supplementing the canon that evolved from Matthiessen's *The American Renaissance* (1941) to Spiller's *Literary History of the United States* (revised 1974), the elevation of Faulkner as an American, not just a Southern, artist testifies to the New Critics' supremacy in the discipline. Despite the left-liberal reservations of Edmund Wilson and Irving Howe on Faulkner's mythmaking, Robert Penn Warren's praise for Faulkner's conscience has succeeded in endowing the novelist with the gift of transcending the color bar. But, ironically, such colorblindness only confirmed the gap between the liberal state which guaranteed formal equality to all and the racially structured civil society: "What Faulkner does is to make the character transcend his sufferings *qua* Negro to emerge not as Negro but as man—man, that is, beyond complexion and ethnic considerations. . . . the final story is never one of social injustice, however important that element may be, but of an existential struggle against fate, for identity, a demonstration of the human will to affirm itself."[4] Viewed from this salvational gesture of discrimination, Faulkner's art redeems plantocratic prejudice and the narcissistic violence of a moribund socioeconomic formation. Through this metamorphosis negotiated by criticism, Faulkner has indeed become an overdetermined signifier serving the claims of U.S. moral supremacy in the world.

Despite this rearguard triumphalist humanism, the rituals of the Faulkner cult have been unable to silence dissenting voices, among them Ralph Ellison's refusal of the religious myth and its drive for racial mastery:

> For it is the creative function of myth to protect the individual from the irrational, and since it is here in the realm of the irrational that, impervious to science, the stereotype grows, we see that the Negro stereotype is really an image of the unorganized, irrational forces of American life, forces through which, by projecting them in forms of images of an easily dominated minority, the white individual seeks to be at home in the vast unknown world of America. Perhaps the object of the stereotype is not so much to crush the Negro as to console the white man.[5]

We can see how Ellison, through a dialectical ruse of counterpointing outside and inside, conceives his task as one of helping black people attain self-definition, that is, "having their ideals and images recognized as part of the composite image which is that of the still forming American people." From the perspective of the reified subject now acquiring self-consciousness, the "American nation" is then articulated as a site of struggle where demarcations and boundaries are redrawn: "The artist is no freer than the society in which he lives, and in the United States the writers who stereotype or ignore the Negro and other minorities in the final analysis stereotype and distort their own humanity."[6] At this point, we anticipate the totalizing principle of structuralism (most pronounced in Lévi-Strauss' anthropology) that would subsequently displace the New Critical doctrine of the self-contained subject with a relational method in which the discovery of identity unfolds through the mediation of the symbolic Other (social codes, laws, taboos).

Following our premise that race as a social construction (where the exploitation and oppression of one group occurs in a hierarchical system of class conflict) is needed for the self-affirmation of the dominant community, we can construe literature as one privileged field of this ideological operation, one of the most efficacious cultural spaces where the subject is racially marked and constituted.[7] Faulkner's texts are powerful interpellations of the black population as a subject race, albeit endowed with saving grace; *Intruder in the Dust*, for instance, can even be described as dialogical or intertextual—if only the voices of Richard Wright, Ellison, and Baldwin can be stilled. There is no space here to explore how Faulkner's texts, like the pioneering film *The Birth of a Nation* by D. W. Griffith (based on a fictional apologia, *The Clansman*, 1905), trace a common descent from racist attitudes thematized in religion, pseudoscientific thinking, and popular lore, discourses which also inform non-Southern writing by Frank Norris and Jack London, among others.

With the end of the Reconstruction followed by a series of economic depressions, the maintenance of fin-de-siècle order required the revitalization of a racist episteme and *habitus*. According to T. Jackson Lears, a historian of this transitional period:

> In America as in Europe, racism intertwined with the recoil from modern softness. Anglo-Saxon racism offered a rationale for imperialist crusades against "inferior" overseas foes and also met less obvious social and psychic needs. Racism reasserted the cultural authority of the WASP bourgeoisie; it may also have provided many WASP Americans with a kind of negative identity—a means of shoring up selfhood by disowning impulses they distrusted in themselves. Defining idleness, irresolution, avarice and other moral shortcomings as "race traits" confined to inferior stock, racists reaffirmed a masterful, virtuous mode of identity for those who had lost a solid sense of self. Private needs had public consequences. In a variety of ways, racism revitalized the hegemony of the dominant WASP culture at a critical historical moment. (1981, 108–9)

In short, the presence of the racial Other sustains and validates the master's identity. Since the social field is a complex articulation of various levels of life activities (political, ideological, economic), the intertextuality between hegemonic sociopolitical discourse and racist social practices and institutions can only be mapped in specific historical conjunctures, a mapping which, for example, may be approximated by Thomas Gossett's survey *Race: The History of an Idea in America* (1963) and Michael Banton's *Racial Theories* (1987). Conceptions of racial contradiction, not just juxtaposed differences (such as those voiced by Hegel, Kant, Taine, Gobineau, Le Bon, and others) are thus articulated with literary/aesthetic, moral, and ethical ideas via the mediation of the underlying public discourse on the identity of American society.

Given this sketchy background on the displacements and sublimations of racist ideology, we may consider next the present conjuncture as a possible turning point in the fraught relations between race and literary theory. This interaction has preoccupied the contributors to two important volumes both edited by Henry Louis Gates, Jr.: *Black Literature and Literary Theory* (1984) and *"Race," Writing, and Difference* (1987). In the latter volume, the theoretician of structuralism Tzvetan Todorov asks the tricky but misleading question: "If 'racial differences' do not exist, how can they possibly influence literary texts?" Ignorant of the subtle dynamics of ideology, Todorov misconceives the issue. He reduces the social categorization of people by racial (phenotypical) markers to legitimize hierarchy (economic and political stratification) to a simple question of cultural diversity. How can tolerance of cultures be equivalent to oppression and exploitation of a group based on a belief in its presumed inferiority? Todorov, moreover, seems innocent of the simplest facts of wage-differentiation and other forms of political and economic subordination based on ethnic/racial identification. Todorov also insists that, in general, European Enlightenment thought was "universalist and egalitarian," thus defending the uses to which such thought was put in sanctioning the enslavement and brutalization of nonwhite/non-Caucasian peoples. Then he adds insult to injury by apologizing for past racist (in his term, "racialist") ideologies as "not all bad" because they coincided with "popular opinion" in their time, and above all they implied "the very idea of shared humanity," the abandonment of which would be more dangerous than "ethnocentric universalism": "All one would have to do in order to 'recycle' these authors [Taine, Gobineau] would be to subject their works to a double 'cleansing' process, first eliminating their now confusing references to 'race' and physical differences (replacing them with 'culture' and its derivatives) and then criticizing their oversimplified classifications and their glaring ethnocentric value judgments" (1985, 373). What a messy salvaging operation for a famous scholar committed to the search for permanent truths![8]

It appears that the structuralist thinker has escaped the dreaded hermeneutic circle through unwitting bad faith. Although Todorov cautions against fetishizing Otherness and mystifying racial difference to thwart the peril of universalism, he himself succumbs to an equally reprehensible essentialism: "We are not only separated by cultural differences; we are also united by a common human identity, and it is this which renders possible communication, dialogue, and, in the final analysis, the comprehension of Otherness— it is possible precisely because Otherness is never radical." History is thereby suppressed, nullified. I agree with the last point insofar as it resembles Bakhtin's historically situated notion of intersubjective dialogue. And I endorse Todorov's caveat on unwarrantedly superimposing the deconstructionist critique of "the truth of identity" on black writing. But he misses the point of the whole controversy which is focused on *who* precisely commands and exercises the power to articulate this "common human identity" and authorize or enforce it in specific times and places. Just like Derrida (in his reply to his critics in the same volume), Todorov warns against reimposing cultural apartheid when he rejects Gates' call that blacks must return to their own literature "to develop theories of criticism indigenous" to it, even though in both volumes all varieties of Western, nonblack approaches were mobilized to interpret and analyze black and other non-European cultural texts. One can conclude that Todorov's philanthropic humanism is purely verbal. It is singularly blind to the complicity of ideas with state violence and the coercive, disciplinary apparatus of class interests—a concern registered particularly in recent socialist-feminist, Third World, and neo-Marxist inquiries.

Without having to suspect the cunning of Hegel's Reason behind all these ratiocinations, we submit that what Todorov intends in the sphere of thought has already been carried out in the "bantustan" policy of canon formation today. Are we witnessing the return of tokenism writ large, integration recuperated, races separate but equal under the same roof? The phenomenon celebrated today as pluralism, heterogeneity, de Man's vertiginous possibilities of meaning, and free play—all safely operating in the realm of rarefied theorizing—can be appraised as a new hegemonic strategy of the ruling bloc following the demise of the New Criticism and the bankruptcy of its successors, archetypal criticism (Frye), phenomenology, structuralism, and other approaches.[9]

One can suggest that in the absence of any powerful mass movement the terms of public discourse tend to be fixed by those who control the ideological means of production. Let me cite a recent case. You can achieve what E. D. Hirsch calls "cultural literacy" and entitle yourself to join the mainstream community if you can consume enough information about Du Bois, racism, apartheid, and a few hundred pieces of knowledge. In the process, Hirsch believes that we shall also recover what has been lost in the past twenty years of social engineering precipitated by urban and student riots, namely "the Ciceronian ideal of a universal public discourse," by expanding the reading list to include the productions of erstwhile marginal groups. This kind of education (and more) has enabled a sophisticated intellectual like Hirsch to appreciate that even members of the Black Panther Party, to his surprise, can write grammatically correct, intelligent English. This programmatic call to return to the basics, part of the conservative revival of the utilitarian individualism alluded to earlier and a reaction to the popular rebellions of the past two decades, pursues the line of universal humanism still prevalent in the mass media and the academies but now retooled and institutionalized in the context of different global contingencies by a predominantly white ruling class and its organic intellectuals. Hirsch's strategy for reconsolidating hegemony proves once more that all discourse becomes intelligible only when we grasp its social mediations and its implicit political agendas.

Of all mediations, race is still the most dangerous and intractable in contemporary American consciousness. While the assimilation into the curriculum of hitherto alien, potentially disruptive innovations (feminist theories of reading, for example) has enlarged but not substantially deepened the parameters of our discipline, the "political" or ideological critique of texts from an ethnic/racial subaltern perspective remains suspect and can only be intermittently tolerated. That is because subjectivity in the present conjuncture, while constituted by racial discourse, has to operate according to jurisprudential norms of equality, due process, and so forth.

What I would call a race-relations mode of metacommentary which also articulates the moments of class and gender (such as those by black women critics like Barbara Smith and Audre Lorde in *This Bridge Called My Back*, 1981; and the contributions of Hazel Carby and Pratibha Parmar in the Centre for Contemporary Cultural Studies' *The Empire Strikes Back*, 1982) is one that would not only position antithetical texts such as Richard Wright's "Blueprint for Negro Writing" (1937) side by side with T. S. Eliot's "Tradition and Individual Talent" (1919), or Frances Beale's "Double Jeopardy: To Be Black and Female" (1969) next to Adrienne Rich's "When We Dead Awaken: Writing as Re-vision" (1972) in order to de-homogenize a liberal arts curriculum modeled after the classic "marketplace of ideas"; it would also insist on highlighting the contradiction of premises, assumptions, principles, and implications between these texts. It would call attention to "the war of position" (Gramsci's term), the dialectical confrontation between texts and practices and their asymmetrical power relations, within the framework of societies still characterized by injustice founded on class division and gender hierarchy—a condition which, for millions of people in our society, is (whether one likes it or not) still primarily lived and experienced as racial oppression. And that is not, to be sure, something undecidable or indeterminate. Ultimately, this approach will help clarify the problematic of race as analogically parallel to that of religion in Marx's well-known formulation in his "Contribution to the Critique of Hegel's *Philosophy of Right*" (1844): it is the "sigh of the oppressed creature, the sentiment of a heartless world, and the soul of soulless conditions. It is the *opium* of the people."

Notes

1. For an oppositional critique of the conservative trend, see Aronowitz and Giroux (1988, 172–94). On the struggle for the empowerment of "subalterns" in Stanford University, see the report in *The Chronicle of Higher Education* (14 Dec. 1988): 1, All.
2. For a new theoretical formulation of the positionality of race as a "decentered complex of social meanings," I recommend Omi and Winant (1986).
3. See Omi and Winant (1983). For an analysis of racist discourse and practices in Britain which could be highly instructive for U.S. students and activists, see Centre for Contemporary Cultural Studies (1982).
4. Warren (1966, 263). Compare Howe (1968, 43–48).
5. Quoted in Minter (1987, 266). Parenthetically, Ellison's remark uncannily antici-

pates Lacan's theory of the Imaginary as the matrix of Manichaean transitivism, and also Fanon's (1963) dialectics of colonized and colonizer.
6. Minter (1987, 267–68). Elaborations of the black identity project can be found in Gayle (1972) and Baraka (1985).
7. For a neo-Marxist articulation of class and race, I recommend Hall (1980). See also Solomos (1986). For a Gramscian orientation, consult Genovese (1971) and West (1988).
8. Kovel (1984, 211–30) describes such an attitude (instanced here by Todorov) as a form of "metaracism."
9. Part of this hegemonic strategy may be located in the ethnicity approach to the humanities, for example Sollors (1980). Current feminist theories of reading persist in being color-blind as well as classless, as evidenced in Flynn and Schweickart (1986). The scandal of racist white feminism has been noted in numerous accounts; the most provocative and challenging are those by Brittan and Maynard (1984) and Bourne (1983). On linguistic racism, see Pratt (1987, 48–66).

2

The Cult of Ethnicity and the Fetish of Pluralism

The media manipulation of the Willie Horton case during the 1988 election might perhaps be indexed as the culmination of a tidal wave of racist resurgence during the Reagan ascendancy which, as far as I can judge, has not yet subsided. Its effects are now being registered in latent and manifest forms: witness the proliferating incidents of racist harassment and violence in the campuses epitomized by the case (27 Oct. 1986) of the notorious white mob of three thousand students at the University of Massachusetts chasing and beating anyone who was black. I won't remind you anymore of the Goetz shooting incident in New York City nor of Purdy's massacre of Indo-Chinese schoolchildren in Sacramento, California, among recent occurrences. Can we describe these incidents as problems of ethnicity and deviance, or mere dysfunctional symptoms of cultural pluralism?

The prevailing sociological dogma enshrined in the *Harvard Encyclopedia of American Ethnic Groups* (1980) conceptualizes all race relations as problems of ethnicity. In the master discourse of the ethnologues (my term for doctrinaire exponents of ethnicity theory), *Ethnicity: Theory and Experience* edited by Nathan Glazer and Daniel P. Moynihan, ethnicity functions like a floating signifier, a synthesizing figure that can codify all narratives of collective life into something like an updated version of Robert Park's archetype of the "race relations cycle"—except for the utopian impulse of valorizing community vis-à-vis the anomie of consumerist, mass society. One of the contributors to this influential textbook, Daniel Bell (1975), acclaimed prophet of the end of ideology, underscores the salience of ethnicity in U.S. society as "a strategic choice by individuals . . . as a means of gaining some power and privilege" (171).

In the *Harvard Encyclopedia* entry on "Concepts of Ethnicity," for example,

31

William Petersen (1980) reduces race to one criteria of ethnicity (where cultural markers predominate), although he concedes the general practice of distinguishing between "racial" minorities (blacks, Asians, etc.) from "ethnic" (European nationalities). Unwittingly he observes that, as in the case of the Nazi program of racist genocide, the "confusion of biological and cultural characteristics, paradoxically, is the hallmark of racism" (236). Underlying this confusion that is reflected in Petersen's text is the paradigm of the white immigrant experience as the controlling model for understanding the plight of all groups; hence, the observation that "the trend has been to define the black subculture not as standard American culture truncated by educational deprivation but as an immigrant way of life with significant transfers from Africa" (241). This accords with the theory of acculturation: "cultural pluralism" replaced the melting pot analogy in order to project a vision of a future assured by "good will on the part of all," a future "either without meaningful ethnicity or at least with little or no ethnic conflict."

This updated liberal version of assimilation/integration has of course been refuted by Harold Cruse and other activists in the sixties, by Robert Blauner in his book *Racial Oppression in America* (1972), and by a whole generation of American Indian, Chicano, black, Puerto Rican, and Asian American artists. The pseudouniversalism of "We are all immigrants, hyphenated Americans, etc.," simply distorts history. It erases the crucial difference between the incorporation of the colonized minorities by force and violence—not only the intensity of their repression but its systematic nature—and that of the European immigrant groups. By this theoretical revision, the ethnicity theorists have destroyed the rationale of affirmative action and reaffirmed instead what Stephen Steinberg (1981) calls the "systematic inequalities" (conquest, slavery, exploitation) that form the basis and lifeblood of "cultural pluralism" (254, 261).[1]

I would like to endorse here the powerful criticism of this ethnicity cult by the anthropologist M. G. Smith in a 1982 review of the *Harvard Encyclopedia*. The Harvard approach, according to Smith, ignores not only group organization and cohesion but also "the severe and sometimes crippling differences that distinguish racial from cultural groups." Denying racial difference will not exclude nor eliminate racism, he contends: "the Jewish holocaust in Nazi Germany involved an ethnic group of the same racial stock as their killers, who were motivated by an ideology of racism despite the lack of objective racial differences between their victims and themselves" (7–8). The absurd logic of the ethnicity school in dividing the dominant Anglo-American population into three regional groups, making everyone ethnics of one sort or another, can be understood as one impelled by the charitable desire to negate racial differences which have served to ground the hierarchies of the de facto American political structure; but in doing so, the ethnologues have simply deluded themselves into playing blind to "the political nature and racial framework of US Census classifications." To relabel race ethnicity doesn't make it so.[2]

From its inception the United States has been structured as a racial order; the history of its population is organized by complex, intricate racialization processes whereby racial differences (polygenic, phenotypical features enabling racial identification of individuals and groups) valorize, and are in turn valorized by, a stratified polity. The value-neutral scheme of ethnic classification as "a substitute for the perduring American split-level system" of classifying racial stocks (old, foreign, out-of-stock) is called by Smith "an example of academic futility and illusion so long as the age-old inequalities and disjunctions persist among racially distinct sectors of the U.S. population" (20–21). This liberal if dangerously obfuscating attempt at a uniform classification is not only scientifically inept but also morally deceptive:

> Now as then the racial and/or ethnic classification of the American people has been generated and governed by political conditions and considerations, and devised for political ends. Under such circumstances it would be silly to expect an impartial, objective or scientifically defensible basis for the identification and grouping together of American collectivities on racial or ethnic lines, now as then. As always, the measure of its social validity indicated the political utility of U.S. ethnic or racial classifications at any point in time. (Smith 1982, 18)

Less discreetly put, theory cannot be divorced from political practice and social reality. This criticism of the ethnicity cult has been formulated earlier, in 1977, by Alexander Saxton in his review of Glazer's book *Affirmative Discrimination* (1975). Saxton emphasized the need for an accurate historical contextualization so as to avoid confusing racial and ethnic differences; blurring them entails blindness to white racism as a causal/historical force in the shaping of U.S. society and a justification of economic and political inequalities sanctioned by "color-blind" state policies:

> Already in the days of Jefferson and the "sainted Jackson" (to use Walt Whitman's phrase) the nation had assumed the form of a racially exclusive democracy—democratic in the sense that it sought to provide equal opportunities for the pursuit of happiness by its white citizens through the enslavement of Afro-Americans, extermination of Indians, and the territorial expansion largely at the expense of Mexicans and Indians.
>   . . . What seems to have mesmerized [Glazer] is the fact that the United States actually did absorb a variety of cultural differences among European migrants at the same time that it was erecting a white supremacist social structure. Moderately tolerant of European *ethnic* diversity, the nation remained adamantly intolerant of *racial* diversity. (Saxton 1977, 145–46)

Ethnologues typically project their conservative vision of a harmonious society at the cost of historical veracity, in effect apologizing for "the disastrous social and economic consequences of three centuries of white supremacy" and exacerbating the cumulative impact of that supremacy by blaming the collective victims.

In a cogent recasting of the terms of the debate, Michael Omi and Howard Winant's book *Racial Formation in the United States* (1986) not only stresses the insidious error of the immigrant analogy but points out the methodological limitations of ethnicism and its program of "cultural pluralism." Glazer and Moynihan (1975) proposed a hypothetical dynamics of group incorporation which located the source of status differences of minorities in their cultural norms or values: "Ethnic groups bring different norms to bear on common circumstances with consequent different levels of success—hence *group* differences in status" (7). Note how the key phrase "common circumstances" hides those historical realities, the concrete sociopolitical dynamics informed by racial discourse and practices that precisely account for the differential positioning of groups. The fallacious claim concerning the "structural assimilation" of racial minorities is just too blatant to dismiss. "Common circumstances" for racial minorities, argue Omi and Winant, "consist in relatively permanent racial difference and nonincorporation" (22). What is more scandalous is the ethnologue's equation of the category "black" with "Jewish" and "Irish," even though the black experience of institutional discrimination is acknowledged; unlike whites whose ethnic identities are finely discriminated, "blacks" are all lumped into one ethnic slot. Again here the imposition of a paradigm based on white ethnic history on racially defined groups (think of how Chinese, Japanese, Filipinos, and other Asians are all lumped together as one by the majority of Americans) produces a not-so-subtle racism—"they all look alike"—which ethnologues are so anxious to overlook!

In a well-known essay "Ethnicity and Stratification in the Urban United States," Leith Mullings (1984) summed up the ideological and analytic implications of the ethnicity paradigm:

> A historical analysis demonstrates that what we call ethnicity in the United States involves qualitatively different experiences. While ethnicity is not analytically reducible to class, at the base of the phenomenon of how ethnicity is differentially expressed in the United States—whether it functions as a set of cultural symbols promoting diffuse solidarity, as a marker for oppression, as an arena for resistance, or as some or all of these—is the division of labor and allocation of resources. . . . To categorize U.S. populations within the same analytic framework as "ethnic" groups, is to obfuscate their very different histories and structural constraints. For social scientists to ignore the evidence that some populations

have been subjected to unusual structural constraints, is to render affirma-tive action "reverse discrimination" and, again, to turn reality on its head. (35–36)

While I would not endorse Mullings' somewhat easy reduction of ideology and its complex constitution of subjects to the level of an unmediated "division of labor" and "allocation of resources" (the mechanical move of an economistic analysis), I concur with her underscoring of historical differ-ences. In fact this stress on historical concreteness and the dialectical mode of linking objective reality with the intervention of historical collective subjects at various conjunctures leads me to agree basically with Omi and Winant's construing of *race* as "an unstable and 'decentered' complex of social meanings constantly being transformed by political struggle" (68).[3]

The virtual hegemony of the ethnicity paradigm in literary studies on the "multi-ethnic" literature of the United States, as shown in issues of *MELUS (Multi-Ethnic Literature of the United States)* and various MLA (Modern Language Association of America) surveys, invariably registers itself in an endless replication of the strategy of what I would call refur-bishing and streamlining the figure of the "melting pot" by way of "cultu-ral pluralism," acculturation, diversity, and so on.[4] One example may be found in the notion of marginality expressed by Katharine Newman (1980), founding editor of *MELUS*. According to Newman, the ethnic or marginal person responds to the hegemonic culture in three ways: by opposing it, constructing a bridge to it, or enriching it. Admittedly hegemonic (since you are forced to relate to it), the dominant (Euro-American) culture is however presented as a neutral or indifferent body. Pluralism results: a parade of types—Puritan minister, black preacher, Jewish shopkeeper, Yankee peddler, the Indian trickster, etc.—evince the humanist *communitas* of an expansive literature where (she quotes Joseph Bruchac) "differences produce similarities," that is, the quintessential American.

Newman of course is not naive to ignore the vast disparities in the historical experiences of various ethnic collectivities and warns against cooptation "in the name of national unity"; nevertheless, the ethnic schol-ar's obsessive drive is to grasp the transhistorical characteristics of Amer-ican literature which she proceeds to enumerate: horizontality, eccentricity, choice-making. Even before the advent of Derrida, neopragmatism, and New Historicism, Newman has already been producing self-deconstructive significations: while she asserts the existence of multiple value systems in America, she observes that the "chief preoccupation of our writers is *the necessity of choice*." This homage paid to difference, however, betrays a hidden but quite obtrusive agenda: that of homogenizing the sheer heter-ogeneity of discourses by Europeans, blacks, Indians, Chicanos, and Puerto

Ricans, among others. Likewise, the characteristic of "horizontality" subsumes the theme of liberation unifying all ethnic writing: "Given that
Liberation is the goal of those excluded from power, and given the insecu-
rity and guilt of those who have the power but have never been able to
bridge the difference between democratic beliefs and practice, the reason for
the contemporaneity of American literature becomes apparent: it is the same
dilemma, the same conflicts, the same tensions" (Newman 1980, 8).[5] How
can we account for these puzzling paradoxes and ironic aporias? Clearly a
sophisticated form of discrimination is resurrected here behind the mask of
liberal tolerance and the celebration of cultural diversity.

We can discern the matrix of the problem in another typical *MELUS*
pronouncement by Jules Chametzky (1984) who pontificates about the
totality called American literature which he discovers in "core cultural ideas
and values," such as the "process of becoming," "a synthesis of pluralistic
and unitary impulses." He defines "certain essentials of the American
experience" as residing in "adaptation," "pluralistic integration," etc.; indeed, "*confrontation of cultures* [has] been a staple of the American experience
from our beginnings." Echoing the notorious slogan of the United States as
"a nation of immigrants," Chametzky proceeds to invoke the imperative of
unity under the hegemony of transcendental myths: "American literature is
full of stories recreating in one way or another this almost archetypal
pattern: confrontations between East and West, North and South, Civilization and the Wilderness, Industrialism and Agrarianism, the vernacular
tradition and the Genteel, country boys and girls in the city, city boys and
girls in the country" (48). Pursuing a homogenizing project that implicitly
invokes Frye and New Critical formalism, Chametzky makes short shrift of
the heterogeneity to which Newman pays lip service. But like Newman,
Chametzky operates within the framework of the ethnicity paradigm and
thus performs its work of essentializing. Ethnicity breeds essentialism.
Essentialism, according to Barry Hindess, "refers to a mode of analysis in
which social phenomena are analyzed not in terms of their specific conditions of existence and their effects with regard to other social relations and
practices but rather as the more or less adequate expression of an essence"
(cited by Wickham 1983).

The essence the *MELUS* orthodoxy cited above is propagating assumes a
now familiar guise: the hegemonic ideology of individualism, mobility,
self-reliance, and free enterprise.[6] But this position should not be construed
as monolithic. As Sacvan Bercovitch (1986) argues, this ideology "reflects a
particular set of interests, the power structures and conceptual forms of
modern middle-class society in the United States, as these evolved through
three centuries of contradiction and discontinuity. So considered, 'America'
is not an overarching synthesis, *e pluribus unum*, but a rhetorical battle-

ground" (636). For the ethnologues, however, the force of "cultural pluralism" (i.e., free enterprise) has already won in that battleground, articulating
the myth of oneness via precisely the empty, all-purpose signifiers of
diversity, pluralism, and so on.

My last example of this essentializing and ultimately apologetic function
that the paradigm of ethnicity enables is the work of Werner Sollors. In his
book *Beyond Ethnicity* (1986), Sollors explicitly subscribes to the sociologist
Abramson's "universalist interpretation" in which race is "merely one
aspect of ethnicity." His scholarly research into ethnogenesis or the process
of group formation and "the naturalization of group relationships" leads
him to set up a binary opposition between the element of "consent," that is,
identity or status by achievement, and identity by ascription or descent.
Free play of the polarities then takes over. His procedure in general conforms to the methodology of structural functionalism with its stress on the
telos of normative assimilation or integration.

One symptomatic result of this approach is eclecticism. Sollors' obsessive
pursuit of analogies and affinities flattens every historical difference and
reduces diachrony to synchrony. Thus, for him, the Marcus Garvey movement can be read as "a 'trendy' ethnocentric movement which actually
modernized its members" (245). Black writers, such as Jean Toomer of
Harlem Renaissance fame, anticipated modernism in that Toomer's art is
distinguished by its "Whitmanesque sense of panethnic and pansexual cosmic wholeness, a return to the alchemical dreams of the ouroboros and the
hermaphrodite" (253). Toomer's masterpiece *Cane*, for Sollors, is "an
experimental search for reality beyond labels and for mankind above race
and nationality," in short, a transhistorical expression of an individual
quest.[7]

I would like to remark at this juncture that this essentializing mode of
ethnicist criticism becomes a starkly reactionary strategy when, in the
chapter on American Indian literature in *The New Pelican Guide to English
Literature* (1988), Jerome Rothenberg qualifies the richness of American
Indian oral culture by a massive barrage of allusions to Pound, Olson,
Ginsberg, Whitman, Rimbaud, Cassirer, Breton, Dadaism and Surrealism,
Rabelais, McClure, Rexroth, Victor Turner, and other Anglo-Saxon
anthropologists, with contemporary American Indian writers mentioned
only at the tail end, completely devoid of any single reference to the
concrete historical specificities of genocide and continuing dispossession of
their homelands which would give credence to the quotation (by Gary
Snyder) he cites at the end attesting to the American Indian as "the vengeful
ghost lurking in the back of the troubled American mind. . . ." Juxtapose
this with Simon Ortiz's statement (1981) that the Indian oral tradition
embodied the "political, armed, spiritual" resistance of his people to the

"experience of colonization" and we immediately apprehend the repressive if unintentional racism of ethnicity-oriented scholarship. Needless to say, this is the hegemonic, officially validated approach in the academy, mass media, and elsewhere.[8]

What is most damaging in Sollors' liberal project of rehabilitating cultural pluralism, a foundational scheme of inventing America as the model polyethnic nation with "a shared sense of destiny" and ethnicization as a form of modernization, can be illustrated by his choice of the single Filipino author he uses to demonstrate the ethnic poet's quest for "freedom and true vision": Jose Garcia Villa. Divorced from any historical context, Villa's avant-gardism, for Sollors, indicates "a radical *formal* response to the ethnic writer's need for a new poetic language." Villa and Toomer, coming from entirely different socioeconomic formations, are drastically coalesced because they show "affinities with Christic imagery of fusion and revelation" (254). Sollors' formalism fails to recognize that for many decades now, Villa has been a "disappeared" artist, a casualty of his quest for metaphysical anonymity and single-minded renunciation of racial, ethnic, or national genealogy (San Juan 1988, 33–34).

It appears that what William Boelhower (1987) calls the American crisis of *habitare*, which generates ethnic semiosis and "the politics of memory" (43–44, 87–90), has been refused by both the Malay exile/émigré (a hybrid species, indeed!) and his German commentator ensconced at Harvard. Foregoing any investigation into the circumstances of Villa's exile to the United States, the long brutal war (the first Vietnam, by consensus) between the revolutionary Filipino insurgents and the American colonizing forces in the first two decades of this century, the forced immigration of Filipino workers to the Hawaiian plantations from 1907 to 1935, their rich culture of resistance from the twenties to the forties in the West Coast vividly chronicled by Carlos Bulosan (in his testimony of racist violence and Filipino resistance, *America Is in the Heart*), and the continuing struggles of Filipinos against racist prejudice and discrimination—all these have escaped Sollors' notice.[9] It is the logic of ethnicity triumphant.

The *Harvard Encyclopedia* for its part devotes nine pages to "Filipinos" as an ethnic group (now close to two million persons). But again the ethnicity paradigm inflicts its havoc when the academic expert diagnoses the cause of the Filipinos' difficulties of adjustment to U.S. society as inherent in their value system, the cultural norms of feudal life in the Philippines, a U.S. colony up to 1946. Even though the résumé of the Filipino immigrant experience alluded to the systematic racial exclusion of the colonized subject in the wake of the forced annexation of the Philippines—the whole bloody decade of imperialist aggression (1898–1915) becomes a blank, a telltale elision here—the ethnologue forgets the structural constraint of state policies and a whole panoply of laws and administrative rules. He remembers only the formula of cultural explanation: "Filipino loyalty to family and regional group has militated against their achieving success in American politics" (362). Why can't these natives adapt? What's wrong with them? Can't they learn from the role model afforded by Villa's ingenious craft?

Literary theory is thus not innocent of political complicity by way of the framework or paradigm that informs it, together with its ethical and moral implications. We need to critique this paradigm as an instance of "hegemony" or hegemonic war of position, to use Gramsci's term. Racism though under erasure will return, like the repressed unconscious, to sabotage the liberal dream of "a democracy of nations."

In assaying the various theories of race and ethnicity competing in the disciplines, John Rex (1986c) concluded that "the major structures in terms of which ethnic quasi-groups interacted involved market relations, including especially relations arising from relationship to the means of production, but also the type of political incorporation which prevailed" (37). In a recent monograph *Race and Ethnicity* (1986c), he reiterated his view that race relations are situations where there is severe conflict, discrimination, exploitation, or oppression; where categories are clearly distinguished and it is difficult for the individual to shift from one category to another; and where the system is justified by some sort of deterministic theory (20).

In his *Racial Oppression in America* (1972) which I cited above, Robert Blauner was one of the first to outline a historical-materialist view of race relations which Rex now tries to systematize. Blauner enunciated the argument that racial minorities suffering "internal colonialism," given the specific modes of their historical incorporation into the U.S. polity, have uninterruptedly produced their own authentic cultures of resistance in the process of life-and-death struggle. This epic of lived experience incarnated in cultural forms registers class and gender exploitation in the modality of racial oppression. But the power of this achievement is neutralized by the liberal consensus and inventoried as merely one specimen of ethnic diversity.

In the context of the dialectics between racial movements and the hegemonic state, I would argue that the peculiar racial dynamics of life in U.S. society, particularly in the past two decades of reaction and conservatism which eludes the ethnicity model, finds a complex, overdetermined mediation in that ideological practice we call literary production. One instance of this is the production of critical discourse, modes of signifying operations whose chief ideological effect is the reproduction of capitalist social relations, that is, the persisting subalternity of racial groups. Earlier I have touched briefly on how the ideological construction of race—how groups are represented, imaged, described, explained, and valorized—may be discerned in selected critical texts. What we have most often been exposed to, what the liberal ethnologues have made unfashionable, are recognizable forms of racist public discourse that are easy to detect and dismantle. What is more challenging for our critical sensibility is the unmasking and repudiation of inferential racism (and other forms of covert racist practices) which Stuart Hall (1981) defines thus: "those apparently naturalized representations of events and situations relating to race, whether 'factual' or 'fictional,' which have racist premises and propositions inscribed in them as a set of *unquestioned assumptions*. These enable racist statements to be formulated without ever bringing into awareness the racist predicates on which the statements are grounded" (36). What is urgent and imperative, I submit, is the drawing up of a research strategy and project to elucidate the operations of inferential racism in all discourse and cultural practice.[10]

In this struggle against overt and inferential racisms, the attention of our colleagues has been narrowly focused on a revision and reform of the literary canon. No doubt there is a need to decenter the Eurocentric dispensation in the choice of curriculum and texts; but I tend to agree with Giroux and Kaye (1989) that the crux of the struggle involves not just which texts (modes of rhetoric and representation) will transmit the classic heritage of the humanities so as to preserve standards and promote excellence (who, after all, defines the criteria of standards and excellence? and whose interests are at stake?). What is more important, I think, is the question: who will articulate the purpose and meaning of a humanities education, and how? Let me reformulate the project in this way: If the goal is to produce "an informed, critical citizenry capable of actively participating in shaping and governing a democratic society"—a citizenry with a historical perspective that grasps the present as possibilities of intervention, and with a critical praxis that de-reifies or reveals the social origins of the political, economic, and cultural order—then in this society where racism and racial politics pervade everyday life and institutions, priority needs to be given to the fight against racism, against racist ideas and practices, of which the application of the ethnicity paradigm in critical discourse is one manifestation—perhaps a weak link in the chain of domination.

Notes

1. David Wellman (1977) argues the thesis that "a position is racist when it defends, protects, or enhances social organization based on racial advantage" in his pioneering study of the U.S. racial formation.
2. See Pierre van den Berghe (1978, xv): "Precisely because a racial, phenotypical definition of group membership is far more stigmatizing than an ethnic definition, and typically gives rise to far more rigid social hierarchies, it is important to keep the analytical distinction clear. . . ."

3. Omi and Winant's approach parallels the neo-Althusserian perspective of the contributors to the volume *The Empire Strikes Back* (Centre for Contemporary Cultural Studies 1982). See also Brittan and Maynard (1984, 95–112). I would qualify Omi and Winant's overpoliticization of race with the structural constraints of any social formation as delineated, for instance, in Hall (1980). For a survey of explorations along this line, see Solomos (1986, 84–109).

4. To cite an early example: In the chapter "The Mingling of Tongues" in the standard reference text *Literary History of the United States* edited by Robert Spiller et al. (1963), Henry Pochman posits "cultural amalgamation" and "the gradual process of Americanization" as the telos of ethnic literary expression (677, 693). An implicit critique of this may be found in Bradbury and Temperley (1981, 134–37).

5. Newman repeats her views in "Introduction," *MELUS* 8 (Summer 1981): 3. See the interesting comment of R. Baxter Miller (1984): "What Prof. Newman . . . really should fear most involves the imminent mystification and assimilation of ethnicity"—already a fait accompli in most institutions.

6. This perennial theme of individualism functions as a collective representation in racial discourse, according to Prager (1987). But see Jameson's qualifications (1987b) which locate the articulation of individualism within the reified and commodified milieu of late capitalism.

7. A corrective to this imperial homogenizing may be drawn from historical research on racist practices (Higham 1971) and its complex genealogy (Gossett 1963).

8. Compare the ethnicist treatment of black writers in the same volume by Frederick Karl with those by Houston Baker and Henry Louis Gates, Jr., in *Black Literature and Literary Theory* (1984) and by Levine (1977).

9. For a résumé of the historical context, see McWilliams (1964) and Daniels and Kitano (1970).

10. I recommend two articles pursuing an emancipatory direction: Wald (1981) and Alkalimat (1988). I review Wald's hitherto neglected interventions in Chapter 4.

3

Problems in the Marxist Project of Theorizing Race

With the nationwide eruption of racist violence in the past ten years—witness the Atlanta City murders, the furor over Bernhard Goetz from 1984 to 1987, the racial confrontations in university campuses from Stanford to Wisconsin to Massachusetts, the Miami ghetto rebellion (Watt *déjà vu?*), and recently the Central Park gang rape which occasioned the outburst of "lynch-mob mentality" and the formulaic invocation of law and order—the centrality of race for any program for socialist transformation can no longer be shirked or dismissed by quoting, for the nth time, Marx's dictum: "Labor cannot emancipate itself in the white skin where in the black it is branded" (Foster 1973, 196). Indeed, class struggle cannot preempt, or leap over, the color line which W. E. B. Du Bois pronounced as the decisive battlefront of this century and surely of the next.

From the thirties to the sixties, Western Marxism has always subsumed racial conflicts into the class problematic. With the post–World War II emergence of Third World nations led by Marxist-inspired vanguards—China, Vietnam, Korea, and later Cuba, Guinea-Bissau, Mozambique, and Angola—and the birth of the Black Liberation movement in the sixties, the dialectic of race and class has been catapulted for the first time onto the center stage of the political-ideological arena. The famous 1968 Kerner Report on Urban Riots, *Report of the National Advisory Commission on Civil Disorders*, in the wake of Martin Luther King's assassination, crystallized the urgency of the issue. Writing about "Marxism and the Negro," Harold Cruse, among numerous protagonists, lambasted orthodox Marxists (particularly Trotskyites) for "failing to deal with the race question in America" (1968, 151), thus succumbing to "mechanistic materialism." Since then, a raft of Marxist-Leninist organizations, progressive intellectuals, and inde-

42

pendent left publications has debated the thematics of the race–class nexus throughout a whole period (see Progressive Labor Party [1970] and Loren [1977], among others). Before a resolution could break the impasse, the reactionary tide of Reaganism swept in just as the Empire's outposts were again being challenged in Nicaragua, El Salvador, the Philippines, and South Africa.

It might be useful to remind ourselves, at the outset, how the standard Soviet manual, *Fundamentals of Marxism-Leninism* (1963), consistently asserts the primacy of class over nation, race, or ethnicity. Gus Hall, general secretary of the Communist Party USA, condemns racism as "a deliberate strategy [of monopoly capital] for super-profits" (1972, 145), so that to overthrow this racist system, blacks and other minorities should unite with the majority white working class.

Radical economists also echoed this sacrosanct doctrine. Michael Reich, for example, noted that "racism is a key mechanism for the stabilization of capitalism and the legitimization of inequality"; racial conflict "obfuscates class interests." Rooted in the capitalist system, racism weakens workers' unity, promotes powerlessness and alienation within "an individualistic and competitive ethos" [Reich 1972, 320]. Clearly race is not the central determinant but class polarization.[1] Even younger radical economists then, perhaps influenced by Paul Baran and Paul Sweezy's *Monopoly Capital* (1966), also subscribed to the primacy of class over race. Howard Sherman, for instance, concluded his survey of the statistics on blacks by asserting that the function of racism was "to justify economic exploitation," to find a scapegoat for all social problems, and to divide the oppressed so that the elite can rule (1972, 180–81). Sherman urged white radicals to unite with their black counterparts to build a viable socialist movement, a call echoed by Michael Lerner, a founder of the New American Movement, who noted that "racism in this country has acquired an independent life" (1973, 201). This was preceded by historian Eugene Genovese's 1968 speech to the Students for a Democratic Society (SDS) where he argued that racism is not just a class question but is implicated with the right of blacks and other peoples to self-determination (Genovese 1971). Amid the protracted crisis of Western Marxism, in particular the privileging of the proletariat as the chief revolutionary agent for socialist transformation, the salience of race manifested itself in the left's rhetorical prioritizing of the democratic principle of self-determination for all peoples, especially those subjugated by racist neocolonial elites (Smith 1979).

I suggest that we can measure the profound mutation of the conventional Marxist tendency to sublate and valorize every social force or phenomenon within a productivist/economistic model, in the past three decades, by comparing the arguments of two Marxists, Oliver Cromwell Cox's *Caste,*

Class and Race (1948) and Robert Blauner's *Racial Oppression in America* (1972), both epochal discourses in the archive of U.S. race relations.

Long acclaimed as the classic Marxist analysis of race relations, Cox's book aimed principally to refute the habitual academic conflation of race with caste (e.g., Montagu 1962), the widely influential Chicago sociology of race relations cycle (Robert Park), and Gunnar Myrdal's thesis of "cumulative causation" propounded in *An American Dilemma* (1944). Cox elaborates his fundamental premise that racial antagonism is essentially political class struggle. Racial categorization arose with the rise of capitalism in order to facilitate the differential commercialization and exploitation of the labor of certain racially marked groups. Ultimately race relations are class conflicts. Shackled by this obsolescent if still canonical view of ideology as epiphenomenal superstructure, Cox discounts racism as "a system of rationalization" not worthy of analysis contrasted with the "material social fact" of class relations. Cognized as race prejudice, racism is "the socio-attitudinal concomitant of the racial-exploitative practice of a ruling class in a capitalistic society" (1948, 321, 470). To the Negro people Cox ascribes an "abiding urge . . . to assimilate" and thus dismisses outright their impulse to solidarity based on religion, culture, or commonality of experience. Michael Banton correctly faults Cox for overestimating "the integration of the capitalist system" and underestimating the "independence of beliefs in social processes" (1987, 152; see also Sweezy 1953).

What is worth exploring, however, is Cox's postulation of an ethnic system (based on culture and physical diversity) coexisting with political and social class conflicts which would allow the analyst to appraise how blacks not only experienced proletarianization but also racialization, and how they responded to these experiences with ethnic/racial solidarity cutting across class barriers. However, as Robert Miles acutely comments, Cox fails to systematically theorize the concrete dynamics of this interaction between two conceptual networks (1980, 175). The reason for this inadequacy, I think, can be attributed to Cox's reductionist reflex which virtually negates the complex mediation of cultural/ideological praxis in *la vie quotidienne*, the overdetermined constitution of subjects (more precisely, subject positions), and conjunctural displacements in the social field. In other words, Cox's limitation inheres in his instrumental conception of racial beliefs and practices, which he immediately links with the extraction of surplus value. Dialectics is sacrificed to the expediency, the utopian dream indeed, of gradual assimilation.

With the autonomous mobilization of the black masses in the sixties under populist leaders critical or suspicious of integration, Cox's otherwise sophisticated conceptual apparatus no longer matched "material social fact" and had to yield to a more totalizing, self-critical registration of specific historical changes then in progress, Blauner's *Racial Oppression in America*. I consider this text a landmark in refining a Marxist phenomenology and political theory of racial formation in U.S. history.[2] Since my main purpose here is not to catalogue in detail the pre-eighties work on this topic, suffice it to describe briefly Blauner's achievement. For the first time, U.S. society is defined as a "racial order" and race as an international political force. Conceived as a site of power and privilege, U.S. racial dynamics is firmly situated within the historical specificity of each people's differential incorporation into the labor-market system. Repudiating the prevailing immigrant model of integration (the mainstream ethnicity school now identified with Glazer, Moynihan, and the *Harvard Encyclopedia of American Ethnic Groups*, 1980), Blauner contends that race cannot be reduced to class, nor can racism be simply viewed as "subjective irrational beliefs" (1972, 28–29); race and class are dialectically intertwined. Racially categorized groups like blacks, Chicanos, Native Americans, and Asians are both exploited as workers and oppressed as colonized peoples. Applying a Third World global perspective never before tried, Blauner devises the concept of "internal colonialism" (ghetto, barrio, reservation) as the mode fusing both moments of the dialectic. More importantly, he focuses on the mechanisms of cultural domination and its response, nationalist or revolutionary cultural resistance, as the key to grasping racism as a "historical and social project" aimed at destroying the humanity of such peoples.

Within this multileveled perspective, Blauner takes the unprecedented move of valorizing black political history as the substantive core of Black Power, the movement for self-determination, a process of nation-building which is paradoxically enabled by racial (not just class) oppression (1972, 142–43). In so doing he cogently disintegrates the traditional received opinion (fostered by Myrdal and structural-functionalist sociology) that the black person is "an exaggerated American" with pathological values. Blauner delineates the genealogy of his insights in the exemplary practice of black intellectuals like Du Bois, Cruse, Carmichael, and others. Not only does Blauner chart sensitively the complex, fluid, open-ended initiatives of Third World peoples for self-emancipation; but he is also self-critical of his role as a white researcher who, whatever his professional guild's apologetics, nonetheless participates in the victimization of his subjects (1973).

From the publication of Blauner's book up to the eighties, Marxist theoretical projects on race were eclipsed by the mainstream sociology of ethnicity and minority group relations. Liberal scholars like Gordon Allport, Richard Schermerhorn, George Simpson, and J. Milton Yinger dominated the field; finally, the 1975 textbook *Ethnicity: Theory and Experience* edited by Nathan Glazer and Daniel P. Moynihan and the 1980 *Harvard Encyclopedia* marked the foundational ascendancy of this school. While the doctrines of ethnicity had been seriously undermined by scholars like Genovese (1971), Saxton (1977), M. G. Smith (1982), and Mullings (1984), it was not until the absorption of Althusserian and Gramsci-inspired critiques that a renewal of Marxist thinking on race could properly begin. One indication may be glimpsed in the entry on "Race" by John Rex in *A Dictionary of Marxist Thought* which positively stresses "the emergence of independent class struggle mobilized around national, ethnic and race ideologies" (1983b, 407; see also Rex 1986c). Given this renaissance of an authentically dialectical or rehistoricized materialism in this decade, and the mixed legacy of research assessed earlier, what new directions should a Marxist theorizing of the race-class nexus take? I offer the following comments as pretexts for further discussion and exchange.

Advances in the analytical power of historical-materialist science since World War II allow us to reaffirm the view that Marxism is a theoretical organon or research praxis operating on two interlocking premises: the materialist one that requires the analysis of political and ideological structures to be grounded in their actual conditions of existence, and the historical one that demands that social relations be understood not as a priori deductions from what has been traditionally conceived as "the base" but as forms with historically determinate *differentia specifica* (Rozat and Bartra 1980). Racism then cannot be understood as an abstract epiphenomenal result of capitalist development (according to an economistic monism which reduces the category of race to class), or as an "ideal type" (after Max Weber) which aggregates societies using racial ascription to organize the division of labor, distribution of goods, etc. Nor can racism be theorized as a universal albeit plural given, each manifestation differing from the other, all of them resistant to any conceptualization because of a pervasive diacritical principle, as one finds in the autonomist approach (more on this later).

I endorse Stuart Hall's (1980) main thesis that the most viable project for a Marxist research into the status of the category of race vis-à-vis the political agenda for the socialist transformation of capitalism as a global system is to posit historically demarcated racisms and then proceed from there.

Using Gramsci's concept of hegemony as an articulating principle of class alliances, Hall proposes this point of departure: "One must start, then, from the concrete historical 'work' which racism accomplishes under specific historical conditions—as a set of economic, political and ideological practices, of a distinctive kind, concretely articulated with other practices in a social formation. These practices ascribe the positioning of different social groups in relation to one another with respect to the elementary structures of society; they fix and ascribe those positionings in on-going social practices; they legitimate the positions as ascribed. In short, they are practices which secure the hegemony of a dominant group over a series of subordinate ones, in such a way as to dominate the whole social formation in a form favourable to the long-term development of the economic productive base" (1980, 338; see also 1978).

Opposing the class reductionism of traditional Marxists who dissolve race to class, Hall suggests that race as a sociohistorical category possesses a distinctive, "relatively autonomous" effectivity, so that defining the economic grounding does not adequately nor fully explain how it concretely functions in a specific formation. Conjoined with the materialist premise, the imperative of historical specificity poses certain questions: "One needs to know how different racial and ethnic groups were inserted historically, and the relations which have tended to erode and transform, or to preserve these distinctions through time—not simply as residues and traces of previous modes, but as active structuring principles of the present organization of society" (1980, 339).

One illustration of this sedimentation and deferred efficacy to which Hall refers is the plight of the Filipino nationality (now more than two million). Filipinos entered the United States for the first time in 1907 as manual workers recruited by the Hawaiian Sugar Planters Association to anticipate any labor shortage caused by the "Gentlemen's Agreement" to restrict the number of Japanese field hands. This came shortly after the ruthless suppression of Filipino revolutionary forces of the first Philippine Republic in 1898–1902. The context then was the violent colonization of six million Filipinos by U.S. military occupation forces. When the racial exclusion of Japanese by the Immigration Acts of 1920 and 1924 occurred, the Sugar Planters Association recruited 45,000 Filipinos more, a practice which continued until the anomalous status of the Filipino colonial subject—neither citizen nor alien—ceased in 1934 with the passage of the Philippine Independence Act and the limitation of immigration to a quota of fifty a year (McWilliams 1964; Quinsaat 1976; Melendy 1977). This historical matrix, coupled with the persistence of a subaltern *habitus* (Bourdieu), may elucidate why Filipinos, compared to other Asian Americans and despite higher educational attainment, continue to be segregated in low-paying jobs (Nee and Sanders 1985).

Concrete investigation of various historical conjunctures is needed to answer how the reproduction of social relations operate through race insofar as capitalism, for example, articulates classes in distinct ways at each level (economic, political, ideological) of the social formation. In effect, the schematics of race and its use to ascribe values, allocate resources, and legitimize the social position/status of racially defined populations (in short, racism) centrally affect the constitution of the fractions of black, Asian, or

Hispanic labor as a class. Put another way, the class relations that ascribe race as social/political/economic positioning of the subject (individual and collective) function as race relations. Hall affirms his key insight thus: "Race is thus, also, the modality in which class is 'lived,' the medium through which class relations are experienced, the form in which it is appropriated and 'fought through. . . .' Capital reproduces the class, including its internal contradictions, as a whole—structured by race" (1980, 341). Within a modified Althusserian positing of society as a complex, contradictory unity structured in dominance (Althusser 1969), Hall's conception of race as an articulating ideological principle deploys Gramsci's notion of hegemony to elucidate its political effectivity, that is, race as the site and stake of class struggle.

What needs to be foregrounded here is that race or racially based political calculations, under specific conditions, may define the content and form of class struggle—if by class struggle we mean the struggle for hegemony. Hegemony here designates participative moral-intellectual leadership, not the reified mechanical consensus that legitimizes bourgeois authority. Consequently, instead of just being equated with ideas or beliefs tied to state apparatuses (either repressive or ideological), race becomes an integral element of a hegemonic strategy. It becomes part of a principle operated by the bourgeoisie to articulate an ensemble of discourses and practices designed to construct subjects (or subject-positions) whose actions will reproduce capitalist relations (Mouffe 1981). Race then should be construed as an epitomizing aspect of social practice which demonstrates an autonomous effectivity, a historically concrete modality in the configuration of everyday experience of groups and individuals. This is what Blauner and others have shown in describing black or Chicano cultural politics.

What Hall and others have reminded us is that race as a concrete social practice can only be grasped in specific historical conjunctures. It has no transhistorical essence. This follows from Marx's axiom that "the concrete is the outcome of multiple determinations" (1968). Circumscribed by a differentiated or decentered totality and overdetermined by heterogeneous (residual, emergent, dominant) tendencies in the formation, race cannot be abstractly conflated with the ideological or political spheres, much less with the economic. Given the extended or integral state of late capitalism, racialization as part of bourgeois hegemonic strategy informs not only state policies but also institutions and activities of civil society, and in so doing suppresses the potential for expansive democracy by reinforcing racist hierarchy and authoritarian statism founded on national chauvinism.

How does this Gramscian *problematique* compare with other competing neo-Marxist approaches to race as a theoretical construct and historical practice?

In his survey of the "Varieties of Marxist Conceptions of 'Race,' Class and the State: A Critical Analysis," John Solomos comments on the race-class dialectic as obfuscating because it "does little to show the specificity of racism" (Rex and Mason 1986a, 103). Hall's influence on the writers of *The Empire Strikes Back* (1982), as well as his specific analysis of Caribbean race/ethnic relations, has perhaps been unjustly underestimated by Solomos.

In his review, Solomos refers to the "autonomy model" associated with John Gabriel and Gideon Ben-Tovim who argue that the issue is not the relation between racism and the social totality but "the conceptualization of racism as the object of struggle in historically defined conditions" (104). Solomos agrees with this view when he stipulates that "there can be no general Marxist theory of racism, since each historical situation needs to be analyzed in its own specificity." Meanwhile, he also concurs with Hall and the proponents of the migrant labor model that the problem of race relations cannot be thought of separately from the structural features of capitalist society. His third desideratum for a satisfactory Marxist analytic framework coincides with Hall's theory of articulation, namely, racial and ethnic divisions cannot be reduced to phenomena completely determined by the structural contradictions of capitalism. Maneuvering between the simple pluralism of the autonomy model where struggle "is not located in any social context," and what he labels as the orthodox determinist models, Solomos settles on the prospect of further theoretical refinement in clarifying with greater specification the social relations of racism in specific societies, its interconnections with class and non-class aspects of complex social realities; in other words, "the construction, mobilization, and pertinence of different forms of racist ideology and structuration in specific historical circumstances" (106). While this compromise between empiricist relativism and deterministic positivism provides a useful disciplinary guideline, it does not seem to me to offer any substantive catalyzing innovation.

While these debates on the crisis of Marxist theory vis-à-vis popular protest and resistance against racism have raged in Britain in the past two decades with the imposition of reactionary state policies on rebellious Asian and West Indian immigrants, the situation in the United States may be said to be characterized by the decline of the civil rights movement, the fragmenting of cultural and left nationalists, and the subsidence of mass struggles (with the notable exception of feminisms) upon the withdrawal of U.S. forces from Indo-China. The significant Marxist studies on race during this period, in my opinion, were made primarily by black and Third World activists (to cite only the most accessible, West 1982, 1988; Marable 1980, 1981, 1983); their polemical if retrospective orientation contributed to establishing the groundwork for a more consistently dialectical reworking of the race/class/gender convergence. Before the phenomenal rise of Jesse

Jackson followed by the redeployment of left energies to the electoral arena (via the Rainbow Coalition), it was remnants of the New Left and a younger generation of activists receptive to the European debates around Althusser who took up the task of "re-inventing" a non-dogmatic Marxism in consonance with the changed milieu and terrain of contestation (Amariglio et al. 1988).[3] In the late seventies, Stanley Aronowitz (1981) and others set the stage for an interrogation of the orthodox understanding of class, the privileging of capital logic over culture, etc., in the wake of the worldwide renewal of a critical but also anti-Eurocentric—nay, antiracist—Marxism. Aronowitz in fact pushed the renovation beyond the autonomist's limit by postulating that racism, with race functioning as a "transhistorical sign" for the castelike underclass, "is rooted in the domination that social and economic hierarchies have attempted to inflict upon nature, including human nature," so that the problematic of racism transcends historical boundaries and seems to demand a prior ontological diagnosis and subsequent ethical resolution.

One of the most innovative and praxis-oriented results of these developments is Michael Omi and Howard Winant's *Racial Formation in the United States From the 1960s to the 1980s* (1986), parts of which first appeared in 1983 in *Socialist Review*. This work is bound to be controversial and deserves extended comment (I have seen only two superficial reviews of the book so far) since I am personally sympathetic to their bold project of giving theoretical primacy to race as "the fundamental axis of social organization in the United States."

The first part of their book sharply criticizes three paradigms of theorizing race: the dominant paradigm of ethnicity, then the class-based and the nation-based ones. I find their critique of ethnicity theory the most useful, though far from original: they point out that the ethnicity school, by ignoring the qualitatively different historical experiences of various minorities, imposes a monolithic immigrant analogy and thus blames the victims. Racial meanings and dynamics are dissolved in a culturalist absolutism: the paradigm is based on white ethnic history, hence its methodological limitation. Of late, the ethnicity ideologues have provided the chief theoretical weapon for the neoconservative policy of the Reagan administration (Bush's election has not signaled any major revision so far) whose impact Omi and Winant rigorously indict as the systematic reversal of the civil rights gains of the sixties and seventies.

As for the class-based paradigm, Omi and Winant discriminate between the market relations approach (neoclassical economics), stratification theory (exemplified by William Wilson's work), and the class-conflict paradigm (classified into the segmentation theory and the split-labor market model of Edna Bonacich). In all these variations, Omi and Winant observe that they lack a theory of racial dynamics which determines class relationships and class identities. They argue from recent findings that sectoral demarcations within and among classes are objects of political struggle so that class formation cannot be fully understood without recognizing the racial identification of subjects or actors. Here they allude to the work of Poulantzas, Przeworski, Laclau, and others. While it is correct to note that class-based theories tend to subsume the category of race into class, it is not quite fair to dismiss the class-conflict theories as totally reductionist, even though Omi and Winant admit that they do call attention to "the necessity of understanding classes as the 'effects of struggles,'" a theme broached by the autonomy model cited earlier.

It is when Omi and Winant summarize the challenging paradigm of the nation-based theory that I find myself provoked into substantial disagreement for the simple reason that they ignore the two cardinal premises of historical materialism I stressed at the beginning. They reject the theory of "internal colonialism" by a somewhat fallacious reduction of the analogy to literal correspondence. Ghetto, reservation, and barrio bear affinities with such colonies as Puerto Rico or the Philippines (a neocolony since 1946) in a political-cultural, not geographical, sense. Moreover, Omi and Winant also reject cultural nationalism and its Marxist variants as limited in explaining the vicissitudes of racial dynamics because "the US political scene allows radical nationalism little space" (50). In this discussion, Omi and Winant can be said to demonstrate "bad faith" since later on, in tracing the origin of their privileged historical agent, "the new social movements," they assert that "the black movement *redefined the meaning of racial identity*, and consequently of race *itself*, in American society" (italics theirs) (93). Not only do they ignore the historical matrix of black nationalism that inflected race as a principle of difference in constructing their collective identity through symbolic (cultural) modes, but they also refuse to specify the structural or materialist parameters, particularly the Third World resistance to U.S. imperialist aggression in Africa, Latin America, and Asia in the sixties and seventies, which precipitated the global crisis of U.S. hegemony consonant with the civil rights movement. Lacking this totalizing perspective of comprehending U.S. imperialism as a worldwide system, Omi and Winant are unable also to appreciate fully the systemic crisis following the U.S. defeat in Indo-China, the Sandinista revolution, and the U.S. retreat from Iran which are the conditions of possibility for reaction in the Reagan period (Horowitz 1977; Davis 1984).

In explaining the "unitary social and historical problematic" of race which they claim has not been adequately theorized by the paradigms they question, Omi and Winant offer their theory of racial formation: "The meaning of race is defined and contested throughout society, in both collective action and personal practice. In the process, racial categories themselves are formed, transformed, destroyed and re-formed. We use the term *racial formation* to refer to the process by which social, economic and political forces determine the content and importance of racial categories, and by which they are in turn shaped by racial meanings" (61). Here they approximate in a discursive way the autonomy model alluded to earlier.

Contending that the system of racial meanings and stereotypes, of racial ideology, is a permanent feature of U.S. culture, Omi and Winant define racialization as a historically specific ideological process, the shifting meanings of race being produced by diverse historical practices of various social groups. Racial meanings pervade the whole society, shaping individual identities and structuring "collective political action on the terrain of the state." Race is thus the organizing principle of social relations; it is not a fixed essence. However, its locus of effectivity seems to gravitate around state apparatuses. Omi and Winant emphasize what is unique in their conception of racial formation: we much understand race *"as an unstable and 'decentered' complex of social meanings constantly being transformed by political struggle"* (italics theirs) (68). To illustrate this, they chart the trajectory of racial politics by focusing on the emergence of the racial state within the U.S. racial order (they allude to neo-Marxist thinking on the state by Bob Jessop [1978], Skocpol, etc.). Nowhere do they state, however, why the state utilizes racial ideology and for what purpose, although they refer to "conflicting interests encapsulated in racial meanings and identities," "political demands," etc. They focus on the mechanisms of articulation and rearticulation of racial ideology, acknowledging in passing the value of the minority project of "self-determination" (the nation-based paradigm). But why and how the state or the dominant/ruling classes employ this racial ideology as a hegemonic principle is not clarified. When we reach the section on "The Reagan 'revolution,'" Omi and Winant describe the techniques of the "color-blind" policy implemented by the bureaucratic apparatus and the legitimizing rationale supplied by Glazer and other ethnicity apologists. But what is the *differentia specifica* of this new application in terms of the exigencies of capital, of the social totality?

In concentrating on the details of how the New Right rearticulates racial ideology, Omi and Winant appear to have lost sight of the global picture and downgraded the highly intractable and recalcitrant position of those racial groups whom they have celebrated as heroes of "the great transformation." Any strategy for maintaining capitalist hegemony necessarily entails its contradiction: the counterhegemonic resistance of the ruled. This dialectical exploration of possibilities, the response of all the subalterns, is absent in the last third of their book. One can grant that indeed, as their conclusion reminds us, their study has underscored race as "a phenomenon whose meaning is contested throughout social life," that "racial meaning and systems are contested and racial ideologies mobilized in *political* relationships" (138). But what effects they produced in recasting the strategy of the power bloc, the global domination of U.S. corporate monopolies, and the whole international system of transnational capital, they do not say. They conclude by stressing the heterogeneity of new and old immigrants as an obstacle to racially based mobilization while at the same time predicting that color-blind policies will insure the persistence of economic and political inequality. The question of historical agency is elided here:

> For Asian American and Latino communities, the liberalization of immigration laws in the mid-1960s has led to a vast influx of both "old" and "new" groups. Koreans, Vietnamese, Laotians and Filipinos are distinct in ethnic and class composition from each other and from more "established" groups such as Japanese Americans. An increasingly variegated "community" makes it difficult to speak of a shared experience, common sensibility, or unified political outlook. [Here the authors somehow betray the logic of their own approach; those items they find missing are surely results or ends to be struggled for in the process as each democratic demand is articulated in a chain of equivalence in a hegemonic project.] In the face of these realities, political mobilization along presumed "racial" lines becomes an ambiguous project, even though state policy, and the majority of the American public, continues to identify the groups mentioned along racial lines (i.e., as "Asians"). (143)

At this juncture, empiricism has superseded dialectical thinking. Perhaps the sudden wobbling of the argumentation here, the abandonment of a processual and heuristic method, may have been induced by the overvalorizing of the power of the racial state in articulating racist ideology and manipulating the institutional apparatuses of consent. Hegemony becomes hypostatized, contrary to Gramsci's caveat (Merrington 1977; Sassoon 1980). A symptom of that error is Omi and Winant's absurd if wishfulfilling notion that minorities now "have achieved significant (though by no means equal) representation in the political system" (83). But does having black mayors or Japanese American senators automatically guarantee that the programs and policies of these officials will promote the welfare of their racial constituents? While emphasizing the centrality of power and conflict, Omi and Winant one-sidedly privilege political institutionalization—the particular weakness of plural society models (Hall 1977)—as the coordinating or legitimizing principle instead of the process of hegemonic class alliance or the dynamics of a historical bloc (Poulantzas 1968). Further, in overemphasizing the interventionist state apparatus, Omi and

Winant may have avoided the real target of their investigation, namely, the discursive construction of racial meanings, what Laclau (1977) calls the interpellation of subjects in discourse.

It might be appropriate to cite at this point a recent essay by Jeffrey Prager entitled "American Political Culture and the Shifting Meaning of Race" which endeavors to theorize the inscription of race in the pursuit of ascertaining functional norms, but this time concentrating on the semiotic function of race. Prager writes: "In place of racism, I prefer to understand race in America as a 'collective' or 'social representation' implying, as Durkheim and neo-Durkheimian social psychologists today suggest, that the racial problem is a function of the American inability to experience blacks in the same way as other members of the political community" (1987; see also 1982). Here we are paradoxically on the margins of psychologistic speculation which can range from the historicized psychoanalysis of Joel Kovel (*White Racism*, 1984) to the existentialist phenomenology of Sartre (*Anti-Semite and Jew*, 1948) and Fanon (*Black Skin, White Masks*, 1967).[4] What Prager does in an idealistic fashion—namely, analyze racial discourse and the ideological semiotics of racism as they rework the elements of hegemonic ideology (for instance, liberal individualism)—needs to be historically contextualized and transcoded (Therborn 1980b; Green and Carter 1988). More useful for our purposes are studies by Wellman (1977) and Gilroy (1982). What Prager succeeds in doing is to reduce everything to "political discourse, or public conversation," as required by the Durkheimian problematic of ideology as collective representations, and precipitates a poststructuralist reductionism which Perry Anderson (1984) calls the "exorbitation" of the linguistic model (see also Pierre-Charles 1980).

The strengths and weaknesses of Omi and Winant's achievement, which I value highly as an original attempt to formulate a nonessentialist or nonreductive theory of racial dynamics within the framework of a broadly progressive coalition politics, stem from the kind of methodological experiment that we find in neo-Marxists like Laclau and Mouffe. One thesis of their book *Hegemony and Socialist Strategy: Towards a Radical Democratic Politics* (1985), if I may rehearse it oversimply, is that we cannot privilege any a priori historical agent of revolutionary change (e.g., the proletariat) apart from the process of actual political/ideological struggles at specific historical conjunctures.

One of the questions raised against this is that if all modes of symbolic articulation are contingent, not necessary, given the polysemous discourse of new social movements (women, youth, racial minorities, etc.), is it conceivable to identify a homogeneous collective subjectivity that would be the effective agent of historical change? What are the points of condensation in this field of mobile heterogeneous drives, the axis where synchronic and diachronic mappings coalesce? What is the criteria, if any, for judging the material adequacy, aptness, or effectiveness of various articulations of democratic demands? Mouffe herself answers by proposing a theory of symbolic articulation (such as rearticulating the aspects of equality and justice in democratic ideology versus the liberal-possessive aspect) within the space of an expansive hegemony. For her, the Gramscian concept of "hegemonic principle" (Bocock 1986) refers to a chain of equivalence which links a plurality of democratic projects/demands on which a democratic will can be built even as the autonomy of different groups is preserved and respected within a milieu of solidarity. Consequently, she treats the notion of "collective will" or the national-popular will manifest in the historic bloc (Gramsci 1971, 202–5) as a metaphor. There is for Mouffe no center or party to embody and represent the collective will, just as for Omi and Winant racial discourse is always decentered, relative to competing articulations and the transvaluations of dispersed forces. However, she insists that discourse is not just language or ideas but concrete social practices which are specific to historically determinate societies, following Gramsci's notion that philosophy (worldviews of varying coherence) permeates all levels of consciousness so that "Philosophy is where the categories of thoughts are elaborated, allowing us to speak about our experience" (1988, 104). That is to say, symbolic contingency can metamorphose to nodes of condensation in the social field, as in definite programmatic goals and actions. Because philosophy as the site of conflicting worldviews constitutes political subjects, Mouffe contends that the field of ideological practices/discourses is the decisive site of political struggle (Hanninen and Paldan 1984, 153–54).

Can everything then be reduced to articulation as a symbolic process, as discourse or signifying practice? Hall for his part points out that while there is no social practice outside ideology, not all practice can be reduced to discourse: for example, the practice of labor which transforms raw materials into a product. While labor is within the domain of representation and meaning it is not reducible to discourse. "It does not follow that because all practices are *in* ideology, or inscribed by ideology, all practices are *nothing but* ideology. There is a specificity to those practices whose principal object is to produce ideological representations. They are different from those practices which—meaningfully, intelligibly—produce other commodities. . . . [Those forms] of practice operate in ideology but they are not ideological in terms of the specificity of their object" [1985, 103–4]. That is astutely expressed. But are there articulations identical with representations, for example, the performative speech that transforms a crowd into a revolutionary agent? Or are there objective articulations preceding their representation (ideological relations of gender, race, nationality; causal relations, etc.)? It has been suggested that to discover such "objective articulations" and to find adequate symbolic representations for them so as to make them effective ideological agents is the task of Marxist theory.

Wolfgang Fritz Haug warns us that in their obsession to purge class-reductionism, the neo-Marxists succumb to a politics of articulation unable to make distinctions so that their efforts mimic Hitler's project of articulating new social movements into a fascist brand of "revolutionary populism." He suggests that we remain within "the problematics of the specificity of a *socialist* articulation, which takes into account the existence of long waves in historical development, 'hard cores' within the changing realm of societal difference" (Hanninen and Paldan 1984). I am not sure if this is not just a matter of discriminating and then reconciling the antithetical demands of short-range (transitional) tactics and of long-range (maximalist) strategy. In any case, Haug also proposes that we adhere to the analytical concept of a "working class" as an overall orientation in forging new empirical tools because in the absence of this differentiating principle, we would not be able to constitute our identity as "socialists" in search of a "structure of hegemony" even though we may subscribe to the anti-essentialist position that there is no unitary revolutionary subject.

What I think Mouffe and other postmodernizing radicals would insist on in the light of those reservations is that the orthodox tradition lacks a theory of the imaginary and symbolic process of signification (theorized by Deleuze, Lacan, etc.) needed to configure the positioning of various subjects vis-à-vis the structuring of production and the reproduction of social relations (Wilden 1972). It is through the process of the symbolic articulation of ideology that race, as well as gender and nationality, can be understood as the defining quality of specific struggles whose necessary autonomy can only be repressed at the sacrifice of the socialist/democratic project. On the other hand, I think Marx's prescient "On the Jewish Question" (1843) already anticipated the need for a nonessentialist inquiry of extra-class determinants long before Gramsci's intervention (Carr 1985).

Can any agenda be extrapolated from this brief, necessarily schematic mapping of what has been done so far?

I suggest that any future Marxist critique of race relations in the United States needs to take as point of departure the following summations of the collective experience of the victims of racism expressed by Marable and West:

> The most striking fact about American economic history and politics is the brutal and systematic underdevelopment of Black people. . . . Nothing less than the political recognition that white racism is an essential and primary component in the continued exploitation of all American working people will be enough to defeat the capitalist class. (Marable 1983, 1, 262)

Racism has been the most visible and vicious form of oppression in American society. . . . American leftists must give first priority to the most explosive issues in American society, namely, the probability of U.S. participation in international war principally owing to imperialist policies . . ., and the plight of the urban black and brown poor primarily due to the legacy of racism in an ever-changing capitalist economy. (West 1984/85, 18–19)

That granted, I would then urge considering as a methodological imperative the need to formulate a conception of U.S. racism (not a sociology of race relations) as part of a complex historical totality—that is, the United States as a racially ordered capitalist system—where the hegemony of the bourgeoisie has been constructed through the articulation of race, through the production of subjects inscribed in racist discursive/institutional practices. In the process, a national-popular collective will has been generated by the bourgeoisie on the terrain of everyday life where "common sense" (intellectual and moral worldview) is inflected to reproduce racially ordered capitalist relations of production. Racism is then not a fixed or unitary mechanism but an articulating hegemonic principle that involves both the practices of civil society and state apparatuses. Its private nuances and public styles alter according to varying historical conjunctures; its ensemble of elements is constantly disarticulated and rearranged according to the changing balance of conflicting forces. Racist practices by the state and by various classes exhibit contradictory properties—as various historians like Higham (1971), Jordan (1974), Kolko (1976) testify—overdetermined by, and transformed with, the larger political-economic structures of the social formation. This follows as a contextual effect of the production and reproduction of U.S. imperialism in the global stage beginning with the genocidal extermination of the Indians, traversing whole epochs marked by the creation of the internal colonies and later the peripheral ones annexed (the Southwest, Puerto Rico, Hawaii) or hitherto neocolonized (the Philippines, Central America, some Caribbean islands). This assumes the analytic priority of the logic of the capital accumulation process occurring within the uneven, combined development of various modes of production in the U.S. social formation.

Without this global framework inaugurating the rise of capitalism, any account of the tactical and strategic reconstitution of the U.S. racial dispensation would be deficient because, right from the onset of chattel-slavery and colonial conquests, the U.S. formation has been conditioned if not determined by its position in the world market of labor, raw materials, etc. Within this parameter, racism as the chief hegemonic articulating principle may be grasped as one mediation between the dynamics of the capitalist world economy and the structural crisis of the U.S. social formation. As John Solomos and his colleagues point out, "the links between racism and capitalist development are complex, and conditioned by the specific socio-political circumstances in which they function" so that "ethnic and racial forms of domination" proceed "not in a linear fashion but are subject to breaks and discontinuities" (1982, 12) particularly during periods of crisis. While the historical trajectory of racism in Britain has been ably charted by A. Sivanandan (1982, 1983), the Centre for Contemporary Cultural Studies (1982), and others, a comparative historical account of U.S. racist practices from an international perspective is still to be written (Daniels and Kitano 1970; Saxton 1971). Omi and Winant have described how, under certain conditions, the capitalist state in the seventies and early eighties functioned as the crucial agency for articulating and reproducing ethnic/racial divisions. But the international context, the imperialist dimension, is scarcely registered in its effects on the internal alignment of political forces.

In a provocative essay, Dominique Lecourt (1980) contends that racism as a specific ideological aspect of class struggle in history arose from the logic of capitalist political economy and its foundation in a unitary social subject. The subject category conceals domination and subordination, the actual relations of class exploitation, by a homogenizing strategy (freedom in individual exchange, in consensus) where differences (shades of plural society? and ethnic pluralism?) are interpreted and evaluated as a consequence of the calculation of personal advantage. Since Marxism privileges the dialectics of contradiction, not nomadic or aleatory difference, situated in historically defined social formations, Lecourt believes that we cannot enunciate a general Marxist theory of racism. For such a theory can only spring from the bourgeois ideology of humanism and its premise of a given human nature; therefore, racism or racialism is "the *reverse* side and the *complement* of bourgeois humanism." Lecourt then concludes that historical materialism enables us to see that racism is not "an aberrant epiphenomenon introducing a dysfunctioning into the regular social order, but a particular aspect of the ideological class struggle in the imperialist era" (284). Whatever the seductive potential of poststructuralist discourse theory (Foucault, Lyotard, Deleuze, Badurillard) to supplement Marxism with a theory of symbolic practice—Pierre Bourdieu's "praxeology" (1977; see also Rossi 1983) seems to avoid the subjectivism of phenomenology and the objectivism of structuralism—as a tool in research strategy, Lecourt's intervention is, at this point in my exploration, salutary.

In any case, I would like to conclude these reflections by submitting for further examination Harold Wolpe's criteria for judging the theoretical and practical value of inscribing the race/class dialectic within the all-encompassing project of global socialist transformation:

The racial order, including "corporate" racial groups, has to be analyzed as the outcome of multiple determinations of which the operation of an economy characterized, in a non-economistic way, by the capital-labor relation and the structure of state power are essential elements—the account cannot be reduced to race, although the process of racial categorization cannot be reduced to "pure" economy. . . . The decisive question for a Marxist analysis is how, in what way and to what extent do the reproduction, transformation and disintegration of the racial order serve to maintain or undermine the relations of capital accumulation? (1986, 129)

This implies that one cannot finally ignore the moment of the totality and its prefigured disintegration in a revolutionary rupture (Lefebvre 1966); but, as this chapter insists, the trajectory of this complicated struggle necessarily has to go through the catharsis of destroying racism in all its protean forms. There is no shortcut or detour. Racial politics indeed is a matter of life and death for millions of blacks, Hispanics, Asians, Native Americans, and other racially defined communities in the United States, so the more it is urgent and mandatory for all progressive forces to confront racism today as probably the hitherto still undiscovered Archimedean point of the class struggle against the domination of capital, against imperialism.

Notes

1. That the program for black capitalism and independent community development cannot succeed unless "the systemic oppression of the economic system is ended," has been persuasively documented again by William Tabb (1988) and others.
2. Despite the provocative criticisms of the "internal colony" model (one motif in Blauner's research) by Wolpe, Burawoy, and others, I find the narrative of his discourse and its synthesizing framework still cogent and viable (with some modifications and updating; see Liu 1976; Wald 1981).
3. The vital contribution of academics like Michael Burawoy (1981) and Edna Bonacich (1980) should also be acknowledged.
4. Saxton (1979) gives an excellent critique of various "historical explanations of racial inequality," together with an inventory of research projects (e.g., comparative history of racist practices in the United States), which are desiderata for formulating a radical democratic political agenda today.
   Symptomatic of a compromising neopragmatism that vitiates their approach, aside from its lack of a micropolitics of agency of long duration, is Omi and Winant's virtual silence on FBI/COINTELPRO's systematic destruction of popular-democratic organizations of people of color (e.g., Black Panther Party, American Indian Movement, etc.) and the mass mobilizations they led. One suspects that this logically follows from their premature dismissal of class- and nation-based paradigms and their over-valorization of the state.

4

Hegemony and Resistance: A Critique of Modern and Postmodern Cultural Theory in Ethnic Studies

I

One of the most incalculably seminal results arising from the recent rediscovery and revaluation of Antonio Gramsci's thought in the past two decades may be discerned in the conceptualization of an interdisciplinary, hybrid field of inquiry linking the traditional humanities and the social sciences, the field of cultural studies. However varied, amorphous, and shifting the current approaches in this field may strike the orthodox academic, they all converge on Gramsci's fundamental insight that the full understanding of social phenomena depends on theorizing their historical specificity in the thickness and density of any given society and culture. Historical specification requires that any conjuncture or cross section of life be analyzed as concretely as possible, concreteness being a function of the multiple determinations that reciprocally interact and so overdetermine each other, marking what Gramsci (1971) calls an ethico-political catharsis, "the decisive passage from the structure to the spheres of the complex superstructures" (180–81). In describing this passage from the obligatory parameters of Marxist theory, the economic "base" or production relations, to the ethico-political and ideological complex where human beings become conscious of their contradictions and begin to fight them out, Gramsci stresses the need for a multilayered, dynamic mode of analyzing the balance of relations of social forces, their tempos and trajectories, at any given period, focusing in particular on circumstances defined in long-range and short-range terms.

60

Gramsci's organon of truth is a radical historicism sensitive to the subtle dialectical interplay of textures and structures. Gramsci argued for theorizing the social formation as a complexly differentiated whole, a historically defined totality structured by mutually interacting levels of articulation of economic, political, and ideological instances leading to different combinations, each combination spelling a unique configuration of social forces, a peculiar type of social development, political struggle, etc. (This demand for "concreteness" has been proposed by Marx in his 1857 introduction to the *Grundrisse* and elaborated by succeeding thinkers like Althusser and Balibar in *Reading Capital*.) There is no predetermined telos or objective law of necessity governing any of the levels or their interdependence. Given this historically specific notion of social formation, Gramsci reconceived politics as a strategic (historicist and programmatic at the same time) mapping of historic possibilities in which the subject, the historical agent (the intellectual, for example, as theoretician of ethnicity and race), participates as a factor in the movement for conjunctural and organic social change. Theory becomes a material force in social practice. Politics, thus, is no longer a mechanical, positivist reflection of changes in the mode of production, the economic base, but rather a mode of articulating the various levels toward the hegemony—the intellectual, moral, and philosophical ascendancy—of a social bloc with a specific agenda of social reconstitution. In the struggle for hegemony, the site of culture—more precisely, the national-popular dimension of social practices ranging from systematized beliefs (religion) to common sense—becomes the paramount arena of struggle, the space of that "decisive passage" earlier referred to where consciousness and subjectivity become problematized, where the catharsis of the economic to the political transpires.

Within this historicizing but not relativistic perspective, Gramsci charts the new relations of social forces in the modern world, especially after 1870 and "the colonial expansion of Europe," when new complex forms of transaction between state and civil society have emerged—the unprecedented elaboration in the structure and processes of "civil hegemony" appearing, to Gramsci, "resistant to the catastrophic 'incursions' of the immediate economic element." While civil society remains the space of heterogeneous and multiple inscriptions of subjectivity, the text of indeterminacy and difference, the modern state serves as the point of condensation of this variety of relations and practices into a definite "system of rule" founded on a system of alliances and the social bloc evolving from them, even as its contradictory structures reflect the divergent tendencies in "the civilization and morality of the broadest masses." This schema of a dialectical interaction between state and civil society foregrounds the primacy of culture and ideology in general as the site where the intellectual and ethical unity of individuals and groups as the prerequisite for forging hegemony can be realized. Premised on the basic instability of "common sense"—a palimpsest of texts without an inventory—and the contradictory tendencies of various practices comprising civil society, whatever hegemony is achieved can only be temporary and open to oppositional challenges. This is also because ideology (which includes all cultural practices including art and literature) is a complex and highly differentiated discursive formation, a terrain of diffused and fractured tendencies locked in conflict, so that the subject of ideological articulation is never a unified, self-identical, permanently coherent class subject. Rather it materializes as a locus of multiple energies and actions circumscribed only by the possibilities of the historic conjuncture.

Stuart Hall (1986) interprets Gramsci's concept of hegemony not "as a moment of *simple* unity, but a process of unification (never totally achieved), founded on strategic alliances between different sectors, not on their pre-given identity." And because there is no automatic correspondence between economic, political, and ideological practices, we can begin to explain "how ethnic and racial difference can be constructed as a set of economic, political or ideological antagonisms, *within* a class which is subject to roughly similar forms of exploitation with respect to ownership of and expropriation from the 'means of production.'"

In this context, Gramsci conceives culture as a historically fabricated terrain where categories of class, gender, race, ethnicity, and other forces intersect; and the self (the monadic agent of thought and action) which contending cultural processes work to identify or fix cannot but be a contradictory and composite subject, a social construction, inscribed in a complex genealogy of incompatibles consisting of "Stone Age elements and principles of a more advanced science, prejudices from all past phases of history . . . and intuitions of a future philosophy" (324). Because the identification of subjects and their social positioning occur in all stages of cultural-ideological mobilization, it is imperative for any social force aspiring for hegemony to grasp the precise value of the culturally specific elements—ethnic, racial, gender, religious, etc.—that coalesce in the formation of classes, elements whose articulation constitutes the historically differentiated and specific forms of labor guaranteeing the accumulation process in the regime of capital.

II

Ever since the inauguration of sociology in the nineteenth century as a discipline addressing the historic challenges to the precarious situation of bourgeois hegemony from 1848 to 1917 and the 1930s depression, questions of culture and ideology have been subsumed in the concern for maintaining consensus (Comte), organic solidarity (Durkheim), and cohesion through an ideological community (Weber). Goran Therborn has cogently demonstrated how classical sociology arose as a response to the inadequacies of liberal political economy in solving what we now call the legitimation crisis of laissez-faire capitalism (1980b, 219–315). A characteristic response was to conceive of the market as a sphere controlled and regulated by values and norms, the "moral milieu" of Durkheim, Sumner's "folkways" or mores, or the collective will and representations of Park and Burgess.

It was Weber's theory, however, which (through the mediation of Parsons and Merton) established the coordinates for theorizing the significance of ethnicity and race in mainstream cultural studies. Weber conceived the market as a system of individuals each rationally calculating available means to acquire goods to satisfy his needs; this prudent self-interested "rational choice" may be seen to derive from a particular historical system of values embodied in cultural institutions and is not simply dictated by compulsive market mechanisms. For Weber, the system of common values and norms underlying self-interest made up the social pattern of determination, the ideological community. Like Durkheim, Weber focused on value integration and normative regulation to endow the market with rationality and maintain the harmonious operations of bourgeois society. From this functionalist perspective, racial conflict then becomes a problem of integration and assimilation of minorities (out-group) in a social system with a widely shared system of common values (see Berting 1980). Park's race relations cycle and its latter-day versions, the "melting pot" metaphor; Parsons' evolutionary notion of adaptive upgrading; Kallen's cultural pluralism; multicultural diversity—all these proposals to resolve the dysfunctional effects of a free market economy hinge on the need to affirm "the integrity of a common cultural orientation" defined not by rational argumentation of various interest groups but presumably by a previous settlement, an earlier negotiated compromise, on the hierarchical distribution of power.

The publication of Gunnar Myrdal's research study *An American Dilemma* (1944), completed by the end of the first systemic crisis of global capitalism, and its interrogation by academic sociology in the classic essay by Robert K. Merton, "Discrimination and the American Creed," mark the phasing out of the norm-centered paradigm, a cultural system in constant equilibrium. While still bound by the premises of a methodological individualism rooted in the utilitarian empirical tradition of European philosophy, Merton calls our attention to the relations individual actors form in the context of communities (hence the possibility of ameliorating racist discrimination by policy regulations), not the social system where alter encounters ego (1977,

26–44). However, both Merton and Parsons despite their differences reject any Hegelian notion of totality that would approximate Gramsci's conception of society as a concretely differentiated configuration, a contradictory synchronic–diachronic articulation of multiple practices. Bound by the problematic of self-interest (where the choosing subject defines the meaning of social action) and of normative unity as the unquestioned "social fact"—the axioms of the twin reductionist poles of economism and humanism, traditional sociology is unable to comprehend the Marxian concept of practice as collective processes of transformation occurring simultaneously on the interacting economic, political, and ideological levels.

The social upheavals of the thirties following the collapse of the laissez-faire market forced the humanities and social science disciplines to rethink the almost unlimited determinism ascribed to social norms and to revise the "oversocialized conception" of individuals in the light of conflict theory. With the withdrawal of the European powers from the colonies, the saliency of racial antagonisms and the resurgence of revolutionary nationalism in the Third World defied the technocratic assumptions of liberal-humanist apologetics. With the stabilization of the Cold War in the framework of "peaceful coexistence" after the Korean War and the onset of the civil rights struggles of the sixties, a new demand to assert the hegemony of the free enterprise system required the invention of new ways to reach a compromise with the subalterns and all peoples of color that need to be pacified. A new principle of exclusion or marginalization had to be invented and deployed. Without renouncing their metaphysics of individualism, proponents of ethnomethodology and symbolic interactionism replaced the "normative paradigm" with an "interpretative" one designed to register the plurality of ways by which dominant values and norms are internalized and interpreted.

It is at this point where Weber's notion of explanatory understanding (*Verstehen*), based on grasping the subjective meaning behind actors' behavior, provides the impetus for Fredrik Barth's influential theory of ethnic identity as a matter of socially constructed boundaries, not an ontological and primordial fact. What is essential in defining ethnicity are the practices and processes engaged in by social actors in specific situations: Barth states that "ethnic groups are categories of ascription and identification by the actors themselves" (1969, 10). Three points may be underscored in this analytical model: first, ethnicity appears only when boundaries are maintained between "us" and "them," a situation self-interpreted by the actors involved; second, ethnic identity depends upon ascription by those inside and those outside; and third, ethnicity is not fixed but situationally defined, influenced by ecological or market factors, with the criteria of the boundary changing according to the needs of group organizing. Given this interpretative approach, it is not difficult to explain why the entry on "Concepts of Ethnicity" by William Petersen in the *Harvard Encyclopedia of American Ethnic Groups* betrays both an eclectic indeterminacy and homogenizing hubris, a latitude of self-interpretation permitting the view that the "black subculture" can be considered "an immigrant way of life with significant transfers from Africa" and that American Indians, with the decline of tribal units, will become a new ethnic group "based ostensibly on cultural remnants that its members half-recall, but more fundamentally on the benefits obtainable from today's ethnic politics" (1980, 240)—Leonard Peltier and survivors of the siege of Wounded Knee, take note!

III

We can observe more clearly the allochronic distortions and ethnocentric excesses that Barth's theory of ethnicity can generate in the writings of Werner Sollors. Sollors' erudite thesis in *Beyond Ethnicity* (1986a) centers on the proposition that "ethnic groups in the United States have relatively little cultural differentiation, that the cultural *content* of ethnicity . . . is largely interchangeable and rarely historically authenticated" (28). Stressing the psychological strategies of contrastive and dissociative behavior, "outsiderism" and "self-exoticization" which anyone can arbitrarily deploy, Sollors concurs with Parsons' notation on the "optional and voluntary component of ethnic identification" (35). By a stroke, ethnic groups suddenly become ghostly, floating monads under the pressure of universalistic norms in industrial society. Sollors discounts "race" as merely one aspect of ethnicity, with slavery construed as one extreme form of social boundary "constructed between people who considered themselves full human beings" (37). Denying historical specificities, Sollors is thus forced to resort to paradoxical, even antinomic, formulations when he defines the American norm or hegemonic ideology as "consent at the expense of descent definitions" for individuals and groups, an achieved rather than ascribed identity, which nevertheless allowed slavery and segregation or descent-based discrimination—part of American exceptionalism.

In demarcating the space for theorizing his notion of ethnogenesis, Sollors privileges the culture of the dominant white majority, centered on New England Puritanism, as the typological matrix of ethnic expression (40–65). If ethnicity functions only as a symbolic construct that evokes blood, nature, and descent while national identity springs from "the order of law, conduct, and consent" (151), then it follows that the racialist rhetoric of Du Bois—in "On the Conservation of Races" which Sollors cites as an example of Royce's notion of "wholesome provincialism"—occupies a dubious if not inferior rank. With ethnic boundary-making as a particular symbolic ploy accessible to everyone who seeks to affirm a particular distinction vis-à-vis the Other, no wonder every writer can be denominated "ethnic," the vehicle of a modernizing, monolithic, all-encompassing world-spirit which happens to be domiciled in the North American continent. This conforms aptly with the universalizing project of modernist art—except that when the book was being written, U.S. imperial power had just suffered an unprecedented defeat in Indo-China and was then retooling itself for new further interventions in Iran, Nicaragua, El Salvador, Grenada, Panama, and now in the Middle East.

Sollors concludes that ethnicity has been transcended with the attainment of consensus, "a shared sense of destiny," American nationalism as "transnationalism": "The language of consent and descent has been flexibly adapted to the most diverse kinds of ends and has amazingly helped to create a sense of Americanness among the heterogeneous inhabitants of the country" (259). But it is difficult to accept the equation of a "sense of Americanness," however this is defined, with the skillful manipulation of formal rhetorical strategies such as "boundary-constructing antithesis, biblically derived constructions of chosen peoplehood, . . . regionalist ethics and generational thinking," and the entire repertoire Barth's theory enables. In fact Sollors' privileging of American "revivalist standards" and his conflation of industrial capitalist modernism with ethnicization tend to infiltrate a substantialist apriorism that logically contradicts his analytic formalist method.

When Sollors attacks critics of the standard sexist, racist, and elitist literary canon in "A Critique of Pure Pluralism" for reproducing the antinomies and inconsistencies of Horace Kallen's doctrine of "cultural pluralism," and for endorsing "sectarian and fragmented histories of American literatures (in the plural) instead of American literary history," he betrays a will to knowledge/power that posits only two alternatives: the modernist dogma of American "cultural syncretism" espoused in *Beyond Ethnicity*, or the chaos of ethnic relativism disguised as the "cultural pluralism" of a racist thinker. Sollors equates "the ethnic perspective" proposed by a *MELUS* (*Multi-Ethnic Literature of the United States*) contributor with the emphasis on a writer's descent in contrast to the polyethnic art movements pervading U.S. consumer society. The group-by-group approach traceable in, for example, the *Heath Anthology of American Literature* edited by Paul Lauter would be flawed—for Sollors—by its unhistorical accounts "held together by static notions of rather abstractly and homogeneously conceived ethnic groups," leading to ethnic insiders claiming authority for being what they are, instead of just "readers of texts" (1986b, 256).

In a fairly latitudinarian spirit, Sollors then tries to advocate what he calls "an openly transethnic procedure that aims for conceptual generalizations and historicity," an approach which he demonstrates in contextualizing the genealogy of Kallen's notion of "cultural pluralism." But Kallen is not, to be sure, an African American, Chicano, American Indian, or Asian American; and Sollors' exemplum illustrating the "dynamic nature of ethnogenesis" cannot afford us any insight into the historic predicament of racial victims, peoples of color, who are still engaged in the praxis of writing and living their histories. By insisting that American literature can be made "recognizable as a productive force that may Americanize and ethnicize readers, listeners and cultural participants" if we follow his method, Sollors suggests a model of transethnic approach—he cites Boelhower's *Through a Glass Darkly: Ethnic Semiosis in American Literature* (1987) and Mary Dearborn's *Pocahontas' Daughters: Gender and Ethnicity in American Culture* (1986) as examples—that would just completely miss the aesthetic and cultural significance of Frederick Douglass' *Narrative* as a historically substantive discourse of popular resistance. Just as Sollors' ethnicity paradigm cannot register the nuances of counterhegemonic subversion when African Americans utilize the forms borrowed from the dominant culture to advance their emancipatory ends, so it cannot do justice to the critique of atomized, market-oriented individualism offered by Mark Twain's *A Connecticut Yankee in King Arthur's Court* which Sollors analyzes in detail in his textbook elucidation of "Ethnicity" in *Critical Terms for Literary Study* (1990, 288–305). One cannot help but suspect that what Sollors really wants is to expunge the term "ethnicity" from the critical lexicon and substitute the vocabulary of a *Weltliteratur* with a civilizing mission, marching under the aegis of triumphalist Eurocentrism.

In general, the practitioners of ethnicity theory applied to cultural studies labor under the limitation of an instrumentalizing, reductive metaphysics that fragments and reifies its objects of study. Within that epistemological framework, they can only reproduce the inadequacies of a *problematique* of resolving the practical antinomies of commodity production—the disjunction of purpose and activity, exchange and use, etc.—by idealizing a unity of bipolar boundaries that conceals internal ruptures, conflicts, and divisions on all levels. By positing ethnicity as a transactional process open to manipulation, and concentrating on the self-perceptions and self-interpretations of the actors, the ethnicity theorists seek to thwart the dangers of determinism and ethnocentrism that vitiate the study of intergroup relations. However, as Richard Jenkins has pointed out, ethnicity theory cannot escape its major shortcomings with its ethical and policy implications: aside from tending to reify ethnic groups as corporate entities, it cannot distinguish the ethnic from the racial and thereby ignores power imbalances since racism occurs in situations of domination and subordination (1986,

176–77). The everyday reality of racist oppression and exploitation for millions of people are bracketed, or explained away. In his entirely subjective criterion for determining ethnicity, for example, Barth's theory ignores power imbalance in structures; it takes for granted the prevailing consensus of power which defines unilateral exchange. Paine points out that Barth's notion of exchange is based more on complementarity (master and slave relation) than on reciprocity or mutuality (1974, 8). Barth's theory is oblivious to the racial oppression that occurs in the "pre-established matrix of statuses" sanctioned by the normative market morality of maximizing self-interest. This limits the range of possible transactions, of alleged reciprocal exchanges, with persisting differences presumably suspended since the theory does not examine the differences in values of the transactors negotiating the boundaries (Moore 1989, 39; see also Rex 1986c, 87–91).

Not only does ethnicity theory disregard race but it also occludes its difference and similarity with class. While ethnicity is supposed to be deemed a social resource, it can also stigmatize when it explains the failings of ethnic minorities in terms of their orientations, values, and goals. Banton for his part has attempted to correct these shortcomings; he suggests that individuals use cultural and physical difference to create groups by the process of inclusion and racial categories by the process of exclusion (1987, 126–27). It is the act of racial categorization that foregrounds power relations, whether one group can impose its categories of ascription upon another group and what resources the categorized collectivity can draw upon to resist that ascription. But when we begin to deal with collective subjects and their positioning in a decentered, asymmetrically structured whole, we are already confronted with distinctions of "class in itself" (categorization of individuals) and "class for itself" (group identification). The phenomenon of power imbalance across ethnic boundaries cannot be accommodated to the ethnicity paradigm except when it makes a provision for racial categorization: a categorical identity based on purported inherent and unalterable differences that mark inferiority to the dominating group is imposed by one group on another in the process of subjugation, colonization, conquest, and so on. This is the area of racial antagonism that other mainstream sociologists—to cite only two: Louis Wirth in his conceptualization of the minority group and Pierre van den Berghe in his distinction between paternalistic and competitive race relations—have tried to explore and problematize further by going beyond the paradigm of ethnic boundary construction.

IV

One of the more persuasive critiques of the ethnicity paradigm employed in literary hermeneutics and ethico-political judgment is that drawn up by Alan Wald. In "The Culture of 'Internal Colonialism': A Marxist Perspective," Wald lays out his premise by succinctly summarizing the findings of previous empirical researches by Blauner and Barrera among others:

> colonized minorities differ from the European immigrant ethnic minorities in at least three respects: historically, the colonized minorities were incorporated into the nation by force and violence (for example, as slaves kidnapped from Africa or as the population of a territory that was invaded by outsiders); economically, the colonized minorities became special segments of the work force (for example, as chattel or immigrant laborers); and culturally, the colonized minorities were subject to repression and misrepresentation on a scale surpassing the experience of any European ethnic immigrant group in the United States (for example, the extirpation of African languages and religions, and the banning of certain Native American Indian religions). (1981, 21)

By conflating the two concretely disparate experiences of white European immigrants and the colonized—slavery (Africans), colonization (Chicanos), racially based exclusion (Chinese, Filipinos), genocidal pacification (Native Peoples), forced relocation (Japanese Americans)—the ethnicity school perpetrated a pseudo-universalism that in effect gutted the progressive gains of the civil rights movement in the conservative Reagan era.

Dissociating himself from the chauvinist nationalist movements of the sixties (with which this "internal colonialism" approach is erroneously allied), Wald invokes Frantz Fanon's and Amilcar Cabral's dialectical strategy of national liberation. He offers Leslie Silko's novel *Ceremony* as an instructive model whose aesthetic perspicuity and philosophic vision lie in its nuanced discrimination between ritual, in "which the false lessons of history are simply re-enacted, and 'ceremony,' a praxis-like activity in which a consciously controlled creative act restores humanity to its correct relation to the world" (1981, 26). In a recent essay "Theorizing Cultural Difference: A Critique of the 'Ethnicity School,'" Wald recapitulates the fundamental principle of demarcating "between the experience of people of color and the European ethnic immigrants in the *mode and consequences* of their incorporation into the social formation, and their subsequent treatment" (1987, 23). Race, not ethnicity, becomes the central analytic category; race as a social (not just cultural) construct sometimes underpinned by a mythology of color, an ideology of racist superexploitation. In recapitulating the theory of internal colonialism, Wald emphasizes the levels of historically interanimating determinations pertinent to understanding the social construction of race: origin, occupation, American apartheid, religion, culture, and history of the U.S. social formation.

Actually Wald's historical materialist critique of doctrinaire ethnicism is not an entirely new approach since early students of race relations and ethnic stratification from Oliver Cox (a critic of the sociology of race-as-caste) and E. Franklin Frazier to Wirth, Schermerhorn, Blalock, Rex, and others have accorded due weight to racial factors in the context of anticolonial struggles (especially in South Africa) before and after World War II. The impact of historical circumstances on theory can be exemplified by the way Roger Daniels and Harry Kitano, in *American Racism: Exploration of the Nature of Prejudice* (1970; the subtitle is perhaps a counterpoint to the classic empirical study of racial prejudice by Theodor Adorno and his colleagues, *The Authoritarian Personality*, 1950), try to concretize their two-category stratification model by making boundary maintenance or permeability contingent on relatively weighted criteria such as color (as racial signifier), numbers, nationality, religion, political ideology, culture, and marginality. Later commentaries like Stanley Lieberson's *A Piece of the Pie: Blacks and White Immigrants Since 1880* (1980) and Stephen Steinberg's *The Ethnic Myth* (1981), to cite just two titles, explicitly contend against the lack of historical concreteness in the "abstracted empiricism" and subjectivist formalism of the ethnicity school.

In any case Wald qualifies his earlier view by noting that the "internal colonialism" analogy (1981, 18–27), which foregrounds the economic and cultural exploitation of peoples of color as part of the general development of Western colonialism, needs to be improved by adopting a comparative approach—instead of the serial cataloguing to which Sollors objects—and addressing more integrally the issues of class and gender founded on the recognition that "the components of a class are produced historically and may be comprised of different genders and diverse races" (1987, 24). Valorizing also the text-specific critical practice of such critics as Henry Louis Gates, Jr., and Houston Baker, this race-class-gender perspective pursues the Gramscian research program I noted earlier in which multiple determinants on interacting levels of a complexly structured social formation need to be articulated in a historic conjuncture in order to disclose its hegemonic specificity. By "hegemonic specificity," I mean that sense of totality which allows the subject, the historical agent of change, to intervene in realigning the iniquitous positioning of social forces. Wald imputes this sense of concrete totality to a wider notion of "class" which, as orientation for cultural studies, implies "redirecting the study of U.S. cultural formation away from myths, themes, symbols, and elitist networks—which are symptomatic, not causal—and focusing more precisely on conquest and invasion, capital accumulation, urbanization, colonial and imperial expansion, and late capitalism, as the framework that nurtures and limits the context in which active agents create culture" (1987, 30).

Except for the peremptory dismissal of symbolic exchange as merely "symptomatic," a vestige of the mechanical base-superstructure logic of economistic Marxism, I agree completely with Wald that the conceptualization of "American Culture" or for that matter American identity, nation, or society, entails the forcing of a premature methodological unity that can only serve to reinforce and intensify the present relations of domination and oppression which have marginalized numerous cultures and obliterated from our disciplines and everyday knowledge the ineluctable contradictions of gender, class, and race. Wald's call for a dialectical rethinking of racial difference implies a challenge to the hegemony of Eurocentric, patriarchal worldviews and global practices whose logocentric imperialism has thrived on the continuous reproduction of subalternity status for the majority of the human species. This is not just a triumphalist affirmation of difference, of Otherness as a gesture of radical solidarity, but a beginning stage of a research program that would articulate complex cultural wholes within the parameters of an internally stratified, fractured world system.

The last phrase might evoke for some the parallel or supplementary investigations of Immanuel Wallerstein and cognate theories of dependency, but I am really alluding more to old-style historical-comparative analysis of the rise of the world market and the conflictive relations between the metropolitan industrial powers and the peripheral colonies made by Harry Magdoff, Gabriel Kolko, and others. A useful textbook synopsis can be found in Eric R. Wolf's *Europe and the People without History* whose concrete historical charting of ethnic segmentation not only undercuts the not-so-disinterested antithesis between the culturally homogeneous European modern nations and the heterogeneous, plural societies of the Third World, but also argues that ethnicity theory wrongly ascribes explanatory power to cultural difference when this difference itself is generated by the organization and mobilization of the labor process itself. Racial designations like "Indian" or "Negro" are valorized as hierarchic markers or devices of categorization to rank workers in the worldwide scale of labor markets, segmenting workers, stigmatizing some to lower levels (the underclass, the "truly disadvantaged") and insulating the higher echelons from competition from below. Racial categorization homogenizes by negating cultural and physical differences within subject populations and thus effectively denies their political, ideological, and economic identity.

Wolf thus gives us a historical-materialist appraisal of the exclusionary function of racial categories within industrial capitalism, usually excluding peoples of color from all but the lower echelons of the industrial labor force;

while ethnic categories serve to express "the ways that particular populations come to relate themselves to given segments of the labor market."
Wolf concludes that ethnicity is not a "primordial" or biologically given
social relation; ethnic groups are conceived as "historical products of labor
market segmentation under the capitalist mode" (1982, 381). Wallerstein's
observations about the "ethnicization" of community life, the world's work
force, in the period he designates as "historical capitalism" also makes the
point that the conceptualization of race and ethnicity cannot be theorized
cogently apart from the historical vicissitudes of capital accumulation
whereby institutional racism, one of its ideological pillars, regulated the
relations between various segments of the work force by socializing/
reproducing groups into their assigned roles, fashioning expectations and
limiting them: "Racism was the ideological justification for the hierarchization of the work force and its highly unequal distributions of reward. What
we mean by racism is that set of ideological statements combined with that
set of continuing practices which have had the consequence of maintaining a
high correlation of ethnicity and work force allocation over time" (1983,
78). While color or physiology offered itself as the "scientific" tag in the
course of the development of physical anthropology, racial typology and
Darwinian evolutionary thinking in the nineteenth century, Wallerstein
maintains that the volatility of any given group's boundaries (whether
drawn up by color or other phenotypical markers) is a function of "the
persistence of an overall hierarchy of groups," the ongoing ethnicization of
the global army of labor.

Using the universalizing claims of Barth's theory of ethnicization as "a
form of boundary-construction" where cultural differentiation is erased,
Sollors' influential book *Beyond Ethnicity* ignores the global historical formation of ethnic groups or peoples traced by Wallerstein, Wolf, and others.
Sollors has elaborated a formalist theory of ethnicity—formalist, it seems,
because it dismisses the historical specificity of various peoples' incorporation
into U.S. society—which actually privileges the European immigrant experience as the paradigm for peoples of color. He contends, for example, that
"Afro-American peoplehood could be fashioned . . . with the help of the
same typological materials that were used to naturalize national identity"
(1986a, 59). This contradicts outright the efforts of critics like Baker and Gates
to found a vernacular black poetics on the conjunctural and organic thickness
of their peoples' histories. A symptomatic aporia, however, decenters Sollors'
synthesizing blueprint. As I have contended earlier, his privileging of American "revivalist standards" and his conflation of capitalist modernism with
ethnicization reinforce an idealist or essentialist tendency in his argument
which logically undermines his claim to historical veracity.

V

In a synoptic account of the transition from modern to postmodern culture, "Postmodernism, or the Cultural Logic of Late Capitalism," Fredric Jameson explores the mutations of expressive cultural forms as homologous or analogical reflections of global changes in contemporary social and economic life. He demarcates three epochs of capitalist expansion: market capitalism (the growth of industrial capital and early nation-states from the seventeenth to the eighteenth century), monopoly capitalism or imperialism (nineteenth century up to 1945), and multinational consumer capitalism (from 1945 on). The last one is "the purest form of capital yet to have emerged" (1984, 78). What distinguishes the postmodern condition is the pervasive commodification of everything, in particular representation as such which involves not only culture but all social and economic practices; everything is transformed into exchange-value, quantified for circulation.

Within this framework, Jameson describes the crisis of representation in modernism, the separation of the sign from its referent, as an effect of alienation and reification. All social relations are reduced to inert objects; fetishes obscure the genuine relations among humans. The self-identical subject, the rational Cartesian ego, of classical liberal thought is problematized, interrogated, and deconstructed. One dimension of this crisis can be witnessed in the colonization of culture itself—art and mass media, information and knowledge, the private sphere or the unconscious—by capital; the reification of social relations initiated in the early stage of capitalism spreads to contaminate discourse and language, hence the divorce of sign and referent in modernism which allows for critique and utopian extrapolation. Jameson pursues the spread of reification in postmodernist culture when capital relieves signs of all referential function, occupies all autonomous spaces, and permits only a "pure and random play of signifiers." This new style of pastiche, collage, and other schizoid decenterings "ceaselessly reshuffles the fragments of preexistent texts, the building blocks of older cultural and social production, in some new and heightened bricolage: metabooks which cannibalize other books, metatexts which collate bits of other texts" (1987a, 222). Postmodernist spectacle, intimations of the sublime, simulacra, then become the locus of the crisis where the play of fragmented and ephemeral intensities, ruptures of synchronic and diachronic sequences, may be read as symptoms of the quest for symbolic capital: new identities in fashion, localism, religious revivals, and myths. Ethnicity here enters as one furniture from a lost primordial era of representation rescued, overhauled, and remodeled to serve the needs of a new posthumanist science to be founded on the rubble of the old metanarratives and "grand theories."

One such attempt may be seen in Michael Fischer's essay "Ethnicity and the Post-Modern Arts of Memory" (1986). To revitalize the practice of ethnography as a mode of cultural criticism, Fischer appeals to ethnic autobiography and autobiographical fiction whose resolutions "tend toward a pluralistic universalism, a textured sense of being American." Of course Fischer subscribes to the pervasiveness of a postmodernist ideology in ethnic writing. Bakhtin's notion of ludic heteroglossia becomes the new legitimizing organon of emergent resistance writing. Fischer celebrates this new mode of textuality shown by blacks, Chicanos, Native Americans, and Asian Americans when their artists deploy a series of formal techniques such as "bifocality or reciprocity of perspectives, juxtapositioning of multiple realities, intertextuality and inter-referentiality, and comparison through families of resemblance" (230). These tactics of postmodernist writing are meant to reconcile the twin currents of universalism and particularism in modernist thinking and afford "an ethical device attempting to activate in the reader a desire for *communitas* with others, while preserving rather than effacing differences" (232–33). But all these innovations in generating personality-centered explorations of ethnic identity, which are paralleled by other nonethnics in the cultural spectrum, are meant for Fischer to demonstrate and reinforce "the tolerance and pluralism of American society," not to transform power relations or the hierarchical order of priorities. This postmodernist strategy of contriving a fetish of the unified but equivocal self, reborn in the womb of ethnic interreference but still operating within the hegemonic system of exchange-value, harnesses the capacity of ethnic writers to forge a moral vision through a modernized Pythagorean arts of memory. Ethnic memory is invoked to restore the "public enactments of tradition" as well as its "ritual·and historical rootedness" gutted by a commodity/consumerist society. Ethnicity, it is hoped, will return us to a precapitalist gemeinschaft where authentic individuality will flourish once again.

Fischer's endeavor privileges the deconstructionist principle of textuality as the matrix of ethnic difference. Spatialization overcomes temporality, the intermittencies of becoming, in the palimpsest of the dream-text of Kingston's *The Woman Warrior*. Unlike the drive of Freud's dream-analysis toward fixing referentiality in the cathexis of historical experience, Fischer's reading displaces the historical subtext that is the condition of intelligibility of Kingston's fragmentary "talk stories." Time collapses into manipulable units of topography, grids, diagrams, and charts where humans are quantified and duly catalogued. The complex project of Kingston's narrative apparatus to articulate the continuity of the Chinese people's resistance against white racist violence amid the discontinuities of several generations, shifts in state policies, alterations in political climate in China itself, etc., is reduced to the problem of finding "clear role models for being Chinese-American" and thus trivialized: "Being Chinese-American exists only as an exploratory project, a matter of finding a voice and style" (210).

What needs to be underscored, according to Fischer, is the polyphony, interreferences, interlinguistic or intertextual modalities, the kaleidoscope of alternative selves that constitute ethnicity. But this ethnicity, dependent on the functionalist paradigm of Barth and others cited previously, ignores those mediations of class, race, and gender required to produce concreteness in the philosophical sense I have mentioned earlier. What is at stake is the overdetermined concept of socially constructed identities of peoples of color. This is the reason why I think Ramon Saldivar (1990) criticizes Richard Rodriguez's media-acclaimed autobiography *Hunger of Memory* for its uncritical acceptance of the dichotomy between private and public spheres in pluralist/liberal democracy, and its effect of reducing "the interplay between these two constitutive realms to the overpowering order of the *private* world" (159), precisely a symptom of the fetishism that converts form itself (divorced from social/use value) into exchangeable, universalizing currency.

In the case of American Indian writing, Fischer sees how "the techniques of transference, talk-stories, multiple voices or perspectives, and alternative selves are given depth or expanding resonances through ironic twists" (224). For the postmodernist critic, Leslie Marmon Silko's novel *Ceremony* illustrates how "the problem of the Indian is analogous to that of whites" in their becoming victims of a commercial, reified society; the Indian protagonist Tayo becomes an archetypal figure of the alienated citizen, confused and deracinated. Valorizing irony, humor, and satirical techniques, the postmodernist ethnographer would erase the struggle of American Indian nations—the official rubric to designate a multiplicity of nations—to preserve their own history of resistance against the genocidal state, conflating their specific predicament with the life situation of others (including their oppressor).

In treating Momaday, Silko, and other American Indian writers as no different than other ethnic postmodernist authors in utilizing comparable discursive strategies, Fischer has ironically undermined his own commitment to a more realistic, textured, nuanced ethnography by his unquestioned assumption that ethnic writers operate like the typical Euro-American author afflicted with an existentialist angst. Ethnic autobiography may display similarities with the Western genre in its dialogic manipulation of *historia* and *poesis*, verifiable events and imaginative fabrication, but this distinction with its genealogy in the divergent lives of St. Augustine and Rousseau cannot apply to the embattled collective predicaments of Native Americans, Chicanos, Asian Americans, and blacks. The two modes of signifying practice are just truly incommensurable.

Arnold Krupat (1989) insists that the Native American narrator cannot be summarily dissolved by postmodernist theory into the figure of the Western white male author because in her vocation she functions as a storyteller with a well-defined, conventional social role. The voice in Silko's *Storyteller*, for example, is one "who participates in a traditionally sanctioned manner in sustaining the community" so that *Storyteller* is presented as a strongly polyphonic "text, in which the author defines herself—finds her voice, tells her life, illustrates the capacities of her vocation—in relation to the voices of other storytellers Native and Non-Native, tale tellers and book writers, and even to the voices of those who serve as the (by-no-means silent) audience for these stories" (163). Silko herself points out that both remembering and retelling of stories in the Native American milieu are parts of an integral "communal process" undergoing change. Applying poststructuralist criteria, Krupat construes *Storyteller* as an attempt to liberate "cultural-semantic and emotional intentions from the hegemony of a single and unitary language" and as a "clear instance of novelized, of dialogic discourse" which rejects the notion of an isolated, independent self central to the dominant utilitarian philosophy of atomized individual agents competing in the "free" market.

Just as it is presumptuous to predicate ethnogenesis of peoples in the North American continent on the basis of a few Puritanical sermons in seventeenth-century New England, it is also an act of supererogation to claim that "the arts of memory" practiced by non-Europeans can be instrumentalized to reinvigorate the ethnographic pursuits of academic anthropology and the social sciences. Mnemonic procedures and methods have traditionally served the colonizing project of Western science and commerce. What peoples of color strive to articulate is an archeology of popular resistance (I exemplify this below with a recent Chicano novel). Instead of memorializing more texts by Puritan men and women, or instigating revisionist readings of Emerson, Hawthorne, James, and Faulkner, we—if I may editorialize for ethnic intellectuals—need texts that would mobilize mass recollections of activists like the chiefs of the Nez Perce, Harriet Tubman, Juan Cortina, anonymous Chinese miners, Filipino farmworkers, and union organizers. Historical discourses of the U.S. "nation" have been precisely constituted by the absence, elision, and silencing of oppositional agents of change. It is clear that certain representations of the national history or one highly selective version of it has achieved centrality, displacing other competing versions in the process of political and economic struggle. There is no question that "political domination involves historical definition. History—in particular popular memory—is at stake in the constant struggle for hegemony" (Johnson 1982, 213).

Popular memory, a sense of history inscribed in the collective resistance against racist, patriarchal, and exploitative forces, is one of the necessary means for oppressed peoples to acquire a knowledge of the larger context of their collective struggles, equipping them to assume transformative roles in shaping history. It is the means by which communities can become self-conscious about the formation of commonsense beliefs that govern the practices of everyday life. These beliefs are products of determinate processes in history. What is imperative is to articulate their "inventory," not in the manner of the antiquarian folklorist intending to preserve quaint traditions for modern consumption, but "in order that, their origin and tendency known, they may be *consciously* adopted, rejected or modified" (214). Popular memory as embodied in ethnic historiography can provide a knowledge of basic social contradictions (on the level of race, gender, class, etc.) that hegemonic liberalism, mediated through the "common sense" of cultural pluralism or individual freedom, easily conceals. It is this knowledge or its possibility that postmodernist critical theory blocks by its spatializing and aestheticizing politics, reducing differences into formalist novelties or "repetition of circularities" in a "unified global space economy of capital flows" (Harvey 1989, 296). The struggle to define and articulate a politics of popular memory on the face of the populist amnesia which consumerism induces occupies center stage in formulating an agenda for an ethnopoetics sensitive to the racial politics of the twenty-first century.

VI

The fundamental importance of a "politics of memory" has been underscored by William Boelhower's pioneering work *Through a Glass Darkly: Ethnic Semiosis in American Literature* (1987), so far the most serious and ambitious attempt to outline a semiotic theory of ethnic sign production with particular reference to the United States. I think the attempt is commendable in its modernist vision of challenging universalist and homogenizing politics which condemns the Other as a false, inferior image of a superior Self. But the argument is flawed by its failure to sustain a putatively synoptic, historicizing project capable of taking into account the multiple determining forces in the formation of the unequally positioned peoples of color in U.S. territory.

The first two chapters of Boelhower's book proposes the centrality of a generic "American" identity crisis in understanding the culture and history of the United States. While the roots of this crisis may be traced to the Cartesian cartographic logic of private property of land and its corollary, the "Great Myth of Nationalism" and an illegitimate claim of one "nation-state" to cultural purity, it centers mainly on the permanent ethnic difference embodied in the historical fact of immigration. In elaborating a "type-scene pragmatics" which performs the repertoire of possible actions provided by a cultural encyclopedia of the immigrant's ancestors, Boelhower asserts that immigrant narratives "represent the legitimizing epicenter, the original authority, of ethnic literature as a whole" (98). By privileging the European immigrant experience as the theoretical paradigm informing the ethnogenesis of diverse peoples in the continent, Boelhower undercuts his initial aim of refuting the validity of both assimilationist and pluralist paradigms. Boelhower's premise assumes that capitalist modernization generates and increases ethnic differences through the mobile distribution of populations; ethnicity, fluid and situational by definition, springs from the confrontation between the native (here personified by Henry James's sensibility) and the immigrant whom he confronts in Ellis Island in 1904. This hermeneutic interrogation of the space juxtaposing native and immigrant produces the "ethnic *topos*," a conjunctural context where both parties are "decentered onlookers, both on the margins. At the center is not an entity or a content or a definable subject, but a dynamic relation, a qualifying energy, in short an ethnic *kinesis*" (23). We are faced here with a version of Barth's concept of boundaries where the unequal power relation between native and immigrant is obscured since both share a European genealogy. In time, however, the problem of American identity or *habitare*, for Boelhower, can be solved in the chorographic map within the national space, more precisely in a local authentic space which can permit the actualizing of the stereoscopic American self: A (non-A).

Boelhower's semiotics mobilizes the destabilizing logic of ethnic kinesis, its principle of "absent presence," against the "assimilationist logic of *reduction ad unum*." How do ethnic signs embedded in the dominant culture come about? It comes about through a strategy of affirming the principle of difference, nonidentity; the "constructive dream of a unique American identity" is founded on the "deconstructive deferment of plural Otherness" (85). But Boelhower, unlike poststructuralist agnostics, believes that the production of ethnic discourse requires a cohesive unitary subject able to deploy a strategy of localizing, of perspectival orientation. He defines ethnic semiotics as "the interpretive gaze of the subject whose strategy of seeing is determined by the very ethno-symbolic space of the possible world he inhabits" (87). This possible world springs from ethnic semiosis, the strategic use of memory realized in "the topological and genealogical interrogation of the originating culture of his immigrant ancestors" (89). An ethnic tradition arises from the tension between the processing content of Memory and an ongoing Project; this project, I take it, is what Boelhower calls "transgression of the national culture of *habitare*" which is fixated to a *patria*, a homogeneous geopolitical unit.

For Boelhower, the task of ethnic semiotics is to redeem the bare present, the reductive *nunc* of present business society, through cultural contrast and comparison, a game of shifting temporal dimensions combining both tenses of Memory and Project whereby the American crisis of identity can be historicized. Ethnic kinesis can transform "the monocultural space of 'twentieth-century cosmopolitanism' into a polymorphic physiognomy of ethnic traces, associations, images, and symbols" by the "insertion of a dialogical 'clash' capable of redimensionalizing the spatio-temporal restrictions of the culture of the national map" (93). The aleatory, nomadic ethnic sign emerges from a situation where the protagonist (in such texts like John Cournos' *The Mask* or Rolvaag's *Their Father's God*) employs "a perspectival strategy of comparison and contrast by means of a genealogical interrogation of his/her *traditio*" (107). This strategy is at the heart of the ethnic narrative program that reinterprets tradition as a cultural encyclopedia, a semantic/pragmatic apparatus which can be used by the ethnic protagonist to yield "ethnic saviors," mobile and free-floating sign sequences. The diagram of the ethnic *habitare*, for Boelhower, is coordinated by the vertical axis of Memory and Encyclopedia, the collective resources of the original community, and the parallel axis of Frame and Project, the individual subject who activates innovative thought by Genealogical Interrogation, moving from Memory to Project; and who activates semantic resources in the Encyclopedia through tactical manipulation of Type-Scenes, an "instructional gestalt" which codifies prefabricated scripts, roles, homologous situations, and so on. Figure 1 shows Boelhower's semiotic diagram which theorizes the continuous production of the ethnic self (112).

Since ethnicity here is tied with the immigrant matrix, Boelhower observes that the cultural encyclopedia tends to lack "the intrinsic and ordering principle" usually ascribed to the ancestral community and its institutions and thus cannot organize the complexity of the immigrant experience into a totality. However, this epistemological weakness of the "primordial sentiments" becomes the semiotic strength of ethnic texts since ethnicity now can "be only optional and symbolic, a micro-strategic and rhizomatic device of double awareness which has no desire to retotalize a buried encyclopedia but which also has no desire to abandon the practice of ethnic semiosis." Predicated on the rupture between the ethnic self and her *traditio*, ethnic textuality can either fashion a local cultural map (the quest for roots in regional places, as in Toni Morrison's *Song of Solomon*) or establish the site or situation for "intercultural performance" where the protagonist experiments, reinvents, interrogates, and disrupts—in short,

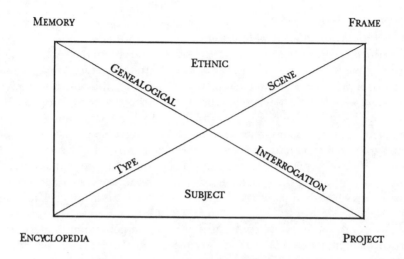

FIGURE 1   Boelhower's Semiotic Diagram of Ethnic *Habitare*

creates the American self as A (non-A), an algorithm projecting identity as basically differential and contextual.

What Boelhower emphasizes, I think, is not just the constraints surrounding the immigrant performance, the conservative and limiting resources of the Encyclopedia (the authority of the community unfolded in Memory) and the limited pragmatics of Type-Scene, but the seemingly uncurbed energy (*ergon*) of the subject signified by the Frame, "the spatio-temporal moment of ethnic semiosis." The role of the Frame in the semiotic diagram is, in my judgment, anomalous because it preempts the functioning of the whole system as the source of ethnic performance. I suspect that it introduces what might be called Freedom of Agency, a gesture of suspending the structural closure so obviously connoted by both processes of Genealogical Interrogation and the operational pressure of Type-Scenes. According to Boelhower, the Frame is "thought in action" versus Type-Scene, thought at rest:

> Instead of trafficking in types, thereby reconfirming the established field of ethnic identity through repetition, the frame proposes actorial roles never evident until then, thus introducing an ethnic *novum* unrepeatable in time and space. It is this fundamentally contractual or dialogical dimension that makes it impossible to explain or predict frame genesis by means of encyclopedic description. Between the semantic stasis of the latter and the pragmatic action of the former there is a qualitative leap. (110–11)

How the Frame is able to succeed in escaping the relational logic of perspectivism and suddenly come up with a qualitatively new act is not explained here.

Following this discussion of the Frame and the semiotic diagram, Boelhower's example of "The Ethnic Feast" as a literary *topoi* only illustrates how the "utopian space of ethnic identity" is achieved through "a genealogical exercise of storytelling, music, and group recollection," an exercise of historical synthesis and integration where Memory and Encyclopedia limit subjective framing. The ethnic feast, it turns out, serves only as an ad hoc device to contrast, say, the American way of life and the Italian, a trivial point which begs the question of exactly how ethnic kinesis relativizes and unbalances the whole field of signs, practices, rituals, and so on. This is the point where Boelhower, attributing a flexible pragmatic astuteness to the framing subject, signals his shift to a postmodernist celebration of ethnic discourse as infinite and ceaseless acts of interpretation, the topic of his concluding chapter.

In returning to the crisis of *habitare* in the postmodernist context, Boelhower now declares that all ancestors are dead, "in place of the real world there is now only a global strategy of possible worlds" (120). At this juncture, the presiding spirits of Deleuze and Guattari are replaced by the invocation of some cosmic technotronic simulacra, courtesy of Baudrillard and Virilio. Encyclopedia, Memory, and topography disappear in the formlessness of the contemporary metropolis celebrated by Le Corbusier, Futurism, and John Dos Passos. Boelhower rightly observes that this urban deterritorialization serves "the mass man's functions of production and consumption," not the possibilities of socialization and communication; the tempo of America as one huge metropolis "requires the self to be a perpetuum mobile in a highly organized culture of profit," of productive circulation (125). In the city of advertisement and publicity, everything has become derealized into fiction, news, image; reality and the subject have dissolved into the simulacrum. Since the original has disappeared, together with the authentic object and the unique and unrepeatable subject, what happens to ethnic discourse?

Forgetting what he has just said about the commodification of all life in late capitalist society, Boelhower now believes that the national map has changed. It is "now capable of realizing an updated version of the American dream, a hyperreal circulation of simultaneous communication in which the human subject, no longer hampered by a physical body, can be everywhere and yet nowhere at the present time" (131). Ethnic kinesis which formerly assumed a differential relation, a temporal spacing, is now inconceivable within the postmodern episteme where past and future are reduced to the present, where synchronic relations supersede diachronic referentiality, juxtaposition causal sequence, and fragmentation perspectivism. Postmodern

ethnic semiosis can no longer deploy the strategy of genealogical interrogation since distinctions of authentic and false, existential and symbolic, are no
longer valid; "authenticity now pertains to the pragmatics of simulation
rather than to a process of literal representation" (132). Ethnic pragmatics
cuts off its mimetic anchorage by valorizing the world of signs, the world of
absence, where possible worlds can be performed by free play:

> After all, the task of ethnic framing is not to name a world already known
> but to produce the same conditions of knowability as that which has
> already been named. Far from being confined to the ethnic encyclopedia
> as a set of fixed cultural contents to be continually reproposed with each
> new generation, the ethnic subject now plays freely with the encyclopedia
> in order to produce an ethno-critical interpretation of the present and of
> his possibilities in it. (133)

The epistemological status of the "Encyclopedia" is, I think, highly suspect
because it could turn out to be merely a simulacrum, not a fixed inventory
of traditional practices.

Boelhower concurs with the postmodernist thesis that the metaphysics of
self as organic, rational, and coherent has been annulled by a notion of the
self as "an effect of the surface," of linguistic stratagems, of "a serious game
of words and possible worlds" (134). The ethnic self is now conceived as a
potentially catastrophic subject: "As a pluralized and multiform self, the
ethnic's very instability as well as his access to an open series of possible
worlds make him unpredictable and aleatory" (135). The ethnic subject is
multiple, polymorphic, protean, allotropic, and ultimately uncodifiable.
Ethnicity is a matter of performance, of role reversibility, a putting into
play of ethno-semiotic competence. This self-reflective game of inhabiting
several possible worlds is not a return to origins but a questioning of limits.

But what seems paradoxical is that underneath this exultant apotheosis of
fiction and fable where history is absent, of the local and marginal,
Boelhower still insists that ethnic semiosis is "a radical questioning of
contemporary American experience." The politics of memory cannot be
repressed:

> Indeed, in a culture without a historical memory, where the crisis of
> identity and the crisis of memory are coterminous, remembering is itself
> a central category of the ethnic project. By interrogating the *traditio* of his
> ancestors, the ethnic subject opens a new inferencing field in which he can
> re-present the crisis of cultural foundations in a critical light. . . . The
> ethnic remains semiotically strong because of his relationship with his
> originating cultural *traditio* which, as an absent presence, solicits ethnic
> interpretation in a metacultural space that is nowhere and everywhere at
> the same time. (140–42)

At this stage, postmodern ethnic wisdom rediscovers the meaning of "the originating cultural tradition." The "absent presence" of the Encyclopedia, the community of origin, resurfaces here as the binary opposite of the simulacra, virtually the "political unconscious" buried by textuality, language games, images, and exorbitant signifiers which characterize the empty now of postmodern America. Nevertheless, we can no longer think of American identity in terms of maps, of a charted and coordinated global space where the Puritan city on the hill and the wilderness surrounding it are clearly demarcated. We can no longer totalize the orbit of our knowledge and experience. Despite this gesture of refusing to generalize, Boelhower sums up with a resolute tone: "Ethnic semiosis, then, is a way of thinking differently by thinking the difference, and in the postmodern American framework this may be all the difference there is: a particular form of discourse, of evaluating the agency of the subject, of holding one's ground against the map of national circulation" (143). To be sure, the postulation of the power of a "map of national circulation," unless this is just another equivalent discourse competing for supremacy, reveals that the ethnic subject knows something else which the theoretician of ethnicity unwittingly elides or deliberately ignores. We are a long way from the "culture of the map" associated with European merchant capitalism examined by Boelhower in the second chapter, and the "sense of the cauldron" which disturbed Henry James. In the unfolding of his text on ethnic semiosis, it seems that Boelhower has forgotten the conditions of possibility of theorizing ethnicity itself so that the concept of postmodernist thinking of difference collapses figure and ground, subject and object, signifier and signified, into itself. Meanwhile, the ethnic self survives this vertiginous adventure in the abyss of postmodernism to carry on its protracted resistance against the power of the American dream.

I am sure that in the course of my summarizing Boelhower's endeavor to characterize ethnic semiosis as postmodernist in form if not in substance, the ethnic discourse becoming *ecriture* or textuality incarnate, one will have noticed a disturbing inconsistency if not aporia undermining the plausibility of the argument. The problem lies in Boelhower's desire to reconcile opposites, to preserve the modernist utopian dream of the monadic subject in the all-absorbing intensity of the postmodernist sublime. Even while endorsing the view that reality has disappeared into the simulacra, Boelhower appears unable to give up the thematics of the individual subject in quest of some coherent identity, albeit one which is in perpetual migration, nomadic and schizophrenic. Paradoxically the Project, a parasite on Memory as it ransacks the collective Encyclopedia, is not really motivated to a future redrawing of the map of different positionalities for the simple reason that representation no longer makes sense. But if there is no old order, not even a vestige of tradition, embedded in Memory and the Encyclopedia, how can the Frame of ethnic pragmatics ever create the New?

Nevertheless, Boelhower still believes in hermeneutics and interpretation even though the diacritical nexus of surface and depth, of outside/manifest and inside/latent, as well as the liaison of signifier and signified in the signifying chain, have all broken down. A pragmatics of simulation now valorizes the here and now, the immediacy of the flux. Boelhower comments on Maya Angelou's *I Know Why the Caged Bird Sings*: "Encyclopedic foundations do fade away into myth and the ethnic genealogical strategy is a *mise en abime*" (102–3). The act of remembering turns out only to be a ludic gesture, a carnivalesque ruse, as empty as the intention of historicizing actions and situations ascribed to the Frame.

Even while Boelhower affirms the necessity of ethnic mimesis or mimetic representation when he says that "ethnic sign production is ultimately an encyclopedia/frame circuit" (117), he posits a catastrophic subject transcending all codes, representation, referents, and figuration. If ethnic equals postmodernist, what was ethnic semiosis in the stage of modernism? I suspect that in the process of constructing his model of ethnic semiosis where the strategic locus of the Frame will guarantee creative novelty, richness, and depth of reflexivity, and utopian plenitude surrounding the genesis of the ethnic Self, Boelhower succumbed to the seduction of the "hysterical sublime" (Jameson 1984, 77), the pleasure of aestheticizing. In brief, the spatializing logic of postmodernism which Boelhower upholds in his final chapter cannot but destroy the essentially temporal dynamics, the historicizing purpose and will, of ethnic *habitare* which his semiotics of ethnic framing was designed to make intelligible in the first place. Ethnic framing cannot just be a valorization of experience as the heterogeneous given because experience, as Adorno has demonstrated in *Negative Dialectics* (1973, 186), acquires intelligibility only when its dense and rich mediations—its specifically historical immanence—are thoroughly concretized in a totalizable temporal pattern.

One might note here how Baudrillard himself, imprisoned by his theory of universal simulation, is forced to indulge in fantasies when he uses the Tasaday tribe in the Philippines as an example of "The Precession of Simulacra." Not knowing that the late Philippine dictator Marcos manipulated this hoax by bribing anthropologists and media/simulation experts in order to promote tourism, grab mineral-rich lands, and sow division among rebellious ethnic minorities in Mindanao, Philippines, Baudrillard (1984) waxes eloquent thus:

> The Indian [a telling misnomer for several indigenous tribes inhabiting Mindanao, Philippines] thereby driven back into the ghetto, into the glass

coffin of virgin forest, becomes the simulation model for all conceivable Indians *before ethnology*. The latter thus allows itself the luxury of being incarnate beyond itself, in the "brute" reality of these Indians it has entirely reinvented—savages who are indebted to ethnology for still being Savages: what a turn of events, what a triumph for this science which seemed dedicated to their destruction! (257–58)

The "Tasadays," colonized by Baudrillard's text as "Indians," become posthumous, "referential simulacra" while ethnology (actually, the bureaucratic machinations of a U.S.–subsidized neocolonial regime) becomes "pure simulation." Culled from different tribes engaged in farming, trade, and crafts in modern society, the "Tasadays" were not savages who lived in virgin forests. The "Tasadays" were contrived and staged by the oligarch Manda Elizalde, a Marcos bureaucrat, for commercial and political purposes. Terrorized and many of them mysteriously murdered after investigations by the government were launched in 1986, the "Tasadays" no longer exist except as a pseudoreferential aberration, perhaps an imploding hypothetical moment, in Baudrillard's self-serving script.

One of the fatal inadequacies of Boelhower's ethnic semiotics inheres in its atomistic individualism, its allocentric Eurocentrism, its failure to recognize that in the case of peoples of color who have experienced violent conquest (Chicanos), slavery (Africans), systematic genocide (Indians), and dehumanizing exploitation (Asians), the problem of *habitare* is a collective one: the loss of homes for Indians and Chicanos, the cultural deprivation and various forms of racist oppression for Africans, Asians, and others. The paradigm or analogy of the European immigrant narrative of success that underpins the mainstream functionalist theory of ethnicity and also to some extent Boelhower's model cannot comprehend the collective project of Indians aspiring for autonomy in their homelands, of blacks demanding self-determination, and so on. Ethnic framing for peoples of color goes beyond mere "genealogical" retrospection, beyond a pragmatic inventory of "ethnic" life-styles. Ethnic framing for the colonized subalterns coincides with the forging or recovery of a historical consciousness that can grasp the experience of resistance to colonial domination, the experience of defeat and survival, of the continuing struggle to assert the integrity of the community against the destructive force of capital.

What is lacking in Boelhower's schema is precisely the concreteness (in Gramsci's sense) of the Project, the multiply determined historical agenda of peoples subordinated to the hegemonic rule of the dominant Euro-American power elite. For Boelhower, this Project is like a primal script, an ontological archive open to self-perpetuating subalterns or outcasts forever trying to assume the masks of an officially repeatable persona. It seems like a formalist exercise in duplicity, at best a parody of Bakhtin's heteroglotic scenario, predicated on the assumption that postmodern society no longer values the traditional norm of individuals sharing common ground and pride in the rituals and sentiments of a historically evolved community. The ethos and principle of a possessive/acquisitive individualism inform Boelhower's semiotic model and make it incapable of understanding the antithesis of a transactional anthropology, namely, the complex and mutable relations of domination and subordination, of hegemony and resistance, which establish complex and productive interdependencies between peoples of color and the Euro-American population in the United States.

VII

I would like to illustrate another way of theorizing the semiotics of ethnogenesis by discussing briefly its embodiment in a recent novel by Chicano novelist Arturo Islas, *The Rain God* (1984).

Within the context of the long history of the Mexican people as a fusion of Hispanic and Indian cultures, decisively punctuated by the loss of Spain's northern territory after the Mexican-American War of 1846–48, Islas charts the vicissitudes of the Angel family largely from the viewpoint of Miguel Chico, a university professor residing in California. This third-generation Chicano intellectual represents the force of a nascent decolonizing agency, an individual in the process of being interpellated into a rebellious Third World subject. Miguel Chico's near-death experience affords him a measure of critical distance in surveying his life intricately enmeshed with his parents, uncles and aunts, siblings and relatives, in particular with his grandmother Mama Chona. In the narrative diachrony, private eschatology becomes inflected with the heterogeneous demands of popular memory.

But this is not just merely a familial narrative of conflict within three generations, a chronicle of misunderstanding between fathers and sons. What is at stake is the patriarchal hubris of Miguel Grande, the "big man" who dominates the Angel family, who tries to establish the proverbial male authority by controlling his household and also his mistress. Lola, his mistress, finds that she cannot give up her friendship with Juanita, Miguel's wife; her role as divisive agent is transformed into a mediating one as she departs for California from the Texas/Mexico borderland, reassuring both husband and wife of her enduring love. In the context of gender and class conflicts, the test performs a cognitive mapping of solidarity among the native subalterns faced with imperial Eurocentric temptations of individualist alternatives.

Observe how the contradiction between monadic imperial power and the subordinated colonized people is overlaid with tensions disrupting the space of patriarchy. What reinscribes the conflict of the sexes on another level and overdetermines it, the level of Anglo masculinity versus Chicano homosexuality or ambivalence, is the killing of Felix (who strongly upholds family pride and racial honor) by a young Anglo soldier in the fourth chapter, "The Rain Dancer," in the center of the narrative. Here the cultural encyclopedia of the colonized provides a mechanism of exchange and compensation. This sacrifice of Felix becomes the symbolic propitiation of the Rain God, the Aztec deity of the cosmic cycle, the cycle of birth and death and resurrection; the retributive justice of the Rain God—whose nihilism can be vanquished only by the artist-writer, by textuality—wreaks havoc on the family, especially on Felix's son JoEl. At the same time it exposes the spiritual cancer corrupting this Chicano family and by extension the whole community in general: the naive, unquestioning submission to Anglo hegemony and its apologetics of success through accommodation or acquiescence. Genealogy is questioned, boundaries redrawn. This is poignantly dramatized in the scene where Lena accompanies her uncle Miguel Grande to the district attorney's office to be confronted by the impotence of this male "hero":

> She waited for her uncle to raise the obvious objections, to express the deep rage she felt at such injustice. Miguel Grande remained silent. He was as helpless as she, and in her ignorance she decided that his love for her father was without conviction, and that once again the family pride had led him to humiliate himself before men who did not give a damn about people like them. She was stunned. Had she been permitted to say anything, she told Miguel Chico many years later—after she had moved to California and could talk about it—she would have asked two questions. "What is the name of the son of a bitch who killed my father? I'll kill him myself since you men can't think about anything but your balls." And to the district attorney: "How many times have you sucked a cock, you prissy fool, or gotten some whore to suck yours?" (87–88)

Shamed and humiliated, Miguel Grande is forced to confess his impotence to his niece who refuses to accept his penitent gesture. Space (instanced in middle-class homes encroaching upon the desert) yields to the time of realizing the cost of alienation and distance from the community:

> She faced him. "Tell it to the judge, you fucking hypocrite." She slammed the door and ran into the house. A few months later she was glad to find out that he had not been selected chief, thinking it might force him to understand what life was really like for "low class" Mexicans in the land that guaranteed justice under the law for all. (88)

Upholding tradition and normative rituals, the proud males collapse under the pressure of this revelation of Felix's homosexuality and his victimization. Metaphorically put, the desert cannot be converted into a garden by a fiat of imitating the bourgeoisie through the grace of material possessions. This peripety or reversal in turn betrays the impotence of the family to demand and get justice from institutional Anglo power for which Felix's tortured body is the figure of propitiatory sacrifice. The pathos of JoEl's insanity attests to the breakdown of the male-centered Chicano family as a refuge from the racist/sexist violence of the free-market milieu. With this patriarchal institution disintegrated, a new praxis of resistance—one no longer fixated on the spatial ideologeme of borders—opens up on the margins of disciplinary regimes.

Miguel Chico, the central protagonist undergoing an existential ordeal, mobilizes a textual apparatus of sign production mindful of racial contradictions. Having survived the threat of death and the pain of enduring physical abnormality, Miguel Chico is faced with the moral dilemma of either completely negating the familial ethos of patriarchal honor as the chief obstacle to self-fulfillment or working through this crisis and resolving it in some dialectical fashion: negating some elements, preserving others, and transforming their value in a new ensemble of everyday relations. This is what the narrative action unfolds: a collective project for the preservation of the schismatic history of this Chicano extended family, a microcosm of the community. This quest is mediated through a critical praxis performed by Miguel Chico's historicizing interrogation of Mama Chona's character and her function as a dis-integrated locus of antagonisms pervading the whole history of the conduct of the Mexican people vis-à-vis Indians and Europeans. The modality of temporal positioning serves to mediate the solitude of suffering individuals with the decolonizing project of the whole community.

I submit that what Islas' text deploys is a paradigmatic unfolding of possibilities divided between the European tradition of Hispanic aristocratic ideology and the Indian vision of reciprocity. The Mexican community is presented here as dialogic: the organic Indian sensibility attuned to the rhythm of nature contrasts with the unitary Faustian self of the European (Spanish Roman Catholic) colonizer. This indigenous duality is then quickly associated with class division: Mama Chona opts for the aristocratic hauteur of the European colonizer against plebeians like Maria. For the grand matriarch, the greatest sin for a mother is to allow her children to be "*malcriado*." But the Aztec vision of life which almost cancels difference and conflict into illusions is vindicated by the Mexican revolution, although it is the occasion of that revolution against the long-entrenched power of land-lords and church which sacrifices Mama Chona's firstborn, the first Miguel Angel, who is the prototype for father and son in the novel. Note that it is not clear whether he was killed by the revolutionaries or the elite oligarchs;

but it is this victim Miguel Angel who transcribes the poetic prayer to the Rain God supposedly written by Netzahualcoyotl, King of Texcoco, in fifteenth-century pre-Columbian America. As pivotal vehicle of national tradition, the 1910 revolution can then be construed as a popular-democratic praxis of resistance against subalternity and its replication in familial totemism and hierarchical religion.

Miguel Chico is the chief protagonist who has been assigned the task of evaluating the functional significance of these two strands in Chicano culture, the Indian inheritance and the Spanish legacy. He confronts the dilemma of choosing between Western "phallogocentrism" and the ecological sensorium of the autochthonous Indian culture. At the beginning of the novel he contemplates a photograph of Mama Chona holding his hand "in a border town's main street on the American side"—a cognitive and aesthetic mapping of possibilities. It is a symbolic portrait of the young being led/guided by the old generation at a juncture where the desert encroaches on homes bought by Mexicans who consider them an index of their improved status. What we find in the last chapter where Mama Chona's personality, her relations with her husband and children, and her physical deterioration are unfolded, is Miguel Chico's coming to terms with the complexity of Mama Chona's figure as domineering matriarch, victimized woman, and finally a mediator between outside and inside, between the conformist and the deviant, the living and the dead. The grandmother can be conceived as an emblem or synecdoche of a dialogic community in emergence. Her dying figure crystallizes the promise of the desert blossoming:

> Days passed during which Mama Chona heard and smelled rainstorms passing over the desert. She longed to see the yucca and ocotillo in bloom, to breathe in their fragrance and praise them for their thorniness and endurance. If only human beings could be like plants. In one of her daydreams, she saw the desert sand filled with verbenas and blooming dandelions, and with the first Miguel by her side, she discovered wild roses. (179)

From a dialectical perspective, this passage articulates an intrinsically utopian vision—in the language of the sixties, the liberation of the Chicano people from Babylonian captivity in the U.S. empire and their exodus to Aztlan. From a structuralist viewpoint, one can read Mama Chona's narrative role as one mode of reconciling the contradictory polarities in Chicano society. This matriarch condenses heterogeneous impulses—residual, dominant, emergent—in the texture of her idiosyncratic life history which Miguel Angel tries to appraise and judge in the context of the limits and possibilities of her gender and class.

And yet, at the end, Miguel Chico relinquishes her hand—the bond of the *familia*—as she enters the realm of the Rain God, choosing the tortuous and tormenting agon of life. We anticipate that choice by the foreshadowing experience in his dream when he was tempted by the monster of a universalizing sameness, the monster who dissolves all differences into one amorphous plenitude; he confronts this demon of absolute pathos and embraces him in his fall: "As he fell, the awful creature in his arms, Miguel Chico felt the pleasure of the avenged and an overwhelming relief" (160). With this sacrifice of his double, Miguel Chico proceeds to perform his ritual of making "peace with his dead" by feasting them with words so that they wouldn't haunt him: the power of writing vindicates the oppressed. At last he is also prepared to face the truths of his family, released by a twofold praxis of demystification and imaginative extrapolation: "He looked, once again, at that old photograph of himself and Mama Chona. The white daisies in her hat no longer frightened him; now that she was gone, the child in the picture held only a ghost by the hand and was free to tell the family secrets" (160).

It is easy to conclude that *The Rain God* is a narrative deconstruction of the myth of the monolithic, sacrosanct Chicano family and the equally fetishized honor of the "fathers" as mirror image of the dominant patriarchal system which is projected here as an apparatus of castration and death. It appears that the paradigm of the heroic male memorialized in the *corrido* tradition has been severely questioned by Lola, Tia Cuca, Mema, Maria, and the brutalization of Felix. But while the family and its articulation with women's labor and sexuality serves as the site of political and ideological struggle, what the narrative foregrounds is the integrative power of the colonized family challenged by the individualist logic and exchange calculus of Anglo hegemony. What the predicaments of Miguel Angel and Antony, of Felix and JoEl disclose are the limits of kinship and familial obligation as well as the reproduction by the family of the dominant society's mechanisms for gender and class oppression. Miguel Chico's self-proclaimed task is a hermeneutic rewriting of the encyclopedia inspired by the secular ideals of Enlightenment modernism which is here transvalued to challenge Western supremacy: "to give meaning to the accidents of life . . . from an earthly, rather than otherworldly, point of view" (28).

In this project of elucidating motives, the narrator's libidinal investment in the portrait of Maria suggests the displacement of the Oedipal crisis onto the dimension of class and racial antagonisms. Maria overturns fixed genealogies and reifying codes of Anglo individualism. She represents the Indian servant class who crosses the border to nurture the children of the ambitious Chicano petty bourgeoisie; she incarnates both the sensual and the mystical, the garden and the desert fused in the instability of her marginal location. The only time in the whole narrative when Miguel Chico registers genuine pleasure is the time when Maria "licked the lashes of his deeply set eyes" (13). When she tells Miguel Chico to respect and love his mother because she is going to die, he believes her: "In that instant, smelling her hair and feeling her voice of truth moist on his ear, love and death came together for Miguel Chico and he was not from then on able to think of one apart from the other" (19). She acquires a symbolic charge that reconciles opposites, collapsing distances, healing rifts and cleavages: "She visited him in dreams, her hair loose and white and streaming to the floor, her immense jaw frozen in a perpetual smile that was alternately loving and terrifying" (23). When Miguel Chico begins to look back in order to disentangle the web of his life, resembling the invoked Rain God who uproots flowers "after having loved and enjoyed them so much," Maria's figure eclipses those of Mama Chona and Juanita in its erotic and didactic impact: "He felt Maria's hand on his face, her hair smelling of desert sage and lightly touching the back of his neck as she whispered in his ear. Every moment is Judgment Day and to those who live on earth, humility is a given and not a virtue that will buy one's way into heaven" (29).

Although a minor character, Maria functions crucially as an overdetermined signifier of change. She is one realization of the actant in which desire and pleasure converge, interrupting the disciplinary regimes of civil society and its internalization by peoples of color. Unlike the fabled *curandera* Ultima in Rudolfo Anaya's classic *Bless Me, Ultima*, however, Maria does not draw on the folkloric mysticism native to the Chicano milieu in the Southwest (although the subtext of the *la llorona* myth may be deciphered in the cathexis of her returning to her "lost son" Miguel Chico in his dreams). As mother surrogate, Maria also neutralizes the seductiveness of Juanita and partly deprives Mama Chona of her deadly charismatic influence on her grandson. Maria's position of being cast out by the patriarch after which she becomes a convert of the Seventh Day Adventist church releases prophetic energies whose most subversive consequence is the knowledge of connections between the plight of peoples of color and that of other deprived, powerless groups: "Years later, wandering the streets of New York, his own bag glued to his side, Miguel Chico saw Maria in all the old bag ladies waiting on street corners in Chelsea or walking crookedly through the Village, stopping to pick through garbage, unable to bear the waste of the more privileged" (14). This nodal passage magnificently transcribes the mutation of ethnic localization beloved by postmodern artists into a totalizing discourse of class (whose inaugural texts are Richard Wright's *Native Son* and, in the Chicano tradition, the performances of Luis Valdez's El Teatro Campesino) which is highly anathema to the doctrinaire advocates of pan-ethnicism.

In that startling epiphany where the synchronic and diachronic lines of the narrative converge, where New York (the Puritan consensus) intersects Los Angeles (the decolonizing imperative), we witness the trajectory of ethnic semiosis from the effort to historicize the seemingly normal and natural condition of subordination lived by peoples of color—the condition of conquest and dispossession of Chicanos—to an attempt at a cognitive mapping of the affinities between the racially oppressed groups whose identities are always in an ambiguous crossroad of simultaneous emergence/ cooptation and the other subaltern, exploited classes and sectors in American society. This is the semantic dimension of the semiotic model I propose here for the production of discourse inscribed in racial formations.

As an example of racially oriented semiosis, *The Rain God* telescopes the act of personal remembering with the affiliative process of shaping a collective future. Memory coalesces with an ethical/political praxis of collective resistance. Constructed around the existential turning points of loss, separation, and death, the narrative frame exhibits the convergence of the synchronic axis of organic duration (long-term patterns) and the conjunctural sequence of punctual events. A vision of a planetary ecosystem may be glimpsed in the novel's historical panorama. Against the background of the neoconservative resurgence after the decline of the antiwar movement in the sixties and early seventies, the protagonist's extended meditation on his life plots the organic scale of temporality from the Aztec period to the advent of the Spanish conquistadors (whose presence is not really challenged until the 1910 revolution), and the 1848 Treaty of Guadalupe Hidalgo up to the Spanish Civil War, and the Vietnam imperial aggression to contain world communism. What the paradigmatic line stages (following Gramsci's prescription to grasp the shifting configuration of forces) is the condensation of these large organic patterns into the conjunctural crisis of punctual events the most important of which is Felix's death.

In those events, recollection precipitates eschatological speculation. We witness the transformation of what has long been deemed necessary or natural—assertion of family honor—as a constraint based on individual decisions. What is regarded a necessity is then revealed as contingent: Miguel Angel could demand the bureaucratic pursuit of Felix's murderer, or his extralegal punishment (as the precedent of Juan Nepomuceno Cortina would warrant). This is the concrete analysis of the alignment of forces performed by the textual apparatus.

In conducting this maneuver of demystification, however, the text recontains the vision of the rupture in Chicano subalternity by way of an aesthetic resolution: the paradigm of a quasi-generic romance where the ritual of sharing pain in a dialogic community envisages a restoration of love and harmony among warring siblings, between conflicting groups. Nonetheless the breakdown in Miguel Chico's routine life signals the activation of a cognitive-aesthetic mapping of his situation, a gesture anticipating the transformation of the colonized subaltern into a differential subject of social change. Abstracting from the theoretical postulates of my metacommentary on Islas' novel, I offer here Figure 2: a diagram of the semiotic model of discourse-production in racial formations which is designed to supplement, correct, and modify Boelhower's formula of ethnic semiosis discussed earlier.

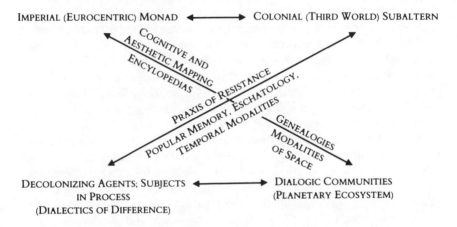

FIGURE 2   Proposed Schema for the Production of Racial Discourse

One can argue that the imposition of ethnic perspectivism in the struggle of the Chicano artist (in this case, Miguel Chico) to face death by raiding his Indian and Spanish heritage distracts from the problem of Chicano dependency. However, it is clear that this thematic of finitude and indigenizing ecology is translated into the crisis of Chicano patriarchal authority and the repudiation of humanism as a solution to racial injustice. While many questions are never completely answered at the end, the ideological closure in *The Rain God* vindicates the anticipated overcoming of repressive feudal vestiges in the Chicano family but only at the expense of sublimating antagonisms of class and race. At best, this index of an absence inscribed in the resilience and pathos of the Angel family displaces those antagonisms to the inchoate resolution of gender conflicts; the power of artistic knowledge—something like the unthinkable "arche-writing" or "trace" of Derrida—surfaces in the triumphalist eulogy of the Rain God. If there is a double writing, a reversal, and recuperation in Islas' text, it might be discerned in the experiences shared by the women (between Lola and Juanita, Mema and her sisters and mother) where the tension between self and Other shows how difference relates, how nonidentity is preserved in community. The artist's duplicity, his solitary individualism, and his empathy with the victims may epitomize also the discontinuity and alterity characterizing certain periods in Chicano history. One can even say that Mama Chona herself, like the artist, is bifurcated and dispersed even as she bridges disparate worlds: the conservative and recalcitrant, the living and the dead. Such imagined reconciliation of opposites with its implied omission or displacement of U.S. racial politics may be taken as the textually fabricated ideology of Islas' novel insofar as we subscribe to Althusser's definition of ideology as a "'representation' of the imaginary relationship of individuals to their real conditions of existence" (1971, 152). Those "real conditions" are textualized in the interweaving of the conjunctural (occasional, accidental incidents) and tactical in the syntagmatic plane with the organic and strategic in the paradigmatic plane. Such is the dynamics of semiotic ethnogenesis in a racial formation generating the novel's semantic and ideological structures.

In *The Rain God*, then, the aleatory and seemingly random disjunctions of postmodern life fall into well-delineated lines of development. It is obvious that the novel's focalization, plot, rhetorical design of characterization, setting, and so forth, still rely on a logic of realist representation and its binary polarity, albeit qualified by folkloric interpellations. But it shifts the center of gravity from the fetishism of *différance* and the hypostasis of performativity which vitiate Boelhower's model to the critique of Roman Catholic dogmatism and male supremacy as the synecdochic signifier of capitalist-racist oppression. The contrasting ideologemes of imperial Eurocentric aggression and Third World colonial subalternity are played out to generate their opposites: decolonizing subjects and dialogic communities in genesis. Whether monological or dialogical, personal identity here seems no longer to be the primary issue; ecology—the relation between the body and its habitat, desire and alienated work, pleasure and death—is.

In his memorable essay "The Storyteller," Walter Benjamin (1978) has pointed out the interdependency between narrative authority and death. In this light, one can perceive some similarity between Miguel Chico's existential quest for meaning and the protagonist's allegorical fantasy in Ron Arias' *The Road to Tamazunchale* (Saldívar 1990, 126–30). But in Islas' rewriting of Chicano ethnogenesis where the constellation of race, class, and gender counterpoints history and geography, the ecological politics of transforming the desert of American society at large into a garden accessible to all, a conjuncture where private and public spheres coalesce, proceeds by way of confronting first the fragile and contingent state of the body, its dispersed memory and its unconscious, where the vicissitudes of genealogy (the past) and liberation (the future) are intertwined.

It is also instructive to remark here that the Chicano aesthetics of the borderland so ably expounded by Ramon Saldivar in *Chicano Narrative: The Dialectics of Difference* cannot be subsumed into the fashionable idiom of postethnic dialogism or transethnic nomadism which would transcend the exclusionary algorithm of identity politics, the logocentric and binary axiology of representation. To believe that we can overcome the capitalist logic of racial categorization of labor power—the reification of the bodies of peoples of color—by rhetorical gestures of glorifying the heterogeneous as such, the eccentric marginals and outcasts, would, I submit, only spell the preemptive triumph of status quo metaphysical idealism.

Whatever their claims to giving priority to historical specificity and to the complex mutations of a multiplicity of factors configuring diverse circumstances, postmodernist theories of ethnicity, on the whole, elide the boundaries marked by the conflict of individuals, classes, and peoples. Contradictions of power are neutralized into a transactional exchange of signs, of symbolic capital. It is precisely by transcoding this communication circuit of supposedly equal subjects into a scenario of multilayered contradictions which produce subjects/agents in process, a scenario where the relations of domination and subordination define will, action, and imagination, that ethnic semiosis contributes to our understanding of the formation of the subject in history. By virtue of its specific genealogy, the racial subject-position is always constituted in a site of polymorphous, fluid, nomadic guerilla resistance; its authority can be glimpsed in strategies of reversal and displacement as it renegotiates unilateral boundaries and questions hierarchies of power. Born in the terrain of U.S. racial politics, this subaltern subject assumes an identity that is necessarily plural, disjunctive, or decentered, not because of some essential biology or fixed essence but because of the varying interpellations addressed to it by contestatory ideological appeals and the conjunctural demands of mass action. In short, this collective subject constructs and legitimates itself in opposing the utilitarian property-centered ethics and pluralist, racializing logic of postmodern late capitalism.

In conclusion I would like to hark back to Gramsci's original philosophical concept of concreteness as a key theoretical guide in articulating and evaluating any future semiotics of ethnic art form. In a passage on theorizing multiple relations of force in *Prison Notebooks,* Gramsci stresses the imperative of analytically discriminating stages, phases, or moments of any sequence, in particular the multifaceted interface between the organic and the conjunctural and the complex mediations implicit between them, in the process of constituting historically formed subjectivities: subject-positions defined by ethnicity, race, class, gender, and so on. What the "concrete analysis of relations of force" imbricated in discourse and in experience finally teaches us, Gramsci points out, is this:

such analyses cannot and must not be ends in themselves (unless the intention is merely to write a chapter of past history), but acquire significance only if they serve to justify a particular practical activity, or initiative of will. They reveal the points of least resistance, at which the force of will can be most fruitfully applied; they suggest immediate tactical operations; they indicate how a campaign of political agitation may best be launched, what language will best be understood by the masses, etc. The decisive element in every situation is the permanently organized and long-prepared force which can be put into the field when it is judged that a situation is favourable (and it can be favourable only in so far as such a force exists, and is full of fighting spirit). Therefore the essential task is that of systematically and patiently ensuring that this force is formed, developed, and rendered ever more homogeneous, compact, and self-aware. This is clear from military history, and from the care with which in every period armies have been prepared in advance to be able to make war at any moment. The great Powers have been great precisely because they were at all times prepared to intervene effectively in favourable international conjunctures—which were precisely favourable because there was the concrete possibility of effectively intervening in them. (1971, 185)

Thus a semiotics of racial discourse acquires its mediating power only when, first, it helps define and consolidate the emergence of self-conscious, self-critical historical agents (peoples of color) seeking empowerment. At this stage, the politics of ethnic difference which has so far underwritten the prevailing system of institutional apartheid yields to a politics of racial formations. And, second, such a semiotics or theory of textuality is valorized when it succeeds in establishing the ground for effective popular intervention, the mediation of political praxis, by pinpointing the "weak link" of an overdetermined, uneven social totality through a master narrative of realizable social emancipation which this chapter has tried to recuperate via the concrete analysis of organic and conjunctural relations, the dialectics of what is necessary and what is contingent, the strategic and the tactical. The goal of racial/ethnic semiotics is after all, as I conceive it, the destruction of racial formations where all peoples are constructed as racialized, historically specific subjects in antagonistic positions. The socially oriented semiotics I have in mind will be committed to the elimination of the hegemonic discourse of race in which peoples of color are produced and reproduced daily for exploitation and oppression under the banner of individual freedom and pluralist, liberal democracy. At this turning point of what Gramsci calls "catharsis," the qualitative leap from the economic to the ethico-political where categories of race, class, and gender are inextricably bound together, we have already traversed the sphere of aesthetics and reached the threshold of substantive political engagement.

5

Beyond Identity Politics

A. The Predicament of the Asian
American Writer in Late Capitalism

With the presumed collapse of the transcendental grounds for universal
standards of norms and values, proponents of the postmodern "revolution"
in cultural studies in Europe and North America have celebrated *différance*,
marginality, nomadic and decentered identities, indeterminacy, simulacra
and the sublime, undecidability, ironic dissemination, textuality, and so
forth. A multiplicity of power plays and language games supposedly
abounds. The intertextuality of power, desire, and interest begets strategies
of positionalities. So take your pick. Instead of the totalizing master narratives of Enlightenment progress, postmodern thinkers valorize the local,
the heterogeneous, the contingent and conjunctural. Is it still meaningful to
speak of truth? Are we still permitted to address issues of class, gender,
and race?

What are the implications of this postmodern "transvaluation" of paradigms for literary studies in general and minority/ethnic writing in particular? One salutary repercussion has been the questioning of the Eurocentric
canonical archive by feminists, peoples of color, dissenters inside and outside. The poststructuralist critique of the self-identical Subject (by conven-
tion white, bourgeois, patriarchal) has inspired a perspectivalist revision of
various disciplinary approaches in history, comparative aesthetics, and
others. To cite three inaugural examples: Houston Baker's text-specific
inventory of the black vernacular "blues" tradition presented in *Blues,
Ideology and Afro-American Literature* (1984), Arnold Krupat's foregrounding
of oral tribal allegory in American Indian autobiographies enabled by a
"materially situated historicism" in *The Voice in the Margin* (1989), and
Ramon Saldivar's dialectical assessment of Chicano narrative as an "oppositional articulation" of the gaps and silences in American literary history, a
thesis vigorously argued in *Chicano Narrative* (1990). Premised on the

notion that everything is sociodiscursively constructed, these initiatives so far have not been paralleled by Asian American intellectuals. Who indeed will speak for this composite group?

One would suspect that the rubric "Asian American," itself an artificial hypostasis of unstable elements, would preemptively vitiate any unilateral program of systematization. In addition, Asian Americans being judged by media and government as a "model minority," some allegedly whiter than whites (see Thernstrom 1983, 252; Lee 1991), makes their marginality quite problematic. Perhaps more than other peoples of color, Asian Americans find themselves trapped in a classic postmodern predicament: essentialized by the official pluralism as formerly the "Yellow Peril" and now the "Superminority," they nevertheless seek to reaffirm their complex internal differences in projects of hybrid and syncretic genealogy. Objectified by state-ordained juridical exclusions (Chinese, Japanese, and Filipinos share this historically unique commonality), they pursue particularistic agendas for economic and cultural autonomy. Given these antinomic forces at work, can Asian American writers collectively pursue a "molecular micropolitics" of marginality? What is at stake if a well-known authority on ethnic affairs like Ronald Takaki (whose recent book affords a point of departure for my metacommentary) tries to articulate the identity-in-difference of this frag-mented and dispersed ensemble of *ethnoi* (see Grigulevich and Kozlov 1974, 17–44)? How does a postmodern politics of identity refract the innovative yet tradition-bound performances of the Chinese Maxine Hong Kingston and the Filipino Carlos Bulosan? Given the crisis of the postmodern politics of identity, can we legitimately propose an oppositional "emergency" strategy of writing whose historic agency is still on trial or, as it were, on reprieve?

My inquiry begins with remarks on Asian American history's textuality as prelude to its possible aesthetic inscription. In composing *Strangers from a Different Shore* (1989) in a period when the planet is beginning to be homogenized by a new *pax Euro-Americana*, a "New World Order" spawn-ing (as I write) from the Persian Gulf, Takaki has performed for us the unprecedented task of unifying the rich, protean, intractable diversity of Asian lives in the United States without erasing the specificities, the ramify-ing genealogies, the incommensurable repertoire of idiosyncrasies of each constituent group—a postmodern feat of reconciling incommensurables, to say the least. There are of course many discrete chronicles of each Asian community, mostly written by sympathetic Euro-American scholars before Takaki's work. But what distinguishes Takaki's account, aside from his empathy with his subject and documentary trustworthiness, is its claim to represent the truth based on the prima facie experiences of individuals. At once we are confronted with the crucial problem plaguing such claims to veracity or authenticity: Can these subalterns represent themselves (to paraphrase Gayatri Spivak, 1988) as self-conscious members of a collectivity-for-itself? Or has Takaki mediated the immediacy of naive experience with a theory of representation that privileges the *homo economicus* as the founding subject of his discourse?[1]

No one should underestimate Takaki's achievement here as elsewhere in challenging the tenability of the received dogma (espoused by Nathan Glazer and other neoconservative pundits) that the European immigrant model of successful assimilation applies to peoples of color in the United States (see Takaki 1987). Europe's Others, hitherto excluded from the canonical tradition, are beginning to speak and *present* themselves so as to rectify the others' mystifying re-presentation of themselves. In this light, Takaki is to be credited above all for giving Asian Americans a synoptic view of their deracinated lives by making them (as protagonists who discover their roles and destinies in the process) perform the drama of their diverse singularities. This is stage-managed within the framework of a chronological history of their ordeals in struggling to survive, adapt, and multiply in a hostile habitat, with their accompanying rage and grief and laughter. By a montage of personal testimony—anecdotes, letters, songs, telegrams, eyewitness reports, confessions, album photographs, quotidian fragments, and clichés and banalities of everyday life—juxtaposed with statistics, official documents, and reprise of punctual events, Takaki skillfully renders a complex, intricate drama of Asians enacting and living their own history. We can perhaps find our own lives already anticipated, pantomimed, rounded off, and judged in one of his varied "talk stories"—a case of life imitating the art of history.

Granted the book's "truth-effects," I enter a caveat. For all its massive accumulation of raw data and plausible images of numerous protagonists and actions spanning more than a century of wars and revolutions, Takaki's narrative leaves us wondering whether the collective life trajectory of Asian Americans imitates the European immigrant success story, spiced with quaint "Oriental" twists—which he clearly implies at the end. If so, it is just one thread of the national fabric, no more tormented nor pacified than any other. If not, then this history is unique in some way that escapes the traditional emplotment of previous annals deriving from the master narrative of humankind's continuous material improvement, self-emancipation, and techno-administrative mastery conceived by the *philosophes* of the European Enlightenment. Either way, there is no reason for Asian Americans to feel excluded from the grand March of Progress. Our puzzlement, however, is not clarified by the book's concluding chapter which exposes

the myth of the "model minority" in an eloquent argument, assuring us
that Asians did not "let the course of their lives be determined completely
by the 'necessity' of race and class" (473).

In the same breath Takaki warns of a resurgent tide of racially motivated
attacks against Asians manifested in the media, in campus harassments, in
the 1982 murder of Vincent Chin mistaken for a Japanese by unemployed
Detroit autoworkers. (And, I might add here, in the January 1989 massacre
of Vietnamese and Cambodian schoolchildren in Stockton, California, by a
man obsessed with hatred for Southeast Asian refugees.) During this same
period, in contrast, the judicial victory of the Japanese concentration camp
internees' demand for redress and reparations as well as the growing visibil-
ity of Asian American artists furnishes convincing proof that what David
Harvey calls the post-Fordist post-Keynesian system (1989, 173–78) still
allows dreams to come true, that is, allows Asians the opportunity in
particular "to help America accept and appreciate its diversity."

Calculating the losses and gains, Takaki prudentially opts for a meliora-
tive closure. In retrospect, the telos of *Strangers from a Different Shore* can be
thematized as the Asian immigrants' almost miraculous struggle for survival and recognition of their desperately won middle-class status. What is
sought is the redemption of individual sacrifices by way of conformity to
the utilitarian, competitive ethos of a business society. Reversing the dis-
maying prospect for Asians forecast in an earlier survey, *American Racism*
(1970) by Roger Daniels and Harry Kitano, Takaki offers a balance sheet for
general consumption:

> Asian Americans are no longer victimized by legislation denying them
> naturalized citizenship and landownership. They have begun to exercise
> their political voices and have representatives in both houses of Congress
> as well as in state legislatures and on city councils. They enjoy much of
> the protection of civil rights laws that outlaw racial discrimination in
> employment as well as housing and that provide for affirmative action for
> racial minorities. They have greater freedom than did the earlier immi-
> grants to embrace their own "diversity"—their own cultures as well as
> their own distinctive physical characteristics, such as their complexion
> and the shape of their eyes. (473–74)

It now becomes clear that despite its encyclopedic scope and archival
competence, Takaki's somewhat premature synthesis is a learned endeavor
to deploy a strategy of containment. His rhetoric activates a mode of comic
emplotment where all problems are finally resolved through hard work and
individual effort, inspired by past memories of clan solidarity and intuitive
faith in a gradually improving future. What is this if not a refurbished
version of the liberal ideology of a market-centered, pluralist society where

all disparities in values and beliefs, nay, even the sharpest contradictions implicating race, class, and gender can be harmonized within the prevailing structure of power relations?

This is not to say that such changes toward empowering disenfranchised nationalities are futile or deceptive. But what needs a more than gestural critique is the extent to which such reforms do not eliminate the rationale for the hierarchical, invidious categorizing of people by race (as well as by gender and class) and their subsequent deprivation. Lacking such self-reflection, unable to problematize his theoretical organon, what Takaki has superbly accomplished is the articulation of the hegemonic doctrine of acquisitive/possessive liberalism as the informing principle of Asian American lives. Whether this is an effect of postmodern tropology or a symptom of "bad faith" investing the logic of elite populism, I am not quite sure.

My reservations are shared by other Asian American observers who detect an apologetic agenda in such liberal historiography. At best, Takaki's text operates an ironic if not duplicitous strategy: to counter hegemonic Eurocentrism, which erases the Asian American presence, a positivist-empiricist valorization of "lived experience" is carried out within the master narrative of evolutionary, gradualist progress. The American "Dream of Success" is thereby ultimately vindicated. This is not to suggest that historians like Takaki have suddenly been afflicted with amnesia, forgetting that it is the totalizing state practice of this ideology of market liberalism that underlies, for one, the violent colonial domination of peoples of color and the rape of the land of such decolonizing territories as the Philippines (my country of origin) and Puerto Rico in the aftermath of the Spanish-American War. It is the social practice of an expansive political economy which converts humans to exchangeable commodities (African chattel slavery in the South) and commodified labor power, thus requiring for its industrial takeoff a huge supply of free labor, hence the need for European immigrants especially after the Civil War, and the genocidal suppression of the American Indians. It is the expansion of this social formation that recruited Chinese coolies for railroad construction (the "fathers" poignantly described in Kingston's *China Men*) and Japanese and Filipino labor (and Mexican *braceros* later) for agribusiness in Hawaii and California and for the canneries in Alaska. It is this same hegemonic worldview of free monopoly enterprise, also known as the "civilizing mission" of Eurocentric humanism, that forced the opening of the China market in the Opium Wars of the nineteenth century and the numerous military interventions in China and Indo-China up to the Vietnam War and the coming of the "boat people." Of course it is also the power/knowledge episteme of the modernization process in Kenya, South Korea, Mexico, Indonesia, Egypt, Grenada, and all the neocolonial or peripheral dependencies of the world-system named by Immanuel Wallerstein as "historical capitalism" (1983, 13–43; see Amin 1989).

It is now generally acknowledged that we cannot understand the situation of Asian Americans in the United States today or in the past without a thorough comprehension of the global relations of power, the capitalist world-system that "pushed" populations from the colonies and dependencies and "pulled" them to terrain where a supply of cheap labor was needed. These relations of power broke up families, separating husbands from wives and parents from children; at present they motivate the "warm body export" of cheap labor from Thailand, the Philippines, and elsewhere. They legitimate the unregulated market for brides and hospitality girls, the free trade zones, and other postmodern schemes of capital accumulation in Third World countries. The discourse of the liberal free market underpins these power relations, constructing fluid georacial boundaries to guarantee the supply of cheap labor. Race acquires salience in this world-system when, according to John Rex,

> the language of racial difference . . . becomes the means whereby men allocate each other to different social and economic positions. . . . The exploitation of clearly marked groups in a variety of different ways is integral to capitalism. . . . Ethnic groups unite and act together because they have been subjected to distinct and differentiated types of exploitation. (1983b, 406–7)

The colonization and industrialization of the North American continent epitomize the asymmetrical power relations characteristic of this world-system.

The sociocultural formation of global apartheid has been long in the making. In studies like Eric Wolf's *Europe and the People without History* (1982) or Richard Barnet and Ronald Muller's *Global Reach* (1974), to mention only the elementary texts, one can see that the migration of peoples around the world, the displacement of refugees, or the forced expulsion and exile of individuals and whole groups (the Palestinian diaspora is the most flagrant) have occurred not by choice or accident but by the complex interaction of political, economic, and social forces from the period of mercantile capitalism to colonialism, from the sixteenth to the nineteenth century, continuing into the imperialism of the twentieth century. This genealogy of domination, the self-reproduction of its mechanisms and the sedimentation of its effects, is what is occluded in Takaki's narrative (see Nakanishi 1976).

Racial antagonism has marked the process of U.S. ethnogenesis from the outset. Since its beginning as Britain's colonial outpost, the evolution of the U.S. social formation has been distinguished by the violent exclusion and subjugation of the American Indians and the subsequent differential incorporation of various racial groups. Takaki is sensitive to this process but assumes it as normal and inescapable, not as an index to subsequent race relations in the metropolitan center. Historians like Genovese, Kolko, Zinn, and others have pointed out that U.S. society has been discriminative from the very beginning. Alexander Saxton (1977) underscores Nathan Glazer's fundamental mistake in assuming that a policy of equal rights characterized U.S. history from its inception:

> Already in the days of Jefferson and the "sainted Jackson" (to use Walt Whitman's phrase) the nation had assumed the form of a racially exclusive democracy—democratic in the sense that it sought to provide equal opportunities for the pursuit of happiness by its white citizens through the enslavement of Afro-Americans, extermination of Indians, and territorial expansion largely at the expense of Mexicans and Indians. (145)

By privileging ethnic difference (chiefly cultural superficialities) as a key sociological factor and ignoring what Michael Banton and Robert Miles call "racism"—the justification of unequal treatment of groups by deterministic ascription of negative characteristics to them (1984, 228)—U.S. disciplinary regimes subsumed the plight of peoples of color into the European immigrant model. Thus they actualized a racial formation with ideological roots in Puritan doctrine and in Enlightenment humanist-scientific rationality.

The concept of racial formation I have in mind originates from the dialectical articulation of state policies, discriminatory practices in civil society, and popular resistance to them. With the rise of the civil rights movement in the sixties, a new historical consciousness precipitated an understanding of such phenomena as "internal colonialism" imposed by the state on subject populations (as cogently argued by Robert Blauner in *Racial Oppression in America*) and the segmentation of the labor market. In the eighties, with the renewed assault on civil rights by the particular brand of neoconservatism represented by the Reagan administration, it became necessary to reassess and correct our theoretical perspective in order to grasp the changed configuration of the U.S. racial state and racial politics; this is the signal accomplishment of Michael Omi and Howard Winant's study *Racial Formation in the United States From the 1960s to the 1980s* (see San Juan 1989a). Lacking a theory of the changing articulation of racial discourse in different historical stages and the mutations of "differential exclusion" in late capitalism (see Davis 1984), ethnic histories like Takaki's find themselves undermined by what Etienne Balibar refers to as the "theoretical racism" of liberal democracy. Meanwhile, the subjects interpellated by such discourses find themselves "decentered" by the seemingly gratuitous pathos of living through the accelerated cyclic boom and bust of a postmodern, schizoid, but still profit-centered economy.

As we live through the aftereffects of Reagan's "authoritarian populism," the rollback of affirmative action programs affecting a wide range of social transfer payments that benefited disadvantaged sectors and the "underclass," and the recent media euphoria over the debacle of "actually existing socialism" in Eastern Europe, what's in store for Asian Americans at the threshold of the twenty-first century?

One thing is predictable: without an alternative or oppositional strategy that can challenge the logic of liberal, possessive individualism and the seductive lure of consumerism (what W. F. Haug calls "commodity aesthetics"), I suspect that the only recourse is to revive versions of individualist metaphysics, the most popular of which is "identity politics," that is, the tendency to base one's politics on a sense of identity, internalizing or privatizing all issues and thus either voiding them of any meaning or trivializing them (see Fuss 1989, 97–112). From a strategic angle, this tactical move recuperates an autochthonous will, an indigenous Otherness if you like.[2] But what is unfortunately lost in the process is the historical density of collective resistance and revolt, the texture of our involvement in our communities that Takaki attempts to capture, together with the necessary concrete knowledge of society and politics—the mutable and highly mediated field of discourses, practices, institutions—on which our sense of responsibility can be nurtured, on which strategies of parody, satire, and expressive disruption can be anchored. But are such questions as "Who am I?" and "Why am I writing and for whom?" irrelevant or counterproductive?

Questions of precisely this sort—interrogating the archaeology of a postmodern, hyperreal auto-da-fé itself—were the ones grappled with by more than a dozen Asian American intellectuals (writers, critics, and social scientists) joined by a handful of African Americans and Euro-Americans in a three-day symposium on "Issues of Identity" held at Cornell University in which I was invited to participate as a representative of the Filipino American "ethnic" category.

In my view, the event recapitulated the problems and lessons of the Asian American experience memorialized by Takaki. What transpired may be conceived as a case study of the identity politics syndrome complicated by the usual group dynamics of local born/expatriate encounters traversing a range of sexual, ethical, and occupational discourses. Not only was identity reduced to the garden variety of egos striking confessional postures, but the assorted group of writers (none of whom commanded the stature of Maxine Hong Kingston whose absent presence, as it were, evoked a peculiar ressentiment from some writers) found themselves privileged somehow as the fountainhead of answers to questions of Asian American personal/collective identity. This privileging of the artist's status, orchestrated by the Hong Kong–born impresario of the symposium, may have ruined any possibility of dialogue. When the critics (all based in such higher institutions of the Empire as the universities of California, Michigan, and Wisconsin) assigned to comment specifically on the solicited texts (mostly essays by six authors) presented their commentaries in the language of contemporary critical theory, most of the writers immediately reacted with disappointment, incomprehension, anger, disgust, and futile rage: "Where are you coming from? Speak simply so common people can understand you!" (Such reactions were addressed to the reading of the comments, not to the written texts.) It culminated in a quasi-Puritanical witch trial where the personal motives of the critics were questioned. One Chinese American poet from Hawaii even derogated Kingston—"Why is she always quoted as an authority on our community?" It reached the point where I was attacked for using obscure, pedantic language; for laying down a political line, for imposing a theory (the vulgar terrorist label to make someone superfluous is, of course, "Marxist"), and—to say the least—for not conforming to the unwittingly self-serving identity politics which, by some insidious operation of shame psychology, had by then become the all-purpose weapon of the embattled *écrivains*. In fact, the writers' responses subsided to the crudest debunking accusation that the critics engaged in such activity only for the sake of tenure, fat salaries, prestige, professional vanity, and so forth. How was all this warranted by the ritual of a seemingly cultivated, polite, formally structured academic exchange?

Let me venture an explanation. Apart from my criticism of liberal ideology such as that presiding over Takaki's popularizing effort and also the writers' self-serving justification of their function, what aroused the most intense hostility was my nuanced indictment of "multiculturalism," the writers' solution to the malaise of "cultural schizophrenia" and a pre-Lacanian hyphenated identity. A Filipino American writer, *inter alia*, observed that for her, multiculturalism in the white media was "just mind-blowing"; witness those black rappers, Asian ethnic fashions and technology, Zen car commercials, and so on. To this now hackneyed glorification of consumer society as the site of creative freedom, spontaneity—you can be whatever you want to be—and seemingly infinite libidinal gratification, I countered that the self-indulgence in this fabled cornucopia of simulacra, replicas, and commodified spectacles—the pastiche offered by yuppie catalogues and antiseptic supermalls cloned from postmodern Las Vegas—is a hallucinatory path not to discovering one's creative alterity, but rather to the suppression of the imagination's potential and unrelenting submission to the monolithic law of a racist dispensation. That cornucopia is really the emblem of what Henri Lefebvre describes as "the bureaucratic society of controlled consumption" (1968, 68). The Asian American citizen who articulates her subjecthood, her subalternity, through multiculturalism (assimilation via acculturation lurks not far behind) betrays an ignorance of the lopsided distribution of power and wealth in a racially stratified society. And so, in what might be a postmodern aporia, binary opposites turn out to be double binds (I am both American and Asian, and many other things)—virtually disabling ruses of complicity, self-incriminating games of cooptation.

Recent scholars have documented the growing mass appeal of a new racist practice based on the language of diverse cultures, life-styles, personal tastes, and free choices, articulated with issues of class, gender, age, and so forth. What the advocates of multiculturalism are innocent of is the concept of hegemony (of which more later), which allows a latitude of diverse trends and tendencies in a putative laissez-faire market system provided these operate within the monadic framework of contractual arrangements and hierarchical property relations. Corporate hegemony precisely thrives on your freedom to shop—until your credit runs out and the right to be bankrupt is invoked. In lieu of moralizing, probably the best retort to this rather premature celebration of the postmodernist orgy of the Emersonian Self is from the manifesto of one of its high priests, Jean-François Lyotard (1984):

> Eclecticism is the degree zero of contemporary general culture: one listens to reggae, watches a western, eats McDonald's food for lunch and local cuisine for dinner, wears Paris perfume in Tokyo and "retro" clothes in Hong Kong; knowledge is a matter for TV games. It is easy to find a public for eclectic works. By becoming kitsch, art panders to the confusion which reigns in the "taste" of the patrons. Artists, gallery owners, critics, and public wallow together in the "anything goes," and the epoch is one of slackening. But this realism of the "anything goes" is in fact that of money; in the absence of aesthetic criteria, it remains possible and useful to assess the value of works of art according to the profits they yield. Such realism accommodates all tendencies, just as capital accommodates all "needs," providing that the tendencies and needs have purchasing power. (76)

My reservation, then, to the assumption by racial subjects of an autonomous identity envisaged by multiculturalism (which I would consider the guilty conscience or "bad faith" of petty suburban liberalism) concerns the orthodox conception of the dominant culture as simply comprising lifestyles that one can pick and wear anytime one pleases. That is just unfeasible since this hegemonic multiculture (practices, discourses), viewed from a historical materialist perspective, is precisely the enabling power of a system produced and reproduced by racial, gender, and class divisions. It coincides with a network of domination and subordination in civil society that prevents one from choosing any life-style, or for that matter refusing alienated work, in order to realize one's social potential, that is, the "species-being" Marx postulates in his *Economic and Philosophic Manuscripts of 1844*. In this context, hegemony implies the reproduction of subordinate Others to confirm the hierarchy, but at the same time, sites of contestation open up where desire, fantasy, and the unconscious begin to erode hierarchy. Here is the blind spot which identity politics cannot apprehend, namely, that the contingencies of a hegemonic struggle can generate a variety of subject-positions which are neither fixed nor shifting but capable of being articulated in various directions according to the play of political forces and the conjunctural alignment of multilayered determinants (see Williams 1977, 108–11; Hall 1986). Oblivious to this deeper analysis, the exponents of identity politics construe "identity" in an abstract formalist fashion: the consumer as prototype. However, this politics conceals its essentialism in its claim of affirming universalizing, humanist goals—one writer expatriated from the Philippines and now domiciled in Greenwich Village extolled her world citizenship as her credential of entitlement.

I believe this escape route of the "Unhappy Consciousness," this catharsis of a poststoic universalism, harbors a genealogy that can be traced all the way back to the Renaissance. One filiation is Goethe's vanguard internationalism which, despite its humanitarian intention, exemplifies pure culinary liberalism (to borrow Brecht's term), though one much ahead of its time. In his "Conversations with Eckerman," Goethe (1962) speculates about the advent of "world literature," multiculturalism on a planetary scale. After reading one Chinese novel, this archetypal European culture-hero tries to impart his wisdom to us benighted denizens from Asia:

> The Chinese think, act, and feel almost exactly like ourselves; and we soon find that we are perfectly like them, except that all they do is more clear, more pure and decorous than with us. . . .
> National literature is now rather an unmeaning term; the epoch of World Literature is at hand, and every one must strive to hasten its approach. But, while we thus value what is foreign, we must not bind ourselves to anything in particular, and regard it as a model. We must not give this value to the Chinese, or the Serbian. . . . if we really want a pattern, we must always return to the ancient Greeks, in whose works the beauty of mankind is constantly represented. All the rest we must look at only historically, appropriating to ourselves what is good, so far as it goes. (48)

And so the Faustian spirit of the Caucasian conscience marches on, with Aphrodite at its vanguard and the postmodern Spirit of Negation trailing behind. Nonetheless it must be said that Goethe's internationalist good sense, in anticipating Hegel's "concrete universal," established the ground-work for conceiving Marx's "species being" and thenceforth Fanon's Third World partisanship and Che Guevara's "New Socialist Person."

To return to the symposium: aside from inadequate logistics and inex-perienced planning, I think the provenance of whatever misrecognitions occurred—the Asian American psyche cannot plead to be exceptional—cannot just be personal and/or bureaucratic. Causality inheres in the political-symbolic economy of liberal exchange. It inhabits the paradoxical space that syncopates structural constraints and conjunctural opportunities: constraints due to the organizers' allowing the writers to monopolize the center of attention and the attendant failure to establish an atmosphere of productive conflict by circulating all the texts and distributing occasions for speech in an egalitarian manner. Both failures consequently fostered an attitude of acknowledging differences sublimated in utterly homogenizing repertoires of communication, that is, in commonsense platitudes and pedantic trivia. In the process, novel conjunctural opportunities were missed: for example, my proposal that we distinguish carefully between experi-ence (almost everyone uncritically endorsed the wonderful "chaos" from which writers drew inspiration—a gesture of "bad faith") and knowledge. "Knowledge," however, was immediately yoked to "theory" and de-nounced as dogmatic, mechanical, rigid, and obscurantist. The opportunity for exploring why writers, tuned to a different level of discourse, could not understand the critics' idiom and theoretical formulations was forfeited. Instead of an ambience of genuine national diversity due to uneven develop-ment of consciousnesses, ironically, a leveling temper supervened in which hierarchy was covertly reinstituted: the writer was deemed a prophet/oracle who speaks truth and purveys sacrosanct knowledge. However, because these oracles needed informed readers and intelligent listeners who would confirm their truths, a profound anxiety haunted them. They craved the critics' attention and approval as though the critics could supply the psychoanalytic cure, thus confirming the fact that they could not find this cure in the mirror images of themselves performing their improvised, minstrel-like roles. And so Narcissus takes revenge in identity politics, which converts dialogue as a pretext for monologue.

While the critics in general tried to follow the path of compromise, engaging in a liberal game of balancing negative and positive quantities discerned in their readings, the distinction between knowledge and experi-ence for whose necessity I argued (inasmuch as this articulation between the two conditions the textualization of identity fought in the battlefields of disciplinary regimes) fell on deaf ears. I argued for the need to posit a wide spectrum of levels of understanding, appreciation, and judgment; for the need to criticize the assumptions of identity politics, which functions as the controlling paradigm in mainstream comparative cultural studies;[3] and for the need to guard against anti-intellectualism or a relapse into the banal pragmatic-instrumentalist humanism which preaches that we are all the same, we can all partake of the wealth of the transnational boutiques, and so on. But all these were missed. A "rectification of names" was thus aborted.

In fairness, I should say that what the writers testified to was the enigmatic power of poststructuralist critical discourse which, to some extent under certain conditions, can be mobilized in the service of an oppositional or alternative politics. Such power perhaps bewildered the writers and provoked defensive panic symptoms. Rejecting the imputation of ill will or narrow self-serving intentions, the critics tried to make the texts of the writers (no one, as far as I can recall, alluded to Sartre's *What Is Literature?* or Barthes and Foucault on the authorship function when the writers began to fondle their own texts like private consumption goods) release a virtue that could communicate with the high cultural productions of the Establishment elite, with the discourse of the canonical authors and their foundational critiques. Our project (if I may stress the positive) also aimed to unleash the potential reach of their texts by affording their reading a degree of intelligibility that would challenge and even displace the canonical texts of Euro-American hegemonic culture.[4] But, unarguably, the writers' reflex of self-justification took over and converted the symposium into a theater of naive and pathetic self-congratulation, with disagreements ironed out for the moment, "faces" saved, suspicions deflected—another day swallowed up in the *mise en abime* of ghetto marginality and ethnic vainglory. Liberalism and identity politics have conquered again. Unfortunately, the handful of outsiders in the scene may have carried away with them the wrong impression that Asian American writers and intellectuals (compared to the astute African Americans and the resourceful Chicanos) have a long way to go in "the long march through the institutions," in forging consensus and solidarity through demonstrated respect for their differences. On the other hand, I think the symposium testified to a recalcitrance and intractability ideal for a counterhegemonic drive against the panoptic, reifying thrust of a "New World Order" managed from Washington, D.C.

Still, the cooptative seductiveness of identity politics cannot be discounted. One way of circumventing it may be illustrated by the signifying practice of the Filipino American writer Carlos Bulosan (1913–53). Cognizant of the risks of textualizing an illegible Filipino identity enveloped in a culture of silence, Bulosan wrote the only extant epic chronicle of Filipino migrant workers in the United States, *America Is in the Heart* (see San Juan 1972, 1979). In this quasi-autobiographical life history of a whole community, Bulosan invented a metamorphic persona, a self disintegrated by the competitive labor market of the West Coast and Hawaii. At the same time, this persona is also constituted by the itinerary of the seasonal labor hired by the farms and the ritualized forms of excess (Georges Bataille sees in excess and in transgression the essence of the sacred, of sociality as such); in those moments, space dissolves into the time of annihilating boundaries together with the ethos of bourgeois decorum. In fiction like "Be American," "Story of a Letter," and "As Long as the Grass Shall Grow," Bulosan successfully projects the "I" of subalternity, a self dispersed and inscribed across the commodified space of the West Coast—its desire (use-value) alienated in the exchange-value of commodities expropriated from the time and energies of bodily life.

In the classic story "As Long as the Grass Shall Grow" (Bulosan 1983), we witness the condensation of fragments of the protagonist's identity occurring in the same trajectory of its displacement: the passage through a racialized terrain bifurcates the character, displaces his naïveté, only to reconstitute it as a metaphor for what has been lost: autonomy, security of home, and organic happiness. The eighteen-year-old Filipino boy of this story lands in the United States to join a nomadic group of migrant workers hired to pick seasonal crops in the state of Washington. He is befriended by an Irish schoolteacher, Miss O'Reilly, who volunteers to teach him and the other workers how to read; her excursions to their bunkhouse provoke threats from racist elements in the town. In exchange for her labor and time, translated into the gift of the capacity to read, the workers give her peas and flowers symbolic of their communion with nature.

Forbidden to visit the workers—the patriarchs of the town consider the workers' learning how to read dangerous to the status quo, an attitude reminiscent of that characterizing the antebellum South—Miss O'Reilly invites them to the schoolhouse instead. One evening, the protagonist begins demonstrating his writing skill: "Suddenly I wrote a poem about what I saw outside in the night [the silent sea and the wide clear sky]. Miss O'Reilly started laughing because my lines were all wrong and many of the words were misspelled and incorrectly used." The protagonist's "I" then goes through a series of interpellations and substitutions as the woman teacher reads the "Song of Solomon" from the Bible:

> I liked the rich language, the beautiful imagery, and the depth of the old man's passion for the girl and the vineyard.
> "This is the best poetry in the world," Miss O'Reilly said when she finished the chapter. "I would like you to remember it. There was a time when men loved deeply and were not afraid to love."
> I was touched by the songs. I thought of the pea vines on the hillside and silent blue sea not far away. And I said to myself: *Some day I will come back in memory to this place and time and write about you, Miss O'Reilly. How*

gratifying it will be to come back to you with a book in my hands about all that we are feeling here tonight! (101)

Immediately after this, the boy is beaten up by racist thugs on his way home to the bunkhouse; regaining consciousness past midnight, he weeps and reflects: "Slowly I realized what had happened." Miss O'Reilly disappears; toward the end of the harvesting season, she reappears and tells the boy she is leaving for the big city. The workers celebrate her return with a farewell party lasting through the night, with the moon and stars above the sea and tall mountains surrounding them. Even as she reads the "Song of Solomon," however, the boy has already anticipated her disappearance (in the narrative diegesis) and staged her fictional resurrection here in this text. His "I" fuses narrator-participant and narrator-artist. The narrative voice synthesizes in the circuit of reading/listening the subject of the text's enunciation and the speaking subject. This semiosis engenders a dialogic persona, not a monadic ego. Synchrony and diachrony, the paradigmatic and the syntagmatic axes, coalesce as memory is transported to the future in order to recuperate the present moment of narration. The "I" becomes a site for registering the present as resistance to forgetfulness, loss of pleasure, reification.

Dispersed and sublimated into the predicament of the Filipino community (about 45,000 strong in the mid-thirties), the "I" of Bulosan's story maps its own itinerary, its recursive passage. It maps a pre–World War II rural geography that urgently evokes the provincial landscape of the homeland (the Philippines, the only Asian colony of the United States then about to be ravaged by the Japanese) and induces an uncanny vision, a moment when the repressed returns, when the maternal and educative function of Miss O'Reilly preempts the space once tabooed by racist violence. At this point her figure, metonymically tied to the cyclic fruitfulness of the land, condenses into a metaphor of home:

> One morning I found I had been away from home for twenty years. But where was home? I saw the grass of another spring growing on the hills and in the fields. And the thought came to me that I had had Miss O'Reilly with me all the time, there in the broad fields and verdant hills of America, my home. (104)

In all of Bulosan's fiction, the migrant folk's residual memory of the national liberation struggle of millions of Filipinos against Spanish colonialism and U.S. imperialism mediates the adolescent protagonist's rite of passage from the archaic ways of the feudal countryside to the modern site of metropolitan commodity fetishism, the brute facticity of racist America, where the labor of colored bodies is reduced to abstract exchange-value (the cash-nexus) and wasted away. The adventure of the youthful narrator, whose nascent self-awareness is fixated on traumatic experiences in child-hood, suffers a displacement: U.S. business society is not what it was presented in the colonial textbooks. In effect, the rational Cartesian ego inhabiting the utilitarian ethos of liberal society never really materializes in the Filipino worker's psyche, shrouded as it is with a nostalgic alterity, branded by an irrecuperable loss.

On the whole, intertextuality overdetermines the "I" of Bulosan's fiction. We see the stark contrast between the pastoral locus of the worker's origin and the alienated milieu of the labor camps on the West Coast; this hiatus decenters the native psyche for which a strategy of refusing self-definition by the racist order and its official, homogenizing monoglossia is the only hope of survival. Bulosan's art refuses identity politics as a refuge because the reality of life for an immigrant cannot be legitimated or rationalized by it. In its indigenous cunning, Bulosan's writing registers the ambiguity of freedom, of democratic opportunity in the United States, by inventing the unrepresentable mutant "I" who exer-cises the sensibility of the pariah, the incorporate outcast, in discriminating between what is merely beguiling appearance and what is suffered daily by the worker's body.

Another strategy of creative disruption that can outflank the lure of identity politics, the lure of the romantic totem of the liberal imagination for writers who overvalorize its demiurgic capacity, is that mobilized by Kingston in The Woman Warrior (1976) and China Men (1980). Suffice it to cite here the ludic, witty colloquium in the last chapter of China Men to illustrate Kingston's mode of problematizing racial identity in the United States.

In "On Listening," the narrator questions a Filipino scholar (wandering from the Philippines to nowhere, Georg Simmel's amphibious "stranger") who captivates her with the quite implausible report that Chinese man-darins came to the Philippines in March 1603 looking for the Gold Moun-tain, specifically a gold needle in a mountain, with a chained Chinese prisoner as guide. Kingston asks: "Gold needle? What for?" A Chinese American ventures the opinion that a Chinese monk also traveled to Mexico looking for the "Gold Mountain." "Gold Mountain" is the mythical name given to the United States by the Chinese in China to symbolize familial aspirations for wealth, freedom, happiness, etc. But in this playful ex-change, the rubric "Gold Mountain" becomes detached from the aura of myth owing to the pressure of painful, dehumanizing experiences under-gone by generations of sojourners and settlers from the 1860s on; it becomes a floating signifier, a charisma-laden mana, which then can be affixed to the Philippines, Mexico, Spain, or to wherever the imagination or Eros cathects its adventurous utopian drive.

So the pursuit of truth is distracted, rechanneled, and left suspended as the coordinates of the mountain shift, depending on the speaker's focalizing stance relative to the questioner, the fictive narrator of *China Men*. Cowboys in California claim to have watched mandarins floating in a "hot air balloon," index of technology and sci-fi fabulation. When the narrator returns to questioning the Filipino scholar, the Chinese fortune-seekers have already drained swamps, raised families, and built homes, roads, railroads, and cities—in other words, accomplished a civilizing task on their way to the Gold Mountain, where they then sifted dirt and rocks. But the upshot of this is that although "they found a gold needle. . . . They filled a basket with dirt to take with them back to China." To which Kingston replies: "Do you mean the Filipinos tricked them? . . . What were they doing in Spain?" Places are reshuffled, confusion ensues; dirt, not the gold needle, is transported to China. The positions of speaker and listener are scrambled; signifiers lose their referents. The Filipino scholar wryly promises to distill the facts and mail them to Kingston: truth/knowledge-production aborts further exchange. In conclusion, Kingston says: "Good. Now I could watch the young men who listen." The joke of reversing positions and demythologizing the "Gold Mountain" explodes the metaphysics of success, the work ethic, and stereotyped images of the United States. We recall how, in the novel, the labor of generations of Chinese immigrants culminated in their being "Driven Out" (decreed by the 1882 Exclusion Act) and subsequently victimized in pogroms and lynchings. Veteran workers become fugitives, temporizing or permanent exiles in the belly of the metropolis. "On Listening" refuses the centralizing intelligence that would mediate discrepancies or reconcile opposites into a hypostatized moment of discovering the truth.

What Kingston executes very subtly in her anecdotal montage is the act of undercutting the formula of the American dream of success by presenting heterogeneous versions of what the Chinese did in pursuit of the Gold Mountain; none of these versions is privileged, so the questions posed by the "I" who seeks an authoritative, official version never receive a definitive answer. Hence, the only recourse is to appreciate the virtue of listening, of being open to the possibilities created by our persevering struggles to subvert a monologic political economy. Kingston's maneuver of disrupting any answer that claims to be authoritative, whether it is the narcissistic speech of liberalism or the assimilationist speech of conservative populism ("*e pluribus unum*"), is one which, I suggest, can serve as a foil to the seduction of multiculturalism in our postmodern milieu. As Hazel Carby (1990) puts it, the politics of multicultural difference can effectively neutralize the response of a racialized subject, thus repressing criticism of a social order structured in dominance by race. The politics of difference is what underwrites the ghettoization and apartheid in pluralist America.

Recently, in line with the deconstructionist trend in the discourse of the humanities and the recurrent if transitional vogue of revitalizing individualist "habits of the heart," the notion of inventing one's ethnic identity has been broached as an alternative to a modernized scheme of integration. One writer participant in the Cornell University symposium, for example, mused about the supposed "multiple anchorages that ethnicity provides" amid the color-blind tolerance of the proverbial marketplace of ideas. This celebrates the form, not the substance, of bourgeois individualism retooled for a "post-revolutionary" era. But can one really invent one's identity as one wishes, given the constraints *de jure* and *de facto* enforced by the racial state? She confesses: "I can make myself up and this is the enticement, the exhilaration. . . . But only up to a point. And the point, the sticking point is my dark female body." Identity betrays its lack in the crucible of difference. Here is where I would finally foreground the phenotypical marker, the brand of the racial stigma, as the politically valorized signifier that cannot be denied in spite of the rules of formal juridical equality. The colored body and its tropes may be the uncanny sites where the repressed— history, desire, the body's needs—returns.

I would like to underscore here the nexus between the constraints on self-identification and the theoretical import of hegemony introduced earlier. In a field of force where the liberal episteme is deeply entrenched, the key principle for the maintenance of a stable, self-reproducing hierarchical order of capital is hegemony, a concept first developed by Antonio Gramsci. Hegemony signifies the ascendancy of a historic bloc of forces able to win the voluntary consent of the ruled because the ruled accept their subordinate position for the sake of a degree of freedom that indulges certain libidinal drives, sutures fissured egos, fulfills fantasies, and so forth (Gramsci 1971, 206–76). In exchange for such limited gratification, the subalterns submit to the status quo on the condition that they have access to "individual freedoms," varied life-styles, differential rewards, and so forth. In the context of the U.S. racial order, this arrangement is known as normative pluralism. A social system presided over by normative pluralism thrives precisely because it ignores the institutional differentiation of interests—we are all equal, each one can do her or his own thing. It also displaces onto quarantined terrain those incompatible, discrepant interests that in fact construct our individual and group positions synchronized to the hierarchical imperatives of the system. Everything is normal: I'm OK, you're OK.

It might be useful, in conclusion, to recapitulate certain propositions formulated earlier in order to highlight the contextual nature of what I would propose as an agenda for the committed imagination of peoples of color. This agenda would challenge pluralism as the discourse and practice of atomistic liberalism. This hegemonic pluralism operates most effectively in the guise of multiculturalism, alias ethnic diversity, within the parameters of a unifying national consensus that privileges one segment as the universal measure: the Euro-American elite. To secure its reproduction together with its basis in existing property relations, the hegemonic racial formation elides the conflictive relations of domination and subordination. It substitutes parallelism, synchrony, or cohesion of interests. It negotiates the acceptance of a compromise, a homogeneous national life-style (innocent of gender or class or racial antagonisms) into which other generalized cultures—Asian, American Indian, Latino, African American—can be gradually assimilated. This liberal approach fails to recognize that the reality of U.S. institutional practices of racism is grounded in the unequal possession of wealth. Such inequality extends to the exercise of politico-economic control over resources and authority over institutions. Predicated on the uneven but combined development of political, economic, and ideological spheres of society, such inequality engenders forms of resistance to the power of the dominant social bloc and its ideology of plural identities.[5]

In this arena of struggle, what can be a realistic but also prophetic agenda for the subalterns, the borderline dissidents, and the migrant insurgent intellects?[6] I acknowledge the concern that it may be exorbitant, even presumptuous, to draw any kind of guideline for "unacknowledged legislators." Whatever the risks, a heuristic call for organized initiatives may be broached to spark reflection and debate. And so, taking inventory of the problems, misrecognitions, even "false consciousness" and alibis plaguing our ranks, I hazard the following "untimely" proposal.

What Asian American writers need to do as a fulfillment of their social responsibility is to pursue the "labor of the negative," that is, to problematize the eccentric "and/or" of their immigrant, decolonizing heritage and of their conjunctural embeddedness in the world-system. Such problematization would insist that their signifying practice dovetail with the emergent strategies of resistance devised by all peoples of color to the U.S. racial state and its hegemonic instrumentalities. Such linkage demands a radical critique of the politics of both dichotomous (private versus public) and unitary identity. It requires a rigorous self-critique of one's vocation catalyzed by a staging of its internal contradictions, contradictions that surface when writer and text are contextualized in specific times and places. In art this may assume the shape of what Brecht calls allegorical distancing, modalities of alienation crafted to trick and destroy the enemy; defamiliarizing the customary modes of expression, baring the devices of ordinary commonsense behavior, exposing the artificiality of the contrivance behind the mystery, and unveiling the stigmata behind the transcendental flag of the Empire. It requires foregrounding the adversarial, the contestatory, the interrogative. Demystify the normal order, the shopper's everyday routine—*"c'est la vie!"* Defetishize the imperial self. In pursuing this duplicitous labor of the negative, we can perhaps forge in the process an Asian American vernacular that will inscribe our bifurcated or triangulated selves on emerging post-national cosmopolitan texts—shades of Goethe's *Weltliteratur!*—with restorative, galvanizing effect. In the womb of these vernaculars we hope a dialectics of the utopian power of the imagination and emancipatory social praxis can materialize in, through, and beyond the boundaries of race, class, and gender.[7]

Notes

1. It might be useful to note here how Marx, in *Capital*, criticized bourgeois political economists for taking Robinson Crusoe as their theoretical model of the "natural man" or *homo economicus*—the classic ideological move to claim universal objectivity for a particular interest (see Tucker 1978, 324–28).
2. Eugene Genovese (1971) and Lawrence Levine (1977), among others, have tried to demonstrate the presence of an autonomous, counterhegemonic culture of the African slave in the antebellum South.
3. See, for example, Sollors (1980; 1986a). In the work of Sollors and other ethnicity experts, the whole Asian American experience and its prototypical expressions exist as gaping lacunae. For a critique of the prevailing ethnicity paradigm, see Wald (1987).
4. The debate on the relevance of poststructuralist theory for the study of ethnic writing has been going on for some years now primarily among African American scholars. I find the controversy surrounding the critical practice of Henry Louis Gates, Jr., provocative and useful in weighing the strengths and liabilities of poststructuralist methodology for a research program investigating racist discourse and practices. See Chapter 1 of this book.
5. I paraphrase here statements from Carby (1980).
6. The category of the ethnic intellectual is still open to further analytic specification, for which the most suggestive beginning has been made by Georg Simmel's essay "The Stranger" (1971). For germinal insights on the phenomenology of immigration and homelessness, see Berger (1984).
7. A provisional example of the "and/or" strategy of disruption may be exemplified by David Henry Hwang's *M. Butterfly* (1986), where the mystique of the exotic Oriental, and its material base, is exploded and the binary opposites East/West deconstructed within certain limits. However, I question the "We" of the playwright's statement in the "Afterword": "We have become the 'Rice Queens' of *realpolitik.*" As for Brecht's *Verfremdungeffekt* and his anti-Aristotelian poetics, see Willett (1964) and Benjamin (1978).

B. *Toward the Production of a Filipino Racial Discourse in the Metropolis*

Although Filipinos will become the largest component of the country's Asian American population—close to more than two million—in the next few years, certainly before this century of wars and revolutions closes its account books, we—and I insert myself into this collective subject of enunciation—are still practically an invisible and silent minority. We have been here a long time, but the early tracks of our itinerary have vanished, have been expunged, rubbed out. Our ethnic genealogy may be traced all the way back to the eighteenth century when Filipino sailors, fugitives from the galleon trade between Mexico and the Philippines, found their way to what is now California and Texas. One can resurrect from the archives a mention of how Filipinos were dispatched by the French pirate Jean Laffitte to join the forces of Andrew Jackson in the Battle of New Orleans in 1812. But it was our colonization by the U.S. military, a primal loss suffered through the Filipino-American War (1899–1902) and the protracted resistance ordeal of the revolutionary forces of the First Philippine Republic up to 1911, that opened the way for the large-scale transport of cheap Filipino labor to Hawaii and California, inaugurating this long, weary, tortuous exodus from the periphery to the metropolis with no end in sight. We are here, but somehow it's still a secret.

Our invisibility has been less a function of numbers than an effect or symptom of that persisting colonial oppression by the United States to which no other Asian immigrant group, with their thousands of years of Buddhist/Confucian culture, has been subjected. We don't have to review Hegel's phenomenology of bondsman and master to understand why Filipinos are quick to identify themselves as "Americans" even before formal citizenship is bestowed. It seems that the loss of autonomy is compensated for by identification with U.S. ego ideals, from Lincoln to Elvis Presley. Filipinos find themselves "at home" in a world they've lived in before—not just in Hollywood fantasies but in the material culture of everyday life, from the American English of commercial music to consumer goods, from U.S. weaponry in military bases to sumptuary rituals at McDonalds to Avon cosmetics to condoms to celluloid dreams of the good life. (Hagedorn's novel *Dogeaters* provides a neat catalogue of these symbols and artifacts syncopated with survivals from the palimpsest tablets of an archaic past.) When they encounter rejection or discrimination here, they are at first puzzled, wounded, feeling culpable for not having read the signs correctly, mutely outraged. The psychological reflex is familiar: they vow to prove themselves twice better than their "tutors."

The Filipino has been produced by Others (Spaniards, Japanese, the *Amerikanos*), not mainly by her own will to be recognized: her utterances and deeds. Four hundred years of servitude to Spanish feudal suzerainty preceded our famous American "tutelage," a racial experience which made us a fortuitous *tabula rasa* for the doctrine of market liberalism and meritocracy which, at the turn of the century, wrote its signature in our psyches in the form of U.S. "Manifest Destiny," the "White Men's Burden" of civilizing the barbarian natives into free, English-speaking, forever adolescent consumers. The traumatic fixations began in those forty years of "compadre colonialism" and patronage. When formal independence was granted in 1946, after the harrowing years of Japanese imperial occupation, U.S. "tutelage"—to use this academic euphemism— assumed the form of a perpetual high-and-low-intensity warfare of "free world" democracy led by the United States over our souls and bodies threatened by the evil forces of communism. Recently the U.S. government's gospel of salvation redeemed us from the evils of its lackeys, Ferdinand and Imelda Marcos. You can read this version of contemporary events in Stanley Karnow's *In Our Image*, now a Pulitzer prize winner, and his three-part TV documentary (San Juan 1989b; Tarr 1989). And you can read an oblique commentary of Karnow's narrative (which Peter Tarr calls the "Immaculate Conception" view of U.S. imperial history) in Hagedorn's *Dogeaters*, the first novel I've read which seeks to render in a unique postmodernist idiom a century of U.S.-Philippine encounters: the novel can be conceived as a swift montage of phantasmagoric images, flotsam of banalities, jetsam of clichés, fragments of quotes and confessions, shifting kaleidoscopic voices, trivia, libidinal tremors and orgasms, and hallucinations flashed on film/TV screens—virtually a cinematext of a Third World scenario that might be the Philippines or any other contemporary neocolonial milieu processed in the transnational laboratories of Los Angeles or New York.

And so, long before the Filipino as immigrant, tourist, or visitor sets foot on the U.S. continent, she—her body and sensibility—has been prepared by the thoroughly Americanized culture of the homeland. This is true in particular for the second and third waves of immigrants, from 1946 to the present. Here I disagree with those who claim that the majority of Filipino immigrants after 1965 carried with them traces of the growing nationalist sentiment in the Philippines before and after the declaration of martial law in 1972 (Occeña 1985). The records show that it was the first wave of immigrants in the twenties and thirties who demonstrated an intransigent recalcitrance, a spirit of militant resistance born, it seems, from "the political unconscious" of the popular mass struggles against Spanish and American aggressors in the last decade of the nineteenth century and the first decade of the twentieth. Popular memory counterpointed the path of migration. Thus Filipino workers in Hawaii (about twenty thousand strong) on 19 June 1920 initiated the first major inter-ethnic strike against the sugar planters; it lasted seven months. Again, in April 1924, about thirty-one thousand Filipino workers staged an eight-month strike which closed down half of the plantations in Hawaii; this bloody confrontation—police killed sixteen workers, wounded four, imprisoned sixty, and black-listed hundreds—earned Filipinos the reputation of being dangerous and rebellious workers. With the birth of the United Farm Workers Union from the historic Delano grape strike of Filipino workers in September 1965, an era ended; this heroic archetype of the Filipino worker (McWilliams 1964; Kushner 1971) is now a nostalgic topic for aging veterans of that class war and their kin in retirement villages, an epoch memorialized in Carlos Bulosan's epic chronicle *America Is in the Heart* (1948). This epic theme of immigration is now anachronistic, displaced by the genre of forced exile, CIA intrigues, and sensationalized court trials (Marcos, Duvalier, Noriega), as well as the "warm body export" of more than a million Filipinos scattered all over the planet.

The 1898 conjuncture in Philippine history—the explosion of revolutionary nationalist passion among workers, peasants, middle strata, and intellectuals—has never been replicated so far, not even by the rise of the First Quarter Storm in 1971 nor the February urban insurrection of 1986. So despite the American tutelage of the first three decades which converted Carlos P. Romulo and his ilk (most of whom sang alleluia in the pages of *Philippine News* when Bush sent airplanes to rescue the beleaguered Aquino) into Taft's "little brown brothers," at least two generations of Filipinos (some of whom immigrated to the U.S. like Bulosan and Manuel Buaken) experienced the vicissitudes of life as subalterns in revolt against white Western domination. When they came to the United States, however, they had to undergo another education, an apprenticeship in disillusionment. Manuel Buaken writes:

> Where is the heart of America? I am one of the many thousands of young men born under the American Flag, raised as loyal, idealistic Americans under your promises of equality for all, and enticed by glowing tales of educational opportunities. Once here we are met by exploiters, shunted into slums, greeted by gamblers, and prostitutes, taught only the worst in your civilization. America came to us with bright-winged promises of liberty, equality, and fraternity—what has become of them? (*The New Republic*, 23 Sept. 1940)

Bulosan for his part witnessed the many faces of racist violence at the heart of liberal free-enterprise society, registering in his sentimental and melodramatic style the fabled shock of recognition:

> I came to know afterward that in many ways it was a crime to be a Filipino in California. I came to know that public streets were not free to my people. We were stopped each time those vigilant patrolmen saw us driving with a car. We were suspect each time we were with a white woman. . . . It was now the year of the great hatred; the lives of Filipinos were cheaper than those of dogs. (San Juan 1972, 1983, 1984)

America Is in the Heart, as everyone knows, ends with a utopian hope. Such a vision is possible only because Bulosan's testimony of growing up, an ethnic bildungsroman, is sedimented with the popular memory of folk resistance and numerous peasant uprisings in Pangasinan where he was born. His roots in the dissident folk tradition and communal life preserved a certain cunning in his years of exile which enabled him, by an autodidact's luck, to forge the "conscience of his race" at a time when Filipino guerillas were fighting the Japanese occupation forces, the very same guerillas (descendants of *Katipuneros* and *Colorum* insurgents)[1] who later joined the Huk uprising and were ruthlessly suppressed by the CIA-supported Magsaysay regime in the heyday of McCarthyism. Today Bulosan, once discovered in the early seventies, has fallen back into oblivion.

Why do I linger on this historical specificity of persisting U.S. domination of the Philippines? Because without fully understanding the process of subjectification of the Filipino psyche (the division of the subaltern into the "I," grammatical subject of the statement which defines the fictional ego positioned by class, gender, race, etc., and the "I" as the speaking subject, matrix, or locus of the free play of signifiers), it is impossible to understand the forms of contradictory or antinomic behavior the Filipino is capable of manifesting as ethnic/racial subject in the terrain of U.S. late capitalism. This analysis of the effect of ideology in defining the position (what others would call "identity") of Filipinos as class, gendered, ethnic agents in the U.S. racial formation who are capable of being mobilized or pacified, depending on varying conjunctures, has not yet been systematically carried out. Research on structural constraints to social mobility preoccupy graduate students. But so far the existing studies on the historical development of the Filipino community in the United States has been sketchy, superficial, and flawed in its methodology and philosophical assumptions. What prevails up to now is a reliance on the expertise of white male sociologists whose strategy of "blaming the victim" is still repeated in numerous textbooks, the commonsense wisdom echoed by opportunistic Filipino leaders themselves when they exhort the community to engage in united political activity for the Democratic or Republican party.

I should like to cite here one example, the explanation offered by the well-known scholar H. Brett Melendy for Filipino marginality. Melendy's entry on Filipinos in the authoritative *Harvard Encyclopedia of American Ethnic Groups* (1980) begins with a description of "Origins." He recites the surface details of history and economics, focusing on the family and kinship structure:

> The [compadrazgo] system required an individual's strong sense of identity with and acceptance by the group, and served to promote beliefs that kin relationships tolerate no disagreement; that an individual should maintain his proper station in society, neither reaching above nor falling below it; and that a person's acts should contribute to his self-esteem but not cause embarrassment to others. (356)

Melendy also reports on the prevalence of gambling as part of barrio celebrations in order to show that this predilection prevented Filipino immigrants from saving money despite their diligence.

It was the power of these "cultural backgrounds and values systems" that, from the structural-functionalist point of view, compelled Filipinos to marry Hawaiian, Portuguese, and Puerto Rican women, not the social taboo nor legal prohibition against miscegenation. While Melendy alludes to the peculiar status of Filipinos as "nationals," neither citizens nor aliens, a twilight zone of indeterminacy which excluded them from naturalization but also prevented their deportation, he does not give this the emphasis it deserves. What is worse is that for Melendy the Filipinos came to the United States burdened with values and attitudes that only encouraged prejudice or caused their unacceptance by the dominant white majority. It also explains their political nullity as citizens today:

> The Filipinos, confronted with prejudice both in Hawaii and on the West Coast, divided their world even more sharply than formerly into compadres and enemies. The alliance system that evolved in most California towns was based upon Filipino traditions of reciprocity, obligation, loyalty, and unity; those outside the group were suspect. As in Hawaii, compang groups developed in camps and cities. In the evenings and on weekends these provincial clans partied together and fought others in the local pool hall, bar, gambling house, or dance hall; most of the drunken battles were over women. In contrast to the plantation Filipinos, the West Coast single men moved around constantly seeking work; there was little semblance of permanent community. . . .
>
> Filipino loyalty to family and regional group has militated against their achieving success in American politics. They see no clear reason to form a Filipino political organization, and their tendency to group exclusiveness makes it difficult for any one Filipino to gain widespread support from the others. . . . Provincial allegiances and personality clashes lead Filipino organizations to multiply rather than coalesce. . . . (360, 362)

Like snapshots or painted tableaux, this authorizing and authoritarian text has frozen thousands of Filipinos in some kind of hermetically sealed ethnographic museum or time warp in the mythology of secular predestination. Unfortunately it is still quoted as textbook wisdom, sophisticated common sense.

Given the advance of Third World demystifying scholarship signaled by Frantz Fanon's writings and Edward Said's *Orientalism* (1978), among others, we can now see that the problem of Melendy and other experts on ethnicity stems from the failure of bourgeois social science in general to grasp the historical specificity of global capitalism in its imperialist phase. This is the source of its failure to comprehend the differential incorporation of racial groups into the social formation of developing U.S. capitalism from the nineteenth—for example, Chinese labor in railroad construction, genocidal campaign against the Indians, annexation of Puerto Rico and the Philippines—to the twentieth century. In the seventies, the project of constructing a theory of "internal colonialism" with specific reference to the Chicanos, blacks, and Indians called attention to this historical specificity, only to be overwhelmed by the cult of pan-ethnicity and the mock-pluralist individualism of the Reagan dispensation. What actually underlies this inability of liberal intellectuals to overcome racist ideology inheres in the paradigm of Cartesian knowledge and its allochronic discourse whereby the West exercised its power of transforming the Other (colonized subjects) into scientific knowledge. In *Time and the Other* (1983), Johannes Fabian demonstrates how Western anthropology in particular, with succeeding theories of evolutionism, relativism, and structuralism, refused coevalness—"the problematic simultaneity of different, conflicting, and contradictory forms of consciousness" (146)—to non-Western peoples. Consequently, Western knowledge about other peoples concealed the historic agenda of imperialist conquest through schemes claiming to promote civilized progress, development, or enlightenment upholding the banner of "freedom," "diversity," "integrity," etc.; relativism, on the other hand, fetishized taxonomy (classification as a mode of essentialism) and homogenized all differences, thereby ignoring time and history altogether.

Here then is the problem of reinventing the Filipino in the United States, articulating her silence and invisibility, for creative artists: the master narrative of the migrant workers' odyssey used by Bulosan and the quasi-existentialist interior monologues of Bienvenido Santos' expatriates marooned in the megalopolis can no longer serve as generic models. The plenitude of classic realist narrative, a mimesis of the bourgeois success story, is bound to distort the heterogeneous initiatives of the past three decades.

In a useful introduction to Filipino American literature, Sam Solberg

(1975) argues that the immigration epic can be renewed by younger writers while, for the older generation, "the Filipino dream of independence fades into the American dream of equality. . . ." Suspended in a metonymy of dreams, otherwise known as the Lacanian realm of the Imaginary, the Filipino cannot possess any identity worth writing about. No loss is experienced; the castration crisis of colonial disruption has been forgotten—nay, it has been repressed. He or she becomes simply a mimicry of the white American, a mock-image born of misrecognition. At this point, a struggle for control of the signifying practice linked to the "I" of the speaking subject, site of the polysemy of representations, becomes imperative.

There is, I think, no alternative: a beginning must be made from the realities of immigrants in the eighties, and from the experience of Filipino Americans born here in the sixties and seventies.[2] And this cannot be done without evoking the primal scene coeval with the present: the neocolonial situation of the Philippines and its antecedent stages, the conflicted terrain of ideological struggle which abolishes the distinction/distance between Filipinos in the Philippines and Filipinos in the United States. Continuities no less than ruptures have to be articulated for an oppositional practice to emerge. The terrain is less geographical than cultural—culture defined as the complex network of social practices signifying our dominant or subordinate position in a given social formation. Nor would the triumphalist rhetoric of *Line of March* claiming the Filipino community as part of the proletarian vanguard provide a viable starting point. I believe that we are still in the stage of recuperating and sublating the gains of the sixties in a time when the U.S. Establishment is celebrating the defeat of "actually existing socialism," the failure of Marxism, and the victory of the giant supermall and the religion of endless consumerism—shop until you drop! To allude to the revolutionary situation in the Philippines and the presence of left guerillas contesting the U.S.-backed regime would sound, for a middle-class audience here, as anachronistic and weird as talking of the Watsonville Riots of January 1930 or the staged blowing-up of the *Maine* in Havana harbor in 1898. This, I think, is the achievement of Hagedorn's novel: the unfolding of the historical crisis of U.S. hegemony in the Philippine context (marked by the Aquino assassination, the hovering presence of the New People's Army, the scandalous decadence and corruption of the elite polluting the whole body politic, U.S. consumerism, and so on) conveyed through a postmodern, inescapably complicitous myth.

Of all the Asian American groups, the Filipino community is perhaps the only one obsessed with the impossible desire of returning to the homeland, whether in reality or fantasy. It is impossible because, given the break in our history (our initiation into the Imaginary or mirror-stage of colonial existence), the authentic homeland doesn't exist except as a simulacrum of

Hollywood, or a nascent dream of *jouissance* still to be won by a national-democratic struggle. Its presence (invoked in Hagedorn's novel as the pre–Oedipal matriarch invested in various characters) is deferred, postponed, the climax of a trajectory of collective and personal transformative projects. One such project can be fulfilled through a reinterpretation of the past: what Ronald Takaki in his chronicle describes as the Filipino addiction to gambling, dancing, and pursuit of white women, could be read as the eloquent realization of what Georges Bataille (1985) calls the principle of expenditure: the fulfillment of the need to lose and destroy, a drama which sublimates the agon of class struggle and subverts the rule of capitalist utility and its calculus of reification. Sacrifice of energy, money, and time engenders the sacred. In such acts of gift-exchange or symbolic reciprocity, the Filipino community reinvents itself in a conjuncture (*kairos*) where structure and event coincide, charting boundaries and affirming its solidarity vis-à-vis the alienating world of commodity-fetishism. Conviviality and carnival (in Bakhtin's sense) replace solitary nostalgia, dissolving guilt into shame. But this is of course not the route pursued by post–World War II Filipino American writers.

I quote a characteristic statement (Chin et al. 1975) from three Filipino American writers who address the hybrid of schizoid sensibility of Filipinos presumably straddling Eastern and Western cultures:

> Being born or reared in America is like being put into a kettle with other ethnic groups, simmered by years of racism, identity crises, and subsequent ethnic rejection, and then coming out with a blend of many influences from that environment. Thus, we have Filipinos who are more versed in other ethnic cultures and who talk, act, and actually believe themselves to be white. . . . Although geographically and racially he is Oriental, the Filipino is so influenced by Western ways that many adopt and imitate anything American. The Filipino-American, aware of the contradictions in American society, is thus confused and dismayed when he visits the Philippines and finds brown faces with white minds. . . . The Filipino American writer is seeing and writing about the myth of the American dream, while the Filipino is drawn by the dream that is perpetuated by the heavy American influences in his country. (49, 54)

Written in the early seventies, this reflects the vocabulary and temper of those days, especially the impulse to assert one's identity to surmount the putative identity crisis (Erik Erikson) and the proverbial "melting pot." Self-assertion is conducted by drawing demarcation lines between Filipino American (who can penetrate through the masks of myth) and the mystified though canny Filipino. This taxonomy not only ignores precisely the problem of colonial subordination and racial victimage, but it also represses the truth that the revolutionary process in the Philippines has far outstripped the counterculture rhetoric of California and Greenwich Village. A spurious identity, "Filipino American," is exhibited here as mere form, without real substance. The lesson of poststructuralism is that all these binary oppositions are inscribed in a field of textuality, of overdeterminations, where meaning is relational and processual. In other words, the Filipino American subject-position cannot be defined without elucidating what the problematic relation is between the two terms which dictates the conditions of possibility for each—the hyphen or nexus which spells a relation of domination and subordination. Let us not so peremptorily elide the differences subsisting at the core of a temporary synthesis. Lacking this totalizing and historical view, the critique of racism and imperialism implied by our writers rests on an unquestioned metaphysics of the subject, seemingly autonomous, universal, and free, which is precisely the philosophical and ideological foundation of imperial hegemony that undermines their collective project, their will to self-determination.

Now it is easy to resolve one's problematic situation of being situated on the borders, or on no man's land, deterritorialized by powers whose operations seem mysterious, by making a virtue of necessity, so to speak. It is easy to perform the unilateral trick of reversing the negative and valorizing that as positive: for example, "Black is beautiful." Or else, taking pride in the fact that we are beneficiaries of both cultures, East and West, and that our multicultural awareness, our cosmopolitanism, enables us to partake of the feast of humanity's accomplishments—from Egyptian funerary art and Plato's ideas to the latest IBM computer. This is in fact the fashionable axiom of postmodern theorizing. The postmodernist technique of pastiche, aleatory juxtaposition, virtuoso bricolage carried to its logical culmination, is what presides in the first part of *Dogeaters*—a flattening of heterogeneous elements approximating Las Vegas simultaneity—until the introduction of Joey Sands, symbol of what is actually meant by "special Filipino American relations," forces the text to generate a semblance of a plot (cause-effect sequence, plausible motivation, etc.) whereby the scenario of sacrifice— Joey's slaughter of Taruk, iconic sign for the surrogate father who also functions as castrator/betrayer, and for all the other patriarchs upholding the code of filial piety—is able to take place and the discourse to end in a prayer to the Virgin "mother of revenge." But that vestige of the traditional art of storytelling, in which irreconcilable victims of a neocolonial regime end up in a revolutionary guerilla camp plotting retribution, finds itself embedded and even neutralized by a rich multilayered discourse (exotic to a Western audience) empowered by what Henri Lefebvre (1971, 1976) calls the capitalist principle of repetition. This culture of repetition (pleonasm, tautology, recycled simulations, in effect Baudrillard's world of pure mediations), of which the telltale index is the Hollywood star system (and its counterpart in the commercial mass culture of the Philippines: the regurgitated routine of clichés, stereotypes, and debased sexual rituals), conditions most postmodernist art, reducing even parody, satire, and irony to aspects of a traumatized and redundant cosmos against which the "Kundiman" or prayer of exorcism concluding *Dogeaters* can only be a stylized gesture of protest. In this sense, the novel becomes a Filipino American testimony of reflexive nihilism.

For Asian American artists in general, not just for Filipino writers, the seduction of postmodernism as an answer to racism and ethnic marginality can be intoxicating and well-nigh irresistible. But we need to address these questions (see Mascia-Lees, Sharpe, and Cohen 1989; Fraser and Nicholson 1990): Does the antifoundational favoring of difference and identity politics abolish prevailing norms and hierarchies? Do polyvocality and positionality erase power differentials? Can the fragmentary, dialogic approach of Euro-American intellectuals (specific and local, as Foucault cautions us) claim to be more faithfully "representative" of people of color than the latter's *métarécits* of justice and liberation? Can pragmatism and new historicism empower the victimized subalterns at the mercy of the corporate elite of northern industrialized nation-states? Can Lyotard's paradigm of the "justice of multiplicities" and heterogeneity eliminate private appropriation of surplus-value and the authority of capital? In the ultimate reckoning, isn't this postmodern strategy of "otherness" a none-too-subtle mode of recuperating the totalizing mastery of liberal, pluralist discourse? For whom is modernist and postmodernist theory constructed? Not only Asian Americans but all artists of color have substantial stakes in how these questions are answered.

Since all art in a commodity-centered society is ultimately reduced to exchangeable value—and literature is no exception—we can see that the style of postmodernism and its philosophical justification in cultural pluralism (floating monads in Bloomingdale?) easily becomes instrumentalized to serve the very ends which it originally sought to counter. A certain form of postmodernist art functions to replicate the commodity as eternal recurrence of the same, the paradigm of repetition. The dialectic of art as a substitute for radically transforming praxis, of aesthetic fantasy as substitute for the body's protean transaction with the real world, may also be perceived in the exploitation of illusion embodied in commodities, a phenomenon analyzed by W. F. Haug in his *Critique of Commodity Aesthetics* (1986):

An innumerable series of images are forced upon the individual, like mirrors, seemingly empathetic and totally credible, which bring their secrets to the surface and display them there. In these images, people are continually shown the unfulfilled aspects of their existence. The illusion ingratiates itself, promising satisfaction: it reads desires in one's eyes, and brings them to the surface of the commodity. While the illusion with which commodities present themselves to the gaze, gives the people a sense of meaningfulness, it provides them with a language to interpret their existence and the world. Any other world, different from that provided by the commodities, is almost no longer accessible to them. How can people behave, or change themselves, when continually presented with a collection of dream-images that have been taken from them? How can people change when they continue to get what they want, but only in the form of illusion? (52)

To paraphrase those urgent questions: How can postmodernist writing, offspring of commodity aesthetics, break off from its narcissistic captivity? One effective way I would suggest is by a return to modernist reflexiveness and self-critique, in particular to the defamiliarizing practices of Bertolt Brecht, Augusto Boal, or the San Francisco Mime Troupe. Expose the mechanisms producing illusions, reveal the anatomy of the production process, bare the devices of erotic sublimation. These guidelines may catalyze the imagination of the nomadic artist crisscrossing the borders toward a fundamental interrogation of itself and its social presuppositions. With the writer's complicity, they may help empower the reader/ audience, even the ethnic community, to thwart the homogenizing and integrative force of hegemonic standards and norms, and perhaps facilitate movements demanding the democratic control of the apparatus of intellectual/cultural production once envisaged by Walter Benjamin.[3] Creative writers are, to be sure, astute fabricators and purveyors of illusions, beleaguered or compromised as they compete with corporate mass media (in particular, movies and television). If Asian American writers are not to be merely unwitting agents for the reproduction of capital and its racializing virulence, is it exorbitant to expect them to study and understand the dynamics of U.S. cultural hegemony and in the process commit themselves to a minimum program of demystification and radical critique? Everyone knows each writer must decide for whom her art is destined, whose sense of civic responsibility she seeks to warrant and instigate.

In conclusion I want to emphasize the necessity for ethnic artists, Asian American writers in this case, to grasp that a liberal democratic society constituted by manifold antagonistic interests can function only when hegemony (consent of subjects to be ruled) obtains—that is, when a particular set of values, attitudes, or beliefs, together with its accompanying complex network of practices I alluded to earlier, is accepted as consensus; when people voluntarily act and think in accordance with a certain worldview or structure of feeling associated with a class or historic bloc of groups who dominate what Althusser calls "Ideological State Apparatuses." Hegemony in the Symbolic Order (in the public sphere, civil society) guarantees not only production for profit but also reproduction of the total structure of society, reproduction of itself—endless repetition, with just enough phenomenal diversity or variety to hide the boredom and produce the impression of orderly, peaceful change toward more improvement, more progress, and more illusory gratification.

In line with this concept of hegemony (borrowed from Gramsci and modified by Raymond Williams), the plurality of cultures or life-styles in any given social formation is a mirage which, while palpable and temporarily satisfying, maintains the political hegemony of a particular group whose view of the world prevails precisely by virtue of this illusion (which Haug discussed above). Culture is nothing else but the complex network of social practices which signify or determine positions of domination, equality, or subordination. U.S. normative pluralism denies this definition of culture by concealing the contradictions and conflicts of interests in society. Through postmodernist articulations of formal differences without substantive changes in the structure of power, it seeks to impose a unity of all groups (sexual, racial, and economic); achieving a temporary harmony of all by marginalizing the dissidents and neutralizing the unfit or deviant, it maintains the hegemony of a particular constellation of groups or interests who benefit from the status quo. However, because uneven and nonsynchronic development informs all levels of society (economic, ideological, and political), a totalizing and permanent hegemony by definition is impossible. Gaps, fissures, and cleavages may be discovered in all spaces where negotiation of positions can be the agenda for struggle. Conjunctural opportunities can be seized by the popular forces even within the confines of rigid structural constraints. Within this framework, even postmodernist strategies of expression and modes of utopian representation can be inflected to some extent for alternative or oppositional ends, hence the ambiguous, equivocal effect of such works as *Dogeaters*.

Ideally the critique of hegemony should precede any exploration of one's racial or ethnic identity—subject position, to be precise—because one's place can be discovered and mapped only in the field of multiple relationships. But I would argue that we should first disabuse ourselves that there is equality of cultures and genuine toleration of differences in a stratified society by bearing in mind this very cogent perspective that Hazel Carby (1980, 64–65) proposes for our careful judgment: "By insisting that 'culture' denotes antagonistic relations of domination and subordination, this perspective undermines the pluralistic notion of compatibility inherent in *multi*culturalism, the idea of a homogeneous national culture (innocent of class or gender differences) into which other equally generalized Caribbean or Asian cultures can be integrated. The paradigm of multiculturalism actually excludes the concept of dominant and subordinate cultures—either indigenous or migrant—and fails to recognize that the existence of racism relates to the possession and exercise of politico-economic control and authority and also to forms of resistance to the power of dominant social groups."

The special predicament of Filipino writers in the United States whose historical roots I have tried to outline here may now be diagnosed as a symptom of the weakening of U.S. hegemony on the face of revolutionary challenges to its continued violent institutionalization in the Philippines. But because of the appeal of acquisitive/possessive liberalism and market-oriented individualist freedom in the context of access to certain goods and satisfactions in the metropolitan center, especially because of the power of commodity aesthetics which pervades all space in capitalist society, the Filipino writer in the United States still cannot escape the pleasure-filled trap of hyphenation. Perhaps she considers herself a special case whose destiny seems incommensurate with the African American, Chicano, American Indian, and so forth; or with her brothers and sisters in the neocolony. Perhaps her signifying practice, the whole repertoire of her *métier*, refuses to register the immense loss, the huge expenditure incurred in the thrall of colonial domination. Such a refusal perpetuates the compulsion to repeat. Her liberation from the postmodern mirage cannot be attained without a historical retrospective settling of accounts with the ghosts of the past—all those workers of Bulosan's generation sacrificed to the potlatch of free enterprise democracy—and the present victims of U.S. low-intensity, counterinsurgency warfare. Of course for the Filipino writers here, the struggle is within and outside the institutions of the racializing state whose imperial foreign policy is the chief source of oppression, misery, and death for millions of Filipinos in the homeland. Spatial distance yields to temporal coevalness: the recognition of the authentic Other as one's possibility. Writing in English, an alienating medium for the majority of 66 million Filipinos, the Filipino writer based in the United States (whether sojourner, expatriate, or permanent resident/citizen) can communicate only to a limited audience in the neocolony. But here she can announce the news that the "dogeaters" will soon take their ultimate revenge when a sacrifice of the patriarchal totem of a dog-eat-dog world is enacted in the presence of all those who dare to risk their lives, who dare to live and suffer through the expenditure and the loss, in order to fashion a less destructive, more liberating ecosystem.

Notes

1. *Katipuneros* refers to members of the Katipunan, the revolutionary organization founded by Andres Bonifacio in 1896 which spearheaded the anticolonial revolt against Spain. *Colorum* refers to peasant millennial groups in the twenties and thirties who staged insurrections in various provinces in the Philippines. For an account of some of these groups, and also an interview of Pedro Calosa, a Filipino strike leader in the twenties in Hawaii, consult Sturtevant (1976).
2. This can begin by taking note of basic facts of U.S. political economy with respect to the positioning of the Filipino community along class, race, and gender lines. See Cabezas and Kawaguchi (1989, 88–106).
3. I am thinking here of Brecht's alienation effect in his epic dramaturgy and chiefly his theory of theatrical production contained in "A Short Organum for the Theater" (Willett 1964, 179–208). See also the essay "The Author as Producer" by Walter Benjamin (1978, 220–38). Kristevan semiotics can also perhaps be used as antidote to reactionary postmodernism (Kristeva 1980). For the application of poststructuralist semiotics to popular culture, see Hebdige (1979).

Afterword: Cultural Diversity, Racial Politics, and Ethnic Studies in the Twenty-First Century

Every time the identity of "the American people" in this continent is celebrated today as a uniquely composite blend of European immigrants who settled in the Atlantic colonies or passed through Ellis Island, a political decision and a historical judgment are being made. A decision is made to represent the Others—American Indians, African Americans, Chicanos, Puerto Ricans, Asians, and other peoples of color—as missing, absent, or supplemental. Whenever the question of the national identity is at stake, boundaries in space and time are drawn; this founding moment then maps out the center and the periphery on the basis of "self-evident truths." In that same gesture, a judgment is made to consider the Others as subsumed—"integrated," "assimilated," or "melted"—in a space with a fixed hierarchy, thoroughly charted and demarcated.

An example of one conventional, self-evident truth called "ethnic pluralism" can be found in Professor S. Thernstrom's (1983) discursive rehabilitation of the "melting pot" metaphor which would homogenize peoples of color into the white middle class even as they are classified at the same time: " . . . today both the Chinese and Japanese groups rank well above American whites on every measure of socioeconomic status. They are as physically distinctive as their ancestors, but no one worries about the Yellow Peril any more. Orientals are no longer a stigmatized racial minority but a rapidly assimilating ethnic group" as evidenced by marriages with whites (252). I discuss below the economic and cultural fallacies of this widely held view.

On the question of national identity and who is allowed to enunciate it and solicit answers, we find a telling figure in the question posed by a white journalist to Jesse Jackson some time ago during a political campaign: whether Jackson is an American first and a black second, or vice versa. This is not just a problem of legitimate representation or ethnic autonomy. It is symptomatic of the crucial problem of racial conflict faced by the hegemonic sector of U.S. society which claims to speak for the "American nation."

131

It is obvious that this game of mapping the territory is a matter of articulating power relations. Self cannot be defined except in dialectical relation to an Other which is represented in a process of exclusion and inclusion. Whenever the "American Dream" seems to dissolve in the fires of urban rebellions of the excluded and marginalized, the slogan of unity-in-diversity (*e pluribus unum*), is revived ostensibly for the sake of every citizen's liberty and pursuit of happiness, regardless of race, color, or creed. One nation indivisible. . . .

Disregarding differences, those who draw the map seek to flatten out the uneven particularities of time and place and impose their own view of the territory. An official version of what happened results. This prevails and forecloses the possibility of Others articulating their identity as part of diverse *ethnoi*, of communities-in-the-making. The emergence of Ethnic Studies from the social upheaval of the sixties was an attempt to uncover the occluded and submerged, to liberate the repressed in the process of shaping peoples' histories. Its project was to redraw the boundaries, to affirm the autonomy of the "internal colonies" (barrio, reservation, inner cities), and thus recover the space for the exercise of popular democracy.

With the gradual academicization of Ethnic Studies, "the cult of ethnicity" based on the paradigm of European immigrant success became the orthodox doctrine. The theoretical aggrandizement of ethnicity systematically erased from the historical frame of reference any perception of race and racism as causal factors in the making of the political and economic structure of the United States. One example is Nathan Glazer's 1975 book *Affirmative Discrimination* which argues for a return to laissez-faire political economy at the price of historical amnesia. Since the time of Jefferson and Jackson, the historian Alexander Saxton writes, the United States "had assumed the form of a racially exclusive democracy—democratic in the sense that it sought to provide equal opportunities for the pursuit of happiness by its white citizens through the enslavement of Afro-Americans, extermination of Indians, and territorial expansion largely at the expense of Mexicans and Indians" (1977, 145).

I suggest that aside from principled refutations of the neoconservative argument against civil rights for disadvantaged peoples, Ethnic Studies can revitalize itself by challenging the orthodoxies of Establishment intellectuals and of state policies. This critique would strive to establish the groundwork for the fusion of theory and practice. It would seek to recapture the activist impulse presiding at its birth, mobilizing the agenda of popular memory by inscribing the historicity of people's struggles at the center of the discipline. As critique and praxis, Ethnic Studies can reshape the configuration of the intellectual landscape and contribute to the empowerment of oppressed groups and sectors.

The case of Asian American Studies illustrates the conjunctural crisis of the discipline. Like Ethnic Studies in general, Asian American Studies was born in the midst of the agitation for racial minority access to higher education, the demand for relevant curriculum and for the linkage of intellectual pursuits with the needs and aspirations of embattled communities (Omi 1988, 31–34). Its original vision of consciousness-raising as part of the decolonizing process and its project of shaping a new political identity for Asians motivated the questioning of the Eurocentric paradigm. It sought a new historical reading of the U.S. social formation. It posed a challenge to the dominant conventional thinking in the humanities and the social sciences. But changes in the political climate and the nature of specific social problems during the past two decades, in particular the increasing diversity of the Asian population, have profoundly transformed the Asian American communities so that the old political label "Asian American," which applied to the shared experiences of Chinese, Japanese, and Filipinos, can no longer apply to the Indo-Chinese refugees, the Korean and Pakistani merchants of New York and other big cities, or to the rich Hong Kong speculators of today. With the drastic alteration of immigration patterns in the past two decades and the persisting effects of the reactionary policies of the Reagan dispensation, Asian American Studies today faces a crisis similar to Ethnic Studies: will it continue to conform to the disciplinary regime of the academy? Or will it try to recuperate its inaugural vision as part of wide-ranging popular movements for justice and equality, for thorough-going social transformation?

At present, a current of Asian American Studies is engaged in a postmodernist project of reclaiming the past by focusing on the heterogeneous, the local and specific. Scholars seek to narrativize and foreground the individual life situations of Asians whose ongoing ethnogenesis, whose differential positioning in the political terrain, is homogenized by racial categorization. I think this is especially urgent because of the power elite's strategy to displace and so defuse intensifying class, gender, and racial contradictions. Since the sixties, Asian Americans have been homogenized into a "model minority" who are presumed to practice the typical values of individualism, self-reliance, the work ethic, discipline, and so on. So established is the symbolism of Ellis Island and the Puritan heritage in mainstream culture that to describe the lifelong struggle of diverse Asians to resist racist violence and institutionalized discrimination through "a culture of silence" and protean forms of solidarity may be a disturbing challenge to common sense and received opinion.

With the precipitous decline of middle-class living standards, the gutting of social services, and the rollback of the gains of the civil rights movement, many suspect that the myth of Asians as a "model minority" or even a "super-minority" was contrived to divide working people, pitting one racial group against the others, in order to displace systemic contradictions. If the Asians can do it, why can't Hispanics and blacks? Praising the high family median incomes of Asian American families compared to the total average in 1979, Reagan and the mass media lauded their "hard work," refusal to depend on welfare, and adherence to utilitarian values.

Numerous studies have cogently shown that when the statistics are analyzed against the realities of number of dependents and of persons working per family, educational attainment, residence in high-cost cities, and other factors, the conclusion is that Asian Americans have not reached equality with Caucasians. Despite their comparatively higher educational attainment than whites or Chinese immigrants, for example, Filipinos have average incomes lower than other Asians, remaining a "disadvantaged minority group" trapped in low-paying jobs (Nee and Sanders 1985, 85; see also Yun 1989, 88–106). In 1979, the per capita Asian income was in fact lower than the U.S. average. Moreover, Asians are overrepresented in low-wage sectors like food services and textiles (Lee 1991, 96). The myth of Asian success quickly evaporates before the reality of labor market segmentation, restricted mobility between sectors, and the "glass ceiling"—covert, subtle, and systemic patterns of racism which effectively exclude Asians from the seats of institutional and political power. What has been projected by the state and the media is a highly selective and distorted privileging of a few successful "Asian" individuals as typical or representative. Ronald Takaki (1989) notes that this myth of Asian American success "offers ideological affirmation of the American Dream in an era anxiously witnessing the decline of the United States in the international economy, the emergence of a new black underclass, and a collapsing white middle class" (478). Ignoring the structural problems of society and the economy, this myth provides a quick-fix cultural explanation: to make America number one again, it is necessary to emulate Asians who have accepted the Puritan "errand into the wilderness," the "habits of the heart" crystallized in "the bedrock values" of hard work, thrift, industry—in short, the utilitarian ethos in which the pursuit of enlightened self-interest is rewarded with material success.

Utilitarianism, the logic of competitive or "possessive individualism" at the heart of market-centered democracy, informs the self-identification of the majority. It functions as the ideology of meritocratic competition in the free market. As such, it constitutes the citizens/subjects of the liberal democratic state. Propagated by the mass media and all the ideological apparatuses of civil society and state, utilitarian individualism functions as a strategic principle of producing and reproducing inequality. It is this principle that underwrites the "model minority" myth. What are the practical implications of this social subjectification? Victims of racist practices are blamed for their failures; nothing is mentioned of structural iniquities and the persisting effects of race-oriented legislation. Meanwhile, blacks and Asians squabble over who controls the ghetto grocery store (vividly dramatized in Spike Lee's film *Do the Right Thing*) instead of cooperating together to question the fairness of bank lending policies and other unjust institutions which breed symptoms of deep social decay. The myth not only sanctions deceptively reformist social practices but denies Asians legal and social protection against institutional discrimination. Mari Matsuda (1990), professor of law at the University of Hawaii, comments on the crisis gripping the country and strategies of displacing it:

> From out of this decay comes a rage looking for a scapegoat, and a traditional American scapegoat is the oriental menace. From the Workingman's Party that organized white laborers around an anti-Chinese campaign in California in 1877, to the World War II internment fueled by resentment of the success of Issei farmers, to the murder of Vincent Chin, to the terrorizing of Korean merchants in ghetto communities today, there is an unbroken line of poor and working Americans turning their anger and frustration into hatred of Asian Americans. Every time this happens, the real villains—the corporations and politicians who put profits before human needs—are allowed to go about their business free from public scrutiny, and the anger that could go to organizing for positive social change goes instead to Asian-bashing. (12)

What the liberal state and the corporate mass media have accomplished is this: a highly selective and distorted privileging of a few successful individuals reduces the diverse Asian population into a monolithic yellow-skinned mass, ignores the large number of disadvantaged minority underclass (see Wilson 1988, 29–36), and thus legitimizes the prevailing system of racially based economic inequality underpinning the powerlessness of peoples of color.

Asian Americans, especially recent immigrants from the Philippines, South Korea, Hong Kong, and other peripheral dependencies of multinational, late capitalism (see Takagi 1983), are slowly occupying the lower echelons of the educated elite stratum. They are extremely susceptible to playing the role of a subordinate racial petty bourgeoisie, compliant and adaptable, mimicking the masters and oppressing the subalterns below them. The distinguished sociologist Edna Bonacich (1988) warns us of the insidious mystique of utilitarianism, its seductive claim to universalism, which has a powerful appeal for recent immigrants:

> Utilitarianism touts itself as beyond culture. It is the universal human form, free of content, each individual defining for himself who he will be.

It is the ultimate in freedom. But, of course, this is sheer rhetoric. The truth is, this is the white man's way only. It is his culture that he is imposing, and the claim to its universality rests only on his power to assert it. He who has power can assert that he speaks for humanity.

To the minorities of this nation, the utilitarian free market is a hollow mockery of universal freedom. It was a market economy that led to the buying and selling of African slaves. It was the expanding free market that drove across the American plains, robbing and slaughtering American Indians and Mexicans. It was the imperialistic drive of capitalism that penetrated Asia and bolstered various forms of tyranny there.

So, in being asked to join the great colorblind American rat race, minorities are not only being asked to negate themselves. They are being asked to join the very system that has oppressed them and continues to oppress them. They are being asked to become lieutenants of their captors. (89)

The future agenda of Ethnic Studies is clear: If we, the Others, who are represented by those in power hope to affirm our right of self-determination as peoples, we need to critique the utilitarian ethic that has become normalized in our everyday practices, part of the "common sense" of everyday life.

I would like to illustrate the above themes in terms of the Filipino community's experience in the United States—Filipinos now comprise the largest component of the Asian American population, more than two million, based on the 1990 census.

What is crucial in understanding the Filipino adventure in the North American continent is its disjunction from the white European immigrant odyssey of success and its affinity with the plight of Chicanos, Puerto Ricans, and other colonized nationalities. We should take account above all of the historical specificity of U.S. colonial domination of the Philippines from 1898 to 1946. More significant are its vestiges in the colonial "habitus" (Bourdieu's term) which determines Filipino vulnerability to the temptation of the utilitarian ideal.

Unlike the generations of Chinese workers memorialized in Kingston's *China Men*, Filipinos as a group did not suffer the excruciating humiliation and ordeal of Angel Island—they went straight to the workers' barracks in Hawaii as colonial wards (Filipinos were labeled "nationals"), their political subordination or ambiguity compounding the rigor of contract labor exploitation. The United States annexed the Philippines through violence: it suppressed the revolutionary forces of the Philippine Republic, victors over Spanish colonialism, in the first "Vietnam," the Filipino-American War of 1899–1902. Occurring after the years 1876–98, when segregation in the South had just consolidated itself, the war against Filipinos was distinctly a racial one. It was carried out under the shibboleth of "Manifest Destiny," which historically signified white Anglo-Saxon supremacy (see Horsman 1981). Inspired by the ethos of social Darwinism, the United States' claim of shouldering "the White Man's Burden"—its civilizing mission—was enforced by the military veterans of the Indian Wars in the wake of the Reconstruction's failure and by soldiers and officials who participated in the pacification campaigns in Cuba and Puerto Rico (McWilliams 1964, 229–49).

The historical incorporation of Filipino as well as Chinese and Japanese workers into the U.S. social formation demonstrates more clearly than other cases the emergence of a racial pattern based on the need of business to manipulate a large, mobile, and low-paid labor force that can be excluded when they are needed, pitted against other groups, and terrorized to submission. A cyclical pattern of recruitment, exploitation, and exclusion of Filipinos, Chinese, and Japanese immigrants, a cycle mediated to some extent by the varying power relations between the United States and their country of origin, operates as a background in understanding the present situation of Asian Americans today.

The emergence of this racial pattern should be comprehended in the perspective of U.S. territorial expansion after the Mexican War of 1845–48, the Civil War, the closing of the frontier, and subsequent indusrial development and crisis, culminating in the Spanish-American War of 1898 and the birth of the United States as an imperial power in the Pacific. In his book *The Asian in the West* (1970), Stanford Lyman distinguishes two epochs in the imposition of white Anglo-Saxon culture on peoples of color: the first consists of the total exclusion of nonwhites (blacks and native Americans), "the total institutionalization of the non-white population on plantations and reservations" which covers the period 1607 to the beginning of the century. The next phase substitutes "segmented, partial, institutionalized racism in a wide variety of arenas of action for the abandoned and moribund method of total incarceration"; "the pivotal group for the study of this transition from total to partial institutionalized racism is the Asian and especially the Chinese" (3–8). In this context, I would suggest that the Filipino community of migrant workers epitomizes the conflation of those two phases where dominative and aversive racisms (as defined by Kovel 1984) succeed each other inasmuch as the Filipino was both a colonized native and putative "free worker" who can alienate or sell his labor power—but only in circumscribed ways. In other words, the Filipino is a clear example of a "free racial subject" who has been historically constituted by evolving U.S. state policies and practices.

But unfortunately this is not how the Filipino has been understood by the disciplinary regimes of the state. Like other subjugated peoples of color, the Filipino immigrant in the United States has been conceptualized for the most part as a social problem—not yet a model minority. Sociologists who claim expertise in unravelling the "text" of Filipino ethnicity ascribe the failure of Filipino recruits to adapt to the working conditions in the sugar plantations to their "cultural baggage." What prevented them from becoming successfully assimilated so that they could then register their claim to the "American dream of success," according to H. Brett Melendy (1980), was precisely their cultural genealogy:

> For a long time, the young Filipinos [in Hawaii], separated from more militant groups and already indoctrinated to submission by the barrio political system known as *caciquismo*, made no attempt to rebel against the plantation system. . . .
> Filipino loyalty to family and regional group has militated against their achieving success in American politics. They see no clear reason to form a Filipino political organization, and their tendency to group exclusiveness makes it difficult for any one Filipino to gain widespread support from the others. (358, 362)

Not only are Melendy's statements factually insupportable, but they also lack historical grounding. Such academic analysis betrays the tendency of functionalist thinking to reify the complex and changing life situations of Filipinos of diverse classes and gender into a single empirical instance. The integrally rich and dense phenomenology of the Filipino community's suffering and struggle for survival and dignity disappears.

The sociological approach illustrated by Melendy may be an improvement over the doctrines of social Darwinism and Anglo-Saxon supremacy that presided over the exercise of violence which appropriated the Philippines for U.S. imperial aggrandizement. But all the same, functionalist empiricism erases the historical context in which racism against Filipinos forms part of a configuration of racial politics indivisible from the growth of transnational capital. As Blauner, Saxton, Lyman, and many other historians have cogently demonstrated, this sociopolitical terrain is marked by the genocidal subjugation of the American Indians, the legal and forcible enslavement of Africans, the dispossession of Chicanos, and the battery of legislative exclusion of Chinese from 1882 on (followed by that of Japanese and Filipinos) which climaxed a series of pogroms and lynchings up to the wholesale incarceration of Japanese Americans in 1942.

Mainstream social science expunges not only this record of victimization but also the capacity of Filipinos to produce changes in their lives, changes which reveal that the Filipino resistance to oppression is part of what Robert Blauner calls the Third World decolonizing process (1972, 83–110). The narrative of resistance against exploitation by capital and oppression by racist institutions can be found in the Filipino writer Carlos Bulosan's epic chronicle of migrant workers, *America Is in the Heart* (1946). We also encounter this narrative in the militancy of labor unions beginning from the first major interracial strike in Hawaii in January 1920 and the April 1924 eight-month strike of thirty-one thousand Filipino workers which closed half of Hawaii's plantations (to cite only two major events), up to the September 1965 strike of Filipino farm workers in Delano, California, which signaled the founding of what later became the United Farm Workers of America.

While Filipinos in general became victims to the "civilizing mission" of the Anglo-Saxon ruling bloc and its utilitarian ideology in more than a century of colonial "tutelage," the centuries-long revolutionary tradition of the Filipino people remained alive in the popular memory of thousands of peasants and workers who immigrated to Hawaii and the West Coast before World War II. This tradition invested their lives with meaning and forged an oppositional culture whose discovery inspired the younger generation to initiate the formation of Ethnic Studies at San Francisco State University in 1968.

In this last decade of the Cold War era, we are witnessing the resurgence of anti-imperialist nationalism in the Philippines amid worsening economic and political conditions. Unable to transform exploitative property relations, the U.S.-patronized elite parasitic on the neocolonial formation can only exacerbate the Filipino diaspora to all parts of the global labor market. This conjuncture should be understood as an instance of intensifying contradictions in the world system of capital between the dependent Third World social formations and the metropolitan centers (Europe, North America, Japan).

In the context of the Philippines as a dependent Third World neocolony, it is instructive to conceive of the culture of the Filipino immigrant as one that reproduces in microcosm the contradictions between the utilitarian ethos of transnational capitalism and the subaltern vision of the "internal colonies" in the metropolis. That is, it contraposes and sublimates personal initiative and collective vision. It reflects the predicament of the Third World native who, despite her bondage to the hallucinations of consumerism and commodity fetishism nourished by the U.S. mass media, knows that her Otherness is not just entirely defined by the imperial apparatus. She rejects the model of Sartre eloquently formulated in *Anti-Semite and Jew* (1948) and explores instead the line of flight taken by Frantz Fanon in *Black Skin, White Masks* (1967), premised on an overdetermined Otherness: "I am the slave not of the 'idea' others have of me but of my own appearance" (116). Because she *desires*, because this negating action inscribes itself not merely in life—a narcissistic aestheticism assumed by some Third World artists—but in a project to create a new human world of "reciprocal recognitions" (218), she distances herself from fixed essences ascribed to her and moves to a zone of provisional instability. This nomadic alienation, I suggest, is what orients the Filipino sensibility to the U.S. scenario. It seems to me something like a totalizing condition shared by other Asians whose present fragmented, dispersed, and heterogeneous pluralities are otherwise well-nigh almost incommensurable. What coalesces them is the radical challenge they pose to the power bloc that for now defines the hegemonic American identity which I interrogated in the beginning of this afterword.

With the U.S. economy in shambles and worsening symptoms of social decay—drugs, homelessness, violence—visible everywhere, a need to assert a version of a homogeneous "American identity" surfaces again. This identity now claims to be based on cultural pluralism or diversity, a new strategy to "manage" racial conflicts in the United States and in the world system of transnational "free enterprise" within the paradigm of unity based on adherence to utilitarian liberalism. But, as Stephen Steinberg (1981) has observed, "Ethnic pluralism in America has its origins in conquest, slavery, and exploitation of foreign labor" (5). I would contend that this drive to assert a national consensus assumes a hierarchization of contradictory interests arrived at through various discursive techniques and negotiated compromises. This consensus translates into ideology in action. We see here the operation of a strategy of domination, hegemony in short, which appears when (according to Hazel Carby) "an apparent unity is imposed upon and subsumes inherent contradictions and conflicting economic and political interests within and between racial, sexual or class groupings" (1980, 64). What results is a normative pluralism that effectively eliminates those cultural and political differences which it claims to be respecting in the first place. At the same time it disallows the view that inequality (stemming from the allocation of privileges and privations through invidious racial categorization) is historically and socially constructed.

From this perspective, I see the emancipatory project of Ethnic Studies to be a theoretical and practical deconstruction of hegemonic rule, an unstable equilibrium of conflicting interests, founded on the ideology of normative pluralism. This hegemonic pluralism seeks to reconcile incompatible interests, class and gender differences, within the idea of a "national culture" or a synthesizing "American identity." If there is any key concept whose meaning has to be struggled over or negotiated, it is that of culture. Following the insights of research in Cultural Studies and of such thinkers as Antonio Gramsci and Raymond Williams, I propose that our manifold conceptualization of culture—together with racial politics which subsumes ethnicity and multicultural diversity—should stage in the foreground of inquiry the antagonistic relations of domination and subordination of social forces and agents (see Hall 1986). A paradigm of cultural pluralism as practiced by the traditional institutions usually excludes the concept of dominant and subordinate cultures (whether indigenous or migrant) by promoting a showcase tolerance of diverse ethnic practices. It propagandistically reduces "ideology" (for example, the contours of racial theories explored by Banton) to a matter of attitudes or ideas that can be changed through education or acculturation. I plead for a holistic, historically informed and praxis-oriented approach to the inquiry into race relations, multiculturalism, and ethnicity situated in specific conjunctures.

In a recent essay, Barbara Jean Fields (1989) stresses the racial ideology that underpins the U.S. hegemonic order, ideology being understood here as a total way of experiencing and making sense of one's life. Fields contends that race is an ideology reproduced every day even by "academic 'liberals' and 'progressives' in whose version of race the neutral shibboleths *difference* and *diversity* replace words like *slavery, injustice, oppression* and *exploitation*, diverting attention from the anything-but-neutral history these words denote" (118). This ideology of race that the interdisciplinary field of Ethnic Studies aims to elucidate involves a complex process of signification, of inclusion and exclusion, which characterizes the dynamics of hegemonic rule. Because this process of representation of Self and Other at the core of racism and racial categorization involves unequal representation, decisions and judgments of worth and eligibility which discriminate between collectivities, Ethnic Studies is committed to the practical task of criticizing institutional operations, policies, laws, and other social practices of stratification informed by class, gender, racial, and ethnic determinants. Perhaps the most important task would be to articulate the fundamental character of racial difference in the United States with class and gender so that difference (a term now almost rhetorically debased by postmodernist chic) becomes concrete, overdetermined, coinciding with popular-democratic demands and mobilization for equality and justice.

As an innovative, cross-cultural inquiry into the signification and representation of peoples, Ethnic Studies would ideally command the resources to analyze the linkage between discourse and authority, knowledge and power. We are concerned here not only with a demystification of ideology but a contextual diagnosis of the hegemonic practices that normalize individuals to accept their assigned positions in society. In a consumerist society, the spectacle, image, or simulacrum exercises a power often decisive in influencing thoughts and inciting collectivities into action. The recent award-winning play *M. Butterfly* by David Henry Hwang has called our attention once again to the reciprocal damage that demeaning stereotypes can inflict on everyone, in particular on those who hold power. Textbooks and the mass media continue to perpetuate the image of Asians as the "inscrutable Oriental," treacherous, evil, lacking any respect for human life. Images of "yellow hordes" committing "hara-kiri" or "banzai attacks" in any number of films dealing with World War II, the Korean and Indo-

China wars, help reproduce the now stereotypical but still influential perception of Asian Americans as the degenerate and barbaric Other which warrants forceful treatment.

What *M. Butterfly*, I think, sought to demystify is not so much any single media distortion of "Oriental" females as exotic sex objects analogous to Puccini's opera heroine or to any number of Hollywood potboilers. What it sought to highlight is the process of Orientalizing, the psychological and phenomenological dialectic which generates the suicidal fantasies of the drama's protagonist M. Gallimard, of any number of "Rice Queens" and "Yellow Fevers." Hwang (1986) confronts the intersection among myths of racism, sexism, and imperialism and their often elusive complicities, but it seems to me rather easy to suggest (as the playwright does in his insightful "Afterword") that we can easily transcend these superficial misperceptions and interact as equal human beings by a gesture of humanistic self-enlightenment. Aside from proclaimed commitment to truth and ritualistic examination of conscience, I think radical changes in the social conditions, in the everyday quality of life linked to the dynamics of the individual psyche, that generate and reproduce such misperceptions are necessary. Only then will the powerfully seductive figure of Madame Butterfly and her protean reincarnations become finally resistible.

Meanwhile, in the theater of late consumer capitalism, mutations of the stereotype are everywhere discernible. I can cite here how the perception of Asians as "coolie laborers," faceless beasts of burden, or docile and subservient workers willing to accept low wages and brutal treatment, has been replaced by the image of Asian "whiz kids" and aggressive Korean merchants who have successfully internalized the utilitarian ethos—an image as misleading as Madame Butterfly, the West's projection of the East as the feminine Other asking to be oppressed, victimized, and silenced. What is needed here again is to historicize these images and contextualize them in the ongoing multilayered process of antagonisms between cultures. It is therefore part of our task to question not only whether the role of the Eurasian pimp in the contested musical *Miss Saigon* should be played by a Caucasian with "taped eyelids and yellowface," whether "the right for equal opportunity" should be compromised, but whether such a musical fabrication which fosters demeaning sexist and racist categorizations should be presented at all without risks. This contested role of the French-Vietnamese pimp who supposedly brings about the reunion of an American soldier and the Vietnamese woman he left behind with his child is the London musical's contribution to smoothing adversarial East-West (or shall we say North-South?) relations. Here is a sample of *Newsweek* (2 Oct. 1989) hype: "In the 'American Dream' number, the pimp (Jonathan Pryce) does a showstopping anthem of sleazoid ecstasy ('I speak Uncle Ho and think

Uncle Sam'), lasciviously embracing a giant pink Cadillac surrounded by a chorus line of blond bimbos" (69).

Sympathetically appraised, *Miss Saigon* may be viewed as an updating of Puccini staged with a more dazzling castrative aura, a connotative force stemming from the erotic violence of the Vietnam War and the spectacle of sensual Asian bodies that tend to induce the aesthetic sublimation of guilt and aggression into pleasurable fantasy. But let me register my awareness here that many who may agree with this assessment would still insist that the substantive issue is discrimination in hiring. Notwithstanding the charge of entirely negative portrayal of Asians in the musical, B. D. Wong (the actor who played Song Liling in *M. Butterfly*) replies: "Because at this time in history, we *have* to claim portrayals of all Asians, negative and positive, from the irresponsible hands of non-Asian producers, actors and Miss America finalist judges who have neither a clue how to portray us, nor indeed how we fit into the image they describe as 'American.' Maybe you gotta be in it to win it" (1990, 14). Wong's point is astutely put: peoples of color have to take control of the intellectual means of production. Granting that, however, I think the decisive importance of what the audience or spectator does with the performance and the conditions governing this interpretation cannot be given short shrift. In other words, our grasp of the levers of artistic production should be complemented with an appreciation of the question of ideological-ethical effects raised by Bertolt Brecht's *Rezeptionaesthetik*, by Balibar and Macherey, and others. This is not the place to articulate all the aesthetic, political, and ethical implications of this controversy. Suffice it for me to conclude by saying that this dispute sums up in microcosm the complex tangle of problems and issues challenging scholars and activists involved in racial/ethnic relations and interdisciplinary cultural studies at the threshold of the twenty-first century.

References

Adorno, Theodor. *Negative Dialectics*. New York: Continuum, 1973.

Alkalimat, Abdul. "Black Marxism in the White Academy." *Sage Race Relations Abstracts* 13 (1988): 3–19.

Althusser, Louis. *For Marx*. New York: Pantheon, 1969.

————. *Lenin and Philosophy*. London: New Left Books, 1971.

Amariglio, Jack, Stephen Resnick, and Richard Wolff. "Class, Power and Culture." In *Marxism and the Interpretation of Culture*, edited by Cary Nelson and Lawrence Grossberg. Urbana: University of Illinois Press, 1988.

Amin, Samir. *Eurocentrism*. New York: Monthly Review Press, 1989.

Anderson, Perry. *In the Tracks of Historical Materialism*. Chicago: University of Chicago Press, 1984.

Appiah, Kwame Anthony. "Race." In *Critical Terms for Literary Study*, edited by Frank Lentricchia and Thomas McLaughlin. Chicago: University of Chicago Press, 1990.

Aronowitz, Stanley. *The Crisis in Historical Materialism*. New York: Praeger, 1981.

Aronowitz, Stanley, and Henry Giroux. "Schooling, Culture and Literacy in the Age of Broken Dreams: A Review of Bloom and Hirsch." *Harvard Educational Review* 58 (1988): 172–94.

Baker, Donald G. *Race, Ethnicity and Power*. London: Routledge, 1983.

Balibar, Etienne. "Paradoxes of Universality." In *Anatomy of Racism*, edited by David Goldberg. Minneapolis: University of Minnesota Press, 1990.

Banton, Michael. *Racial Theories*. New York: Cambridge University Press, 1987.

Banton, Michael, and Robert Miles. "Racism." In *Dictionary of Race and Ethnic Relations*, edited by E. Ellis Cashmore. London: Routledge, 1984.

Baraka, Amiri. "The Revolutionary Tradition in Afro-American Literature." In *Poetry and Politics*, edited by Richard Jones. New York: Quill, 1985.

Baran, Paul, and Paul Sweezy. *Monopoly Capital*. New York: Monthly Review Press, 1966.

Barker, Martin. "Biology and the New Racism." In *Anatomy of Racism*. Minneapolis: University of Minnesota Press, 1990.

Barth, Fredrik. *Ethnic Groups and Boundaries*. Boston: Little, Brown, and Co., 1969.

Barthes, Roland. *The Eiffel Tower and Other Mythologies*. New York: Hill and Wang, 1979.

Bastide, Roger. "Color, Racism and Christianity." In *Race, Ethnicity and Social Change*, edited by John Stone. North Scituate, Mass.: Duxbury Press, 1977.

Bataille, Georges. *Visions of Excess: Selected Writings, 1927–1939*. Minneapolis: University of Minnesota Press, 1985.

Baudrillard, Jean. "The Precession of Simulacra." In *Art after Modernism: Rethinking Representation*, edited by Brian Wallis. New York: The New Museum of Contemporary Art, 1984.

Bell, Daniel. "Ethnicity and Social Change." In *Ethnicity: Theory and Experience*, edited by Nathan Glazer and Daniel P. Moynihan. Cambridge, Mass.: Harvard University Press, 1975.

Benjamin, Walter. *Reflections.* New York: Harcourt, 1978.

Bercovitch, Sacvan. "The Problem of Ideology in American Literary History." *Critical Inquiry* 12 (1986): 631–53.

Berger, John. *And Our Faces, My Heart, Brief as Photos.* New York: Pantheon, 1984.

Berting, Jan. "An Appraisal of Functionalist Theories in Relation to Race and Colonial Societies." In *Sociological Theories: Race and Colonialism.* Paris: UNESCO, 1980.

Blauner, Robert. *Racial Oppression in America.* New York: Harper and Row, 1972.

Blauner, Robert, and David Wellman. "Toward the Decolonization of Social Research." In *The Death of White Sociology,* edited by Joyce Ladner. New York: Vintage, 1973.

Bocock, Robert. *Hegemony.* London: Tavistock, 1986.

Boelhower, William. *Through a Glass Darkly: Ethnic Semiosis in American Literature.* New York: Oxford University Press, 1987.

Bonacich, Edna. "Class Approaches to Ethnicity and Race." *The Insurgent Sociologist* 10 (Fall 1980): 9–23.

———. "Teaching Race and Class." In *Reflections on Shattered Windows,* edited by Gary Okihiro et al. Pullman: Washington State University Press, 1988.

Bourdieu, Pierre. *Outline of a Theory of Practice.* Cambridge: Cambridge University Press, 1977.

Bourne, Jenny. "Towards an Anti-racist Feminism." *Race and Class* (Summer 1983): 1–22.

Bradbury, Malcolm, and Howard Temperley. *Introduction to American Studies.* London: Longman, 1981.

Brittan, Arthur, and Mary Maynard. *Sexism, Racism and Oppression.* New York: Blackwell, 1984.

Buaken, Manuel. "Where Is the Heart of America?" *The New Republic* 103 (23 Sept. 1940): 410–11.

Buci-Glucksmann, Christine. "Hegemony and Consent." In *Approaches to Gramsci,* edited by Ann Sassoon. London: Writers and Readers, 1982.

Bulosan, Carlos. *Bulosan: An Introduction with Selections.* Edited by E. San Juan, Jr. Manila: National Book Store, 1983.

Burawoy, Michael. "The Capitalist State in South Africa: Marxist and Sociological Perspectives on Race and Class." *Political Power and Social Theory* 2 (1981): 279–335.

Cabezas, Amado, and Gary Kawaguchi. "Race, Gender and Class for Filipino Americans." In *A Look beyond the Model Minority Image,* edited by Grace Yun. New York: Minority Rights Group, Inc., 1989.

Carby, Hazel. "Multi-culture." *Screen Education* 34 (Spring 1980): 62–70.

———. "The Politics of Difference." *MS.* (Sept.–Oct. 1990): 84–85.

Carr, J. "On the Racism of Colorblindness." *The Eighties* 5 (Winter 1985): 66–96.

Cashmore, Ellis. "Ethnicity." In *Dictionary of Race and Ethnic Relations.* London: Routledge, 1984.

Centre for Contemporary Cultural Studies, ed. *The Empire Strikes Back.* London: Hutchinson, 1982.

Chametzky, Jules. "Some Notes on Imagination: Ethnicity, Acculturation." *MELUS [Multi-Ethnic Literature of the United States]* 11 (1984): 44–49.

Chin, Frank, et al., eds. *Aiiieeeee! An Anthology of Asian-American Writers.* New York: Doubleday, 1975.

Clifford, James, and George Marcus, eds. *Writing Culture*. Berkeley: University of California Press, 1986.

Connor, Steven. *Postmodernist Culture*. New York: Blackwell, 1989.

Cox, Oliver Cromwell. *Caste, Class and Race*. New York: Monthly Review Press, 1948.

Cruse, Harold. *Rebellion or Revolution*. New York: William Morrow, 1968.

Daniels, Roger, and Harry Kitano. *American Racism: Exploration of the Nature of Prejudice*. Englewood Cliffs, N.J.: Prentice Hall, 1970.

Davis, Mike. "The Political Economy of Late Imperial America." *New Left Review*, no. 143 (Jan.–Feb. 1984): 6–38.

———. *Prisoners of the American Dream*. London: Verso, 1986.

Dearborn, Mary V. *Pocahontas's Daughters: Gender and Ethnicity in American Culture*. New York: Oxford University Press, 1986.

Delacampagne, Christian. "Racism in the West: From Praxis to Logos." In *Anatomy of Racism*. Minneapolis: University of Minnesota Press, 1990.

Dews, Peter. *Logics of Disintegration*. London: Verso, 1987.

Dumont, Louis. "Caste, Racism, and Stratification: Reflections of a Social Anthropologist." In *Homo Hierarchus: The Caste System and Its Implications*. Chicago: University of Chicago Press, 1966.

Edgar, David. "Reagan's Hidden Agenda: Racism and the New American Right." *Race and Class* 22 (Winter 1981): 221–38.

Fabian, Johannes. *Time and the Other*. New York: Columbia University Press, 1983.

Fanon, Frantz. *The Wretched of the Earth*. New York: Grove Press, 1963.

———. *Black Skin, White Masks*. New York: Grove Press, 1967.

Farber, Samuel. "Racism over Three Decades." *Against the Current* 26 (May–June 1990): 31.

Faulkner, William. *The Sound and the Fury*. Edited by David Minter. New York: W. W. Norton, 1987.

Fields, Barbara Jean. "Slavery, Race and Ideology in the United States of America." *New Left Review* (1989): 95–118.

Fischer, Michael. "Ethnicity and the Post-Modern Arts of Memory." In *Writing Culture*, edited by James Clifford and George Marcus. Berkeley, Calif.: University of California Press, 1986.

Flynn, Elizabeth, and Patrocinio Schweickart, eds. *Gender and Reading*. Baltimore: The Johns Hopkins University Press, 1986.

Foster, William. *The Negro People in American History*. New York: International Publishers, 1973.

Fraser, Nancy, and Linda Nicholson. "Social Criticism without Philosophy: An Encounter between Feminism and Postmodernism." In *Feminism/Postmodernism*, edited by Linda Nicholson. New York: Routledge, 1990.

Fuss, Diana. *Essentially Speaking*. New York: Routledge, 1989.

Gates, Henry Louis, Jr., ed. *Black Literature and Literary Theory*. New York: Methuen, 1984.

———. *"Race," Writing, and Difference*. Chicago: University of Chicago Press, 1987.

Gayle, Addison, Jr., ed. *The Black Aesthetic*. New York: Doubleday, 1972.

Genovese, Eugene. *In Red and Black*. New York: Pantheon, 1971.

George, Herman. *American Race Relations*. Lanham, Md.: University Press of America, 1984.

Gilroy, Paul. "Steppin' Out of Babylon—Race, Class and Autonomy." In *The*

Empire Strikes Back, edited by the Centre for Contemporary Cultural Studies. London: Hutchinson, 1982.

———. "One Nation Under a Groove: The Cultural Politics of 'Race' and Racism in Britain." In *Anatomy of Racism*. Minneapolis: University of Minnesota Press, 1990.

Giroux, Henry, and Harvey Kaye. "The Liberal Arts Must Be Reformed to Serve Democratic Ends." *The Chronicle of Higher Education* (29 March 1989): A44.

Glazer, Nathan, and Daniel P. Moynihan, eds. *Ethnicity: Theory and Experience*. Cambridge, Mass.: Harvard University Press, 1975.

Goethe, Johann Wolfgang von. "Conversations with Eckermann." In *Modern Continental Literary Criticism*, edited by O. B. Hardison, Jr. New York: Appleton, 1962.

Goldberg, David Theo. "The Social Formation of Racist Discourse." In *Anatomy of Racism*. Minneapolis: University of Minnesota Press, 1990.

Gosset, Thomas. *Race: The History of an Idea in America*. Dallas: Southern Methodist University Press, 1963.

Gramsci, Antonio. *Selections from the Prison Notebooks*. Edited and translated by Quintin Hoare and Geoffrey Nowell Smith. New York: International Publishers, 1971.

Green, M., and B. Carter. "'Races' and 'Race-makers': The Politics of Racialization." *Sage Race Relations Abstracts* 13 (May 1988): 4–29.

Grigulevich, I. R., and S. Y. Kozlov, eds. *Races and Peoples*. Moscow: Progress Publishers, 1974.

Hall, Gus. *Imperialism Today*. New York: International Publishers, 1972.

Hall, Stuart. "Pluralism, Race and Class in Caribbean Society." In *Race and Class in Post-Colonial Society*, edited by UNESCO. Paris: UNESCO, 1977.

———. "Racism and Reaction." In *Five Views of Multi-Racial Britain*, edited by Commission for Racial Equality. London: Commission for Racial Equality, 1978.

———. "Race, Articulation and Societies Structured in Dominance." In *Sociological Theories: Race and Colonialism*, edited by UNESCO. Paris: UNESCO, 1980.

———. "The Whites of Their Eyes: Racist Ideologies and the Media." In *Silver Linings*, edited by George Bridges and Rosalind Brunt. London: Lawrence and Wishart, 1981.

———. "Signification, Representation, Ideology: Althusser and the Post-Structuralist Debates." *Critical Studies in Mass Communication* 2 (June 1985): 87–90.

———. "Gramsci's Relevance for the Study of Race and Ethnicity." *Journal of Communication Inquiry* 10 (Summer 1986): 5–27.

Hanninen, Sakari, and Leena Paldan, eds. *Rethinking Marx*. Berlin: Argument-Verlag, 1984.

Harvard Encyclopedia of American Ethnic Groups, edited by Stephan Thernstrom et al. Cambridge, Mass.: Harvard University Press, 1980.

Harvey, David. *The Condition of Postmodernity*. London: Blackwell, 1989.

Haug, W. F. *Critique of Commodity Aesthetics*. Minneapolis: University of Minnesota Press, 1986.

———. *Commodity Aesthetics, Ideology and Culture*. New York: International General, 1987.

Hebdige, Dick. *Subculture*. New York: Methuen, 1979.

Higham, John. *Strangers in the Land*. New York: Atheneum, 1971.

Horowitz, I. *Ideology and Utopia in the United States 1956–1976*. New York: Oxford University Press, 1977.

Horsman, Reginald. *Race and Manifest Destiny: The Origins of American Racial Anglo-Saxonism*. Cambridge, Mass.: Harvard University Press, 1981.

Howe, Irving. "The Southern Myth and Faulkner." In *The American Culture*, edited by Hennig Cohen. Boston: Houghton Mifflin, 1968.

Hwang, David Henry. *M. Butterfly*. New York: New American Library, 1986.

Islas, Arturo. *The Rain God*. Palo Alto, Calif.: Alexandrian Press, 1984.

Jameson, Fredric. "Postmodernism, or the Cultural Logic of Late Capitalism." *New Left Review*, no. 146 (1984): 53–92.

———. "Reading without Interpretation: Postmodernism and the Videotext." In *The Linguistics of Writing*, edited by Nigel Fabb et al. New York: Methuen, 1987a.

———. "On *Habits of the Heart*." *South Atlantic Quarterly* 86 (1987b): 545–65.

Jenkins, Richard. "Social Anthropological Models of Inter-ethnic Relations." In *Theories of Race and Ethnic Relations*, edited by John Rex and David Mason. New York: Cambridge University Press, 1986.

Jessop, Bob. "Marx and Engels on the State." In *Politics, Ideology and the State*, edited by S. Hibbin. London: Lawrence and Wishart, 1978.

Johnson, Richard. "What Is Cultural Studies Anyway?" *Social Text* 16 (Winter 1986–87): 38–80.

Johnson, Richard et al., eds. *Making Histories*. Minneapolis: University of Minnesota Press, 1982.

Jordan, Winthrop. *The White Man's Burden: Historical Origins of Racism in the United States*. New York: Oxford University Press, 1974.

Kingston, Maxine Hong. "Statement." *North American Review* 272–73 (September 1988): 42.

———. *China Men*. New York: Vintage, 1980.

Kolko, Gabriel. *Main Currents in Modern American History*. New York: Harper and Row, 1976.

Kovel, Joel. *White Racism*. New York: Columbia University Press, 1984.

Kristeva, Julia. *Desire in Language*. New York: Columbia University Press, 1980.

Krupat, Arnold. *The Voice in the Margin*. Berkeley, Calif.: University of California Press, 1989.

Kuper, Leo. "Theories of Revolution and Race Relations." In *Race, Ethnicity and Social Change*. North Scituate, Mass.: Duxbury Press, 1977.

Kushner, Sam. *Long Road to Delano*. New York: International Publishers, 1971.

Kushnick, L. "Parameters of British and North American Racism." *Race and Class* 23 (Autumn–Winter 1981–82): 187–206.

Laclau, Ernesto. *Politics and Ideology in Marxist Theory*. London: Verso, 1977.

Lawrence, Errol. "Just Plain Common Sense: The 'Roots' of Racism." In *The Empire Strikes Back*. London: Hutchinson, 1982.

Lears, T. Jackson. *No Place of Grace: Anti-Modernism and the Transformation of American Culture 1880–1920*. New York: Pantheon, 1981.

Lecourt, Dominique. "On Marxism as a Critique of Sociological Theories." In *Sociological Theories: Race and Colonialism*, edited by UNESCO. Paris: UNESCO, 1980.

Lee, Thea. "Trapped in a Pedestral." In *Race and Ethnic Relations 91/92*, edited by John Kromkowski. Guilford, Conn.: The Dushkin Publishing Group, Inc., 1991. (First published in *Dollars and Sense* [March 1990]: 12–15.)

Lefebvre, Henri. *The Sociology of Marx*. New York: Vintage, 1966.

———. *Everyday Life in the Modern World*. New York: Harper, 1971.

———. *The Survival of Capitalism*. London: Allison and Busby, 1976.

Leone, Bruno, ed. *Racism.* St. Paul, Minn.: Greenhaven, 1978.

Lerner, Michael. *The New Socialist Revolution.* New York: Dell, 1973.

Levine, Lawrence. *Black Culture and Black Consciousness.* New York: Oxford University Press, 1977.

Liu, John. "Toward an Understanding of the Internal Colonial Model." In *Counterpoint*, edited by Emma Gee. Los Angeles: UCLA Asian American Studies Center, 1976.

Loewenberg, Peter. "The Psychology of Racism." In *Rereading America*, edited by G. Colombo et al. New York: St. Martin's Press, 1989.

Loren, Charles. *Classes in the United States.* Davis, Calif.: Cardinal Publishers, 1977.

Lyman, Stanford. *The Asian in the West.* Reno: University of Nevada Press, 1970.

Lyotard, Jean-François. *The Postmodern Condition: A Report on Knowledge.* Minneapolis: University of Minnesota Press, 1984.

Marable, Manning. *From the Grassroots.* Boston: South End Press, 1980.

———. "The Third Reconstruction: Black Nationalism and Race in a Revolutionary America." *Social Text* 4 (Fall 1981): 3–27.

———. *How Capitalism Underdeveloped Black America.* Boston: South End Press, 1983.

———. "Racist Politics Victimize Minorities." *Bowling Green State University News*, 17 Jan. 1991, 2.

Marx, Karl. "On the Jewish Question." In *Early Writings.* New York: Vintage, 1975.

Marx, Karl, and Fredrick Engels. *Selected Works.* New York: International Publishers, 1968.

Mascia-Lees, Frances, Patricia Sharpe, and Colleen Ballerino Cohen. "The Postmodernist Turn in Anthropology: Cautions from a Feminist Perspective." *Signs* 15.d (1989): 7–33.

Matsuda, Mari. "Are Asian Americans a Racial Bourgeoisie?" *Katipunan* (September 1990): 12.

McWilliams, Carey. *Brothers under the Skin.* Boston: Little, Brown, and Co., 1964.

Melendy, H. Brett. "Filipinos." In *Harvard Encyclopedia of American Ethnic Groups.* Cambridge, Mass.: Harvard University Press, 1980.

———. *Asians in America.* New York: G. K. Hall and Co., 1977, reissued by Hippocrene Books, 1981.

Merrington, John. "Theory and Practice in Gramsci's Marxism." In *Western Marxism*, edited by New Left Review. London: Verso, 1977.

Merton, Robert K. "Discrimination and the American Creed." In *Race, Ethnicity and Social Change.* North Scituate, Mass.: Duxbury Press, 1977.

Miles, Robert. "Class, Race and Ethnicity: A Critique of Cox's Theory." *Ethnic and Racial Studies* 3 (April 1980): 169–87.

———. *Racism.* London: Routledge, 1989.

Miller, R. Baxter. "Who Knows But, That on the Equal Frequencies, We Speak for Ourselves? A response to a Statement by Katharine D. Newman, MELUS Editor Emeritus." *MELUS* 11 (Spring 1984): 75–79.

Montagu, Ashley. *The Humanization of Man.* New York: Grove Press, 1962.

———. "The Concept of Race." In *Anthropology Contemporary Perspectives*, edited by David Hunter and Phillip Whitten. Boston: Little, Brown, and Co., 1982.

Moore, Sally Falk. "The Production of Cultural Pluralism as a Process." *Public Culture* 1 (Spring 1989): 26–48.

Mouffe, Chantal. "Hegemony and the Integral State in Gramsci." In *Silver Linings.* London: Lawrence and Wishart, 1981.

————. "Hegemony and New Political Subjects: Toward a New Concept of Democracy." In *Marxism and the Interpretation of Culture*. Urbana: University of Illinois Press, 1988.

Mullings, Leith. "Ethnicity and Stratification in the Urban United States." In *Racism and the Denial of Human Rights: Beyond Ethnicity*, edited by Marvin Berlowitz and Ronald Edari. Minneapolis: MEP Publications, 1984.

Muwakkil, Salim. "Black Leaders Favor 'Self-help' over Integration." *In These Times* (10–16 Oct. 1990): 2.

Myrdal, Gunnar. *An American Dilemma*. New York: Harper, 1944.

Nakanishi, Don T. "Minorities and International Politics." In *Counterpoint*. Los Angeles: UCLA Asian American Studies Center, 1976.

Nee, Victor, and J. Sanders. "The Road to Parity: Determinants of the Socioeconomic Achievements of Asian Americans." *Ethnic and Racial Studies* 9 (January 1985): 75–93.

Newman, Katharine D. "An Ethnic Literary Scholar Views American Literature." *MELUS* 7 (1980): 3–19.

Occeña, Bruce. "The Filipino Nationality in the U.S.: An Overview." *Line of March* (Fall 1985): 35–40.

Omi, Michael. "It Just Ain't the Sixties No More: The Contemporary Dilemma of Asian American Studies." In *Reflections on Shattered Windows*, edited by Gary Okihiro et al. Pullman: Washington State University Press, 1988.

Omi, Michael, and Howard Winant. "By the Rivers of Babylon: Race in the United States." *Socialist Review* 71 (Sept.–Oct. 1983): 31–65.

————. *Racial Formation in the United States from the 1960s to the 1980s*. New York: Routledge, 1986.

Ortiz, Simon J. "Towards a National Indian Literature: Cultural Authenticity in Nationalism." *MELUS* 8 (1981): 7–12.

Outlaw, Lucius. "Toward a Critical Theory of 'Race.'" In *Anatomy of Racism*. Minneapolis: University of Minnesota Press, 1990.

Paine, Robert. *Second Thoughts about Barth's Models*. Occasional Paper No. 32. London: Royal Anthropological Institute, 1974.

Petersen, William. "Concepts of Ethnicity." In *Harvard Encyclopedia of American Ethnic Groups*. Cambridge, Mass.: Harvard University Press, 1980.

Pierre-Charles, G. "Racialism and Sociological Theories." In *Sociological Theories: Race and Colonialism*, edited by UNESCO. Paris: UNESCO, 1980.

Pochman, Henry. "The Mingling of Tongues." In *Literary History of the United States*, edited by Robert Spiller et al. New York: Macmillan, 1963.

Poliakov, Leon. "Racism from the Enlightenment to the Age of Imperialism." In *Racism and Colonialism*, edited by Robert Ross. The Hague: Martinus Nijhoff, 1982.

Popkin, Richard H. "The Philosophical Bases of Modern Racism." In *Philosophy and the Civilizing Arts*, edited by Craig Walton and John Anton. Athens: Ohio University Press, 1974.

Poulantzas, Nicos. *Political Power and Social Classes*. London: Verso, 1968.

Prager, Jeffrey. "American Racial Ideology as Collective Representation." *Ethnic and Racial Studies* 5 (January 1982): 99–119.

————. "American Political Culture and the Shifting Meaning of Race." *Ethnic and Racial Studies* 10 (1987): 62–81.

Pratt, Mary Louise. "Linguistic Utopias." In *The Linguistics of Writing*, edited by Nigel Fabb et al. New York: Methuen, 1987.

Progressive Labor Party. *Revolution Today: U.S.A.* New York: Exposition Press, 1970.

Puzzo, Dante. "Racism and the Western Tradition." *Journal of the History of Ideas* 30 (Oct.–Dec. 1964): 579–86.

Quinsaat, Jesse, ed. *Letters in Exile.* Los Angeles: UCLA Asian American Studies Center, 1976.

Reich, Michael. "The Economics of Racism." In *The Capitalist System: A Radical Analysis of American Society*, edited by R. Edwards, M. Reich, and T. Weisskopf. Englewood Cliffs, N.J.: Prentice Hall, 1972.

Rex, John. *Race Relations in Sociological Theory.* 2nd ed. London: Routledge, 1983a.

———. "Race." In *A Dictionary of Marxist Thought*, edited by Tom Bottomore. Cambridge, Mass.: Harvard University Press, 1983b.

Rex, John, and David Mason, eds. *Theories of Race and Ethnic Relations.* Cambridge: Cambridge University Press, 1986a.

Rex, John. "The Role of Class Analysis in the Study of Race Relations—A Weberian Perspective." In *Theories of Race and Ethnic Relations.* New York: Cambridge University Press, 1986b.

———. *Race and Ethnicity.* Milton Keynes: Open University Press, 1986c.

Rodney, Walter. *How Europe Underdeveloped Africa.* London: Bogle l'Ouverture, 1972.

Rossi, I. *From the Sociology of Symbols to the Sociology of Signs.* New York: Columbia University Press, 1983.

Rothenberg, Jerome. "American Indian Poetry and the 'Other' Traditions." In *The New Pelican Guide to English Literature*, edited by Boris Ford. Vol. 9. London: Penguin, 1988.

Rozat, G., and R. Bartra. "Racism and Capitalism." In *Sociological Theories: Race and Colonialism*, edited by UNESCO. Paris: UNESCO, 1980.

Saldivar, Ramon. *Chicano Narrative: The Dialectics of Difference.* Madison: University of Wisconsin Press, 1990.

San Juan, E., Jr. *Carlos Bulosan and the Imagination of the Class Struggle.* Quezon City: University of the Philippines Press, 1972.

———. "Introduction" [Carlos Bulosan Special Issue]. *AmerAsia Journal* 6 (May 1979): 3–29.

———, ed. "Introduction." In *Bulosan: An Introduction with Selections.* Manila: National Book Store, 1983.

———. *Toward a People's Literature.* Quezon City: University of the Philippines Press, 1984.

———. *Only by Struggle: Reflections on Philippine Culture, Politics and Society in a Time of Civil War.* Quezon City: Kalikasan Press, 1988.

———. "Problems in the Marxist Project of Theorizing Race." *Re-thinking Marxism* 2 (Summer 1989a): 58–80.

———. "Pax Americana on the Boob Tube." *Solidaridad* (First and Second Quarters 1989b): 65–66.

Sartre, Jean-Paul. *Anti-Semite and Jew.* New York: Schocken, 1948.

Sassoon, Ann. *Gramsci's Politics.* New York: St. Martin's Press, 1980.

Saxton, Alexander. *The Indispensable Enemy: Labor and the Anti-Chinese Movement in California.* Berkeley: University of California Press, 1971.

———. "Nathan Glazer, Daniel Moynihan and the Cult of Ethnicity." *AmerAsia Journal* 4 (Summer 1977): 141–50.

———. "Historical Explanations of Racial Inequality." *Marxist Perspectives* (Summer 1979): 146–68.

Shafer, Felix. "New Faces of Racism." *Breakthrough* (Winter 1990): 5–9, 17.

Sherman, Howard. *Radical Political Economy*. New York: Basic Books, 1972.

Simmel, Georg. "The Stranger." In *On Individuality and Social Forms*, edited by Donald Levine. Chicago: University of Chicago Press, 1971.

Sivanandan, A. *A Different Hunger: Writings on Black Resistance*. London: Pluto Press, 1982.

―――. "Challenging Racism: Strategies for the 80s." *Race and Class* 25 (Autumn 1983): 1–11.

Smith, Anthony. *Nationalism in the Twentieth Century*. New York: New York University Press, 1979.

Smith, M. G. "Ethnicity and Ethnic Groups in America: The View from Harvard." *Ethnic and Racial Studies* 5 (1982): 1–22.

―――. "Pluralism, Race and Ethnicity in Selected African Countries." In *Theories of Race and Ethnic Relations*. New York: Cambridge University Press, 1986.

Solberg, Sam. "An Introduction to Filipino-American Literature." In *Aiiieeeee!* edited by Frank Chin et al. Washington, D.C.: Howard University Press, 1975.

Sollors, Werner. "Literature and Ethnicity." In *Harvard Encyclopedia of American Ethnic Groups*. Cambridge, Mass.: Harvard University Press, 1980.

―――. *Beyond Ethnicity*. New York: Oxford University Press, 1986a.

―――. "A Critique of Pure Pluralism." In *Reconstructing American Literary History*, edited by Sacvan Bercovitch. Cambridge, Mass.: Harvard University Press, 1986b.

―――, ed. *The Invention of Ethnicity*. New York: Oxford University Press, 1989.

―――. "Ethnicity." In *Critical Terms for Literary Study*, edited by Frank Lentricchia and Thomas McLaughlin. Chicago: University of Chicago Press, 1990.

Solomos, John. "Varieties of Marxist Concepts of 'Race,' Class and the State: A Critical Analysis. In *Theories of Race and Ethnic Relations*. New York: Cambridge University Press, 1986.

Solomos, John, B. Findley, S. Jones, and P. Gilroy. "The Organic Crisis of British Capitalism and Race: The Experience of the Seventies." In *The Empire Strikes Back*. London: Hutchinson, 1982.

Spivak, Gayatri. "Can the Subaltern Speak?" In *Marxism and the Interpretation of Culture*. Urbana: University of Illinois Press, 1988.

Steele, Shelby. "The Recoloring of Campus Life." *Harper's Magazine* (February 1989): 47–55.

Steinberg, Stephen. *The Ethnic Myth*. Boston: Beacon Press, 1981.

Sturtevant, David. *Popular Uprisings in the Philippines 1840–1940*. Ithaca: Cornell University Press, 1976.

Sweezy, Paul. *The Present as History*. New York: Monthly Review Press, 1953.

Tabb, William. "What Happened to Black Economic Development?" *Review of Black Political Economy* 17 (Fall 1988): 65–88.

Takagi, Paul. "Asian Communities in the United States: A Class Analysis." *Our Socialism* 1 (May 1983): 49–55.

Takaki, Ronald. "Reflections on Racial Patterns in America." In *From Different Shores*, edited by Ronald Takaki. New York: Oxford University Press, 1987.

―――. *Strangers from a Different Shore*. Boston: Little, Brown, and Co., 1989.

Tarr, Peter. "Learning to Love Imperialism." *The Nation* (5 June 1989): 779–84.

Therborn, Goran. *The Ideology of Power and the Power of Ideology*. London: Verso, 1980a.

―――. *Science, Class and Society*. London: Verso, 1980b.

Thernstrom, S. "Ethnic Pluralism: The U.S. Model." In *Minorities: Community and Identity*, edited by C. Fried. Berlin: Springer-Verlag, 1983.

Todorov, Tzvetan, "Race, Writing, and Culture." In *"Race," Writing, and Difference*, edited by Henry Louis Gates, Jr. Chicago: University of Chicago Press, 1987.

Tucker, Robert, ed. *The Marx-Engels Reader*. New York: Norton, 1978.

UNESCO, ed. *Sociological Theories: Race and Colonialism*. Paris: UNESCO, 1980.

van den Berghe, Pierre. *Race and Racism*. New York: John Wiley, 1978.

Wald, Alan. "The Culture of 'Internal Colonialism': A Marxist Perspective." *MELUS* 8 (Fall 1981): 18–27.

———. "Theorizing Cultural Difference: A Critique of the Ethnicity School." *MELUS* 14 (Summer 1987): 21–33.

Wallerstein, Immanuel. *Historical Capitalism*. London: Verso, 1983.

Warren, Robert Penn. "Faulkner: The South, the Negro, and Time." In *Faulkner: A Collection of Critical Essays*. Englewood Cliffs, N.J.: Prentice Hall, 1966.

Watts, Jerry. "Racial Discourse in an Age of Social Darwinism." *Democratic Left* 18, no. 4 (July–Aug. 1990): 3–5.

Wellman, David T. *Portraits of White Racism*. Cambridge: Cambridge University Press, 1977.

West, Cornel. *Prophesy Deliverance! Toward a Revolutionary Afro-American Christianity*. Philadelphia: Westminster Press, 1982.

———. "Reconstructing the American Left: The Challenge of Jesse Jackson." *Social Text* 11 (Winter 1984–85): 3–19.

———. "Marxist Theory and the Specificity of Afro-American Oppression." In *Marxism and the Interpretation of Culture*. Urbana: University of Illinois Press, 1988.

———. "Toward a Socialist Theory of Racism." In *Socialist Perspectives on Race*. New York: Democratic Socialists of America, 1990.

Wickham, Gary. "Power and Power Analysis: Beyond Foucault?" *Economy and Society* 12 (1983): 468–97.

Wilden, Anthony. *System and Structure*. London: Tavistock, 1972.

Willett, John. *Brecht on Theater*. New York: Hill and Wang, 1964.

Williams, Raymond. *Marxism and Literature*. New York: Oxford University Press, 1977.

Wilson, William Julius. "American Social Policy and the Ghetto Underclass." In *Democratic Promise*, edited by Robert Kuttner and Irving Howe. New York: Foundation for the Study of Independent Social Ideas, Inc., 1988.

Wirth, Louis. "The Problem of Minority Groups." In *The Science of Man in the World Crisis*, edited by Ralph Linton. New York: Columbia University Press, 1945.

Wolf, Eric. *Europe and the People without History*. Berkeley: University of California Press, 1982.

Wolpe, Harold. "Class Concepts, Class Struggle and Racism." In *Theories of Race and Ethnic Relations*. Cambridge: Cambridge University Press, 1986.

Wong, B. D. "Helicopter Lands on Atlantic City Runway." *AAJA [Asian American Journalists Association] Newsletter* (Fall 1990): 14–15, 22.

Yun, Grace, ed. *A Look beyond the Model Minority Image*. New York: Minority Rights Group, Inc., 1989.

Index

155